Creative Acrylics

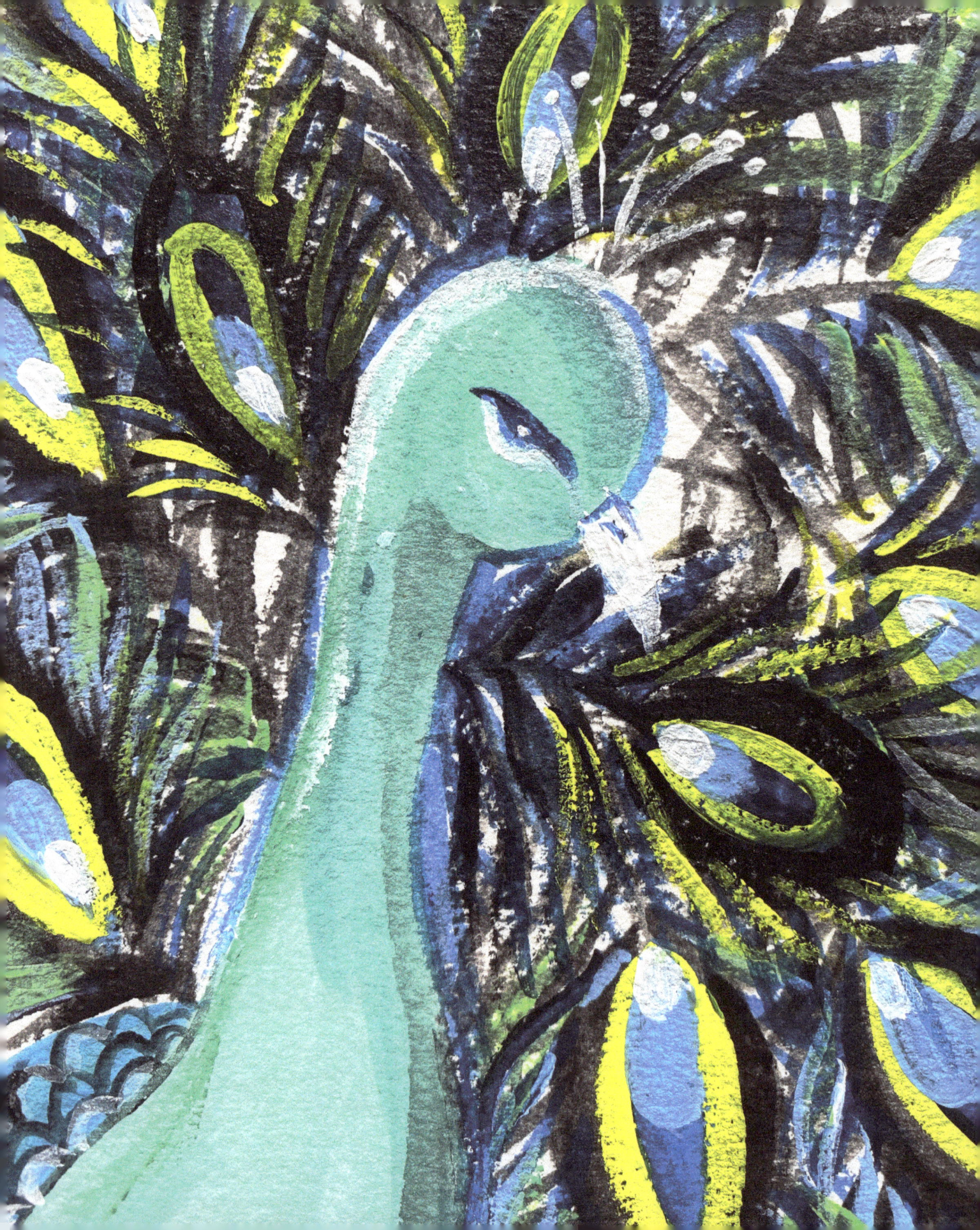

Creative Acrylics

A STEP-BY-STEP BEGINNER'S GUIDE TO CREATING WITH PAINT & MEDIUMS

Carla Co Chua

QUARRY

Quarto.com

© 2022 Quarto Publishing Group USA Inc.
Text and images © 2022 Carla Chua

First Published in 2022 by Quarry Books, an imprint of The Quarto Group,
100 Cummings Center, Suite 265-D, Beverly, MA 01915, USA.
T (978) 282-9590 F (978) 283-2742

Quarry Books titles are also available at discount for retail, wholesale, promotional, and bulk purchase. For details, contact the Special Sales Manager by email at specialsales@quarto.com or by mail at The Quarto Group, Attn: Special Sales Manager, 100 Cummings Center, Suite 265-D, Beverly, MA 01915, USA.

ISBN: 978-0-76037-327-9

Digital edition published in 2022
eISBN: 978-0-7603-7328-6

Library of Congress Cataloging-in-Publication Data

Names: Co Chua, Carla, author.
Title: Creative acrylics : a step-by-step beginner's guide to creating with paint & mediums / Carla Co Chua.
Description: Beverly, MA : Quarry, 2022. | Includes index. | Summary: "Creative Acrylics features the best beginner techniques for painting with acrylics, with lessons on painting vibrant florals, animals, landscapes, and still lifes and skill-building projects on a variety of surfaces"—Provided by publisher.
Identifiers: LCCN 2021037397 (print) | LCCN 2021037398 (ebook) | ISBN 9780760373279 (trade paperback) | ISBN 9780760373286 (ebook)
Subjects: LCSH: Acrylic painting—Technique.
Classification: LCC ND1535 .C6 2022 (print) | LCC ND1535 (ebook) | DDC 751.42/6—dc23
LC record available at https://lccn.loc.gov/2021037397
LC ebook record available at https://lccn.loc.gov/2021037398

Page Layout: Megan Jones Design

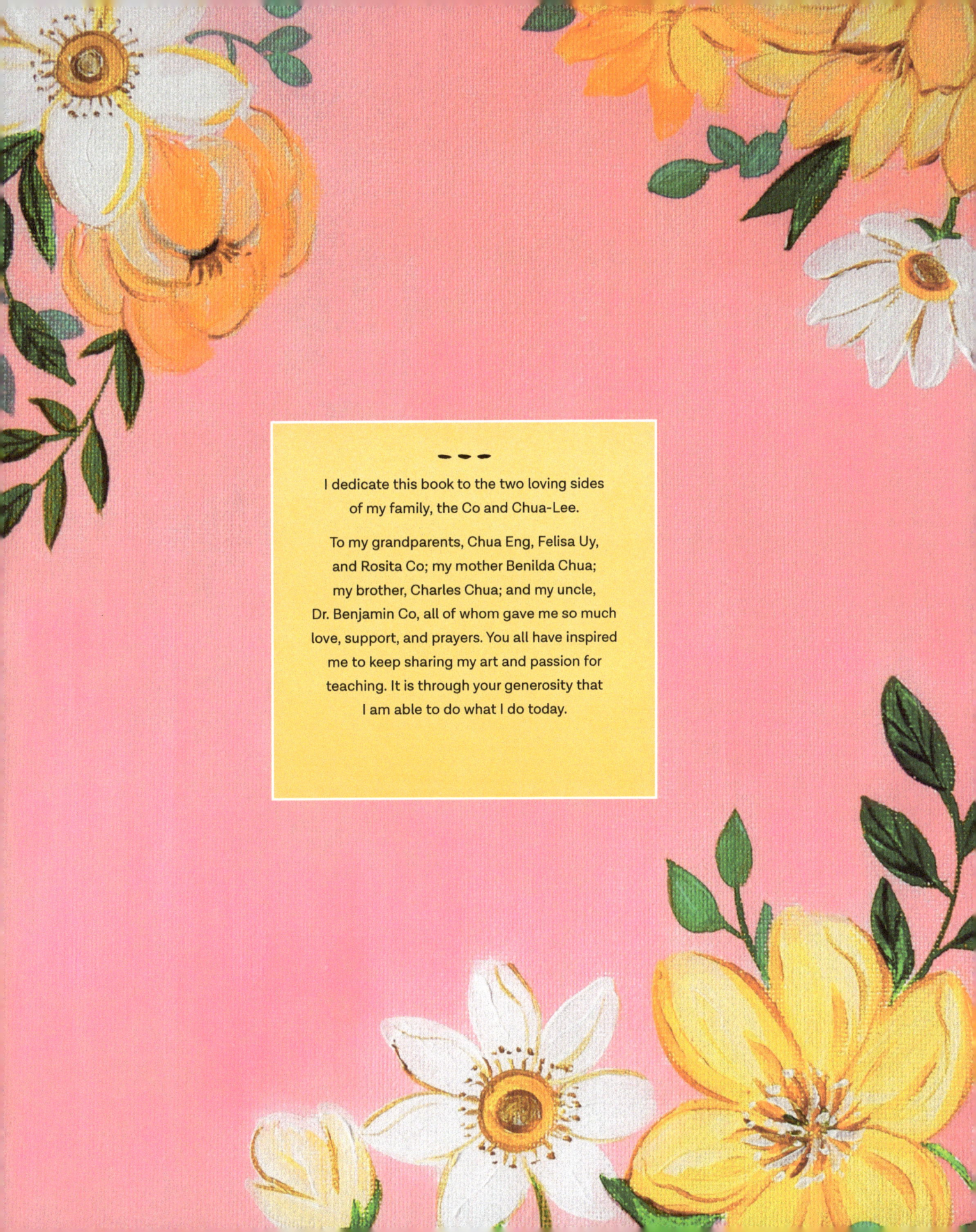

I dedicate this book to the two loving sides
of my family, the Co and Chua-Lee.

To my grandparents, Chua Eng, Felisa Uy,
and Rosita Co; my mother Benilda Chua;
my brother, Charles Chua; and my uncle,
Dr. Benjamin Co, all of whom gave me so much
love, support, and prayers. You all have inspired
me to keep sharing my art and passion for
teaching. It is through your generosity that
I am able to do what I do today.

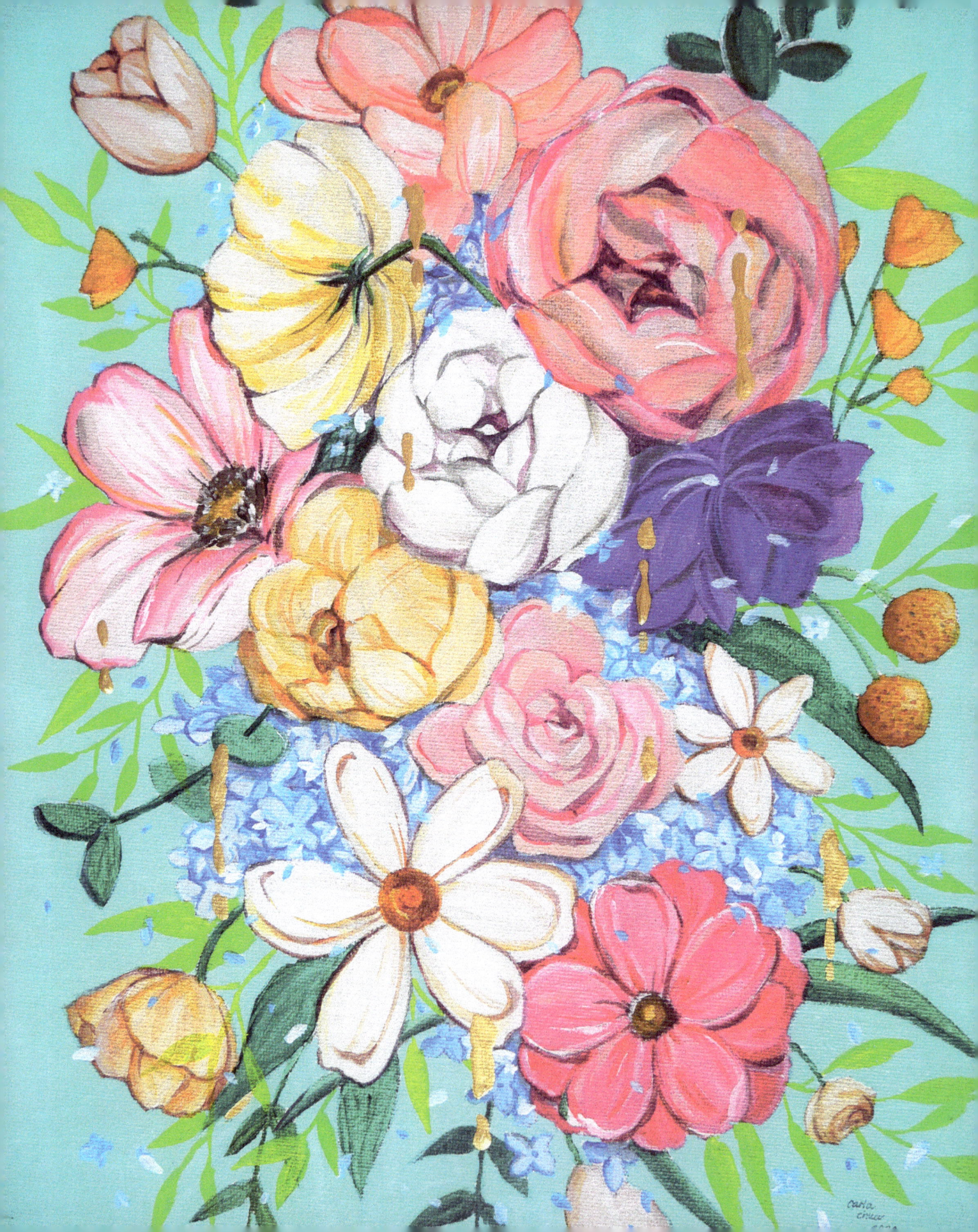

CONTENTS

INTRODUCTION

Painting is one of the most relaxing and fulfilling hobbies a person could ever enjoy. So many possibilities exist for what you can create, and I love how anyone can bring their imagination to life in a unique way. Painting, no matter how simple an activity it may seem, can leave a positive effect on a person's well-being. In my years of teaching, I've always emphasized how painting is a skill that can be learned and improved on through constant practice. Nobody is born an artist.

When people ask me to name the easiest medium for beginning painters, my answer is always acrylics. Acrylics are so easy to work with and so versatile. The paint adheres to a variety of surfaces, and you can achieve different effects with various techniques. Frankly, they're just a lot of fun to use!

I'll show you how to paint with acrylics using simple methods and demonstrations. My goal is to make it easy for anyone to follow along and get a feel for how they can use this fantastic medium. I chose subjects and exercises that are suitable for beginners and for those with some experience who just want to paint for the fun of it. I'm a self-taught artist, and the exercises and lessons in this book show you my thought processes as I work my way through a painting, from start to finish. Because I mostly learn through practical application, the tips and instructions I've chosen to include in the book are easy to understand, even if you don't have any formal art training.

I'm also excited to share the special projects that reveal the seemingly limitless potential of acrylics. These projects are very close to my heart, as they led to the writing of this book! Working with acrylics has enabled me to put my paintings on different substrates, making the pieces practical and interesting. I'm always taken by surprise when people ask me to paint on items I never would have dreamed of painting on.

As I tell students in my art workshops in the Philippines, try not to focus too much on the final painting, as we all interpret subjects in unique ways. Your orange painting might turn out different from mine, and that's perfectly okay!

I hope that the lessons in this book will inspire you to experiment further with acrylics. This is something you'll cherish for the rest of your life. My wish is that this book will be a stepping-stone for you as you begin your creative journey.

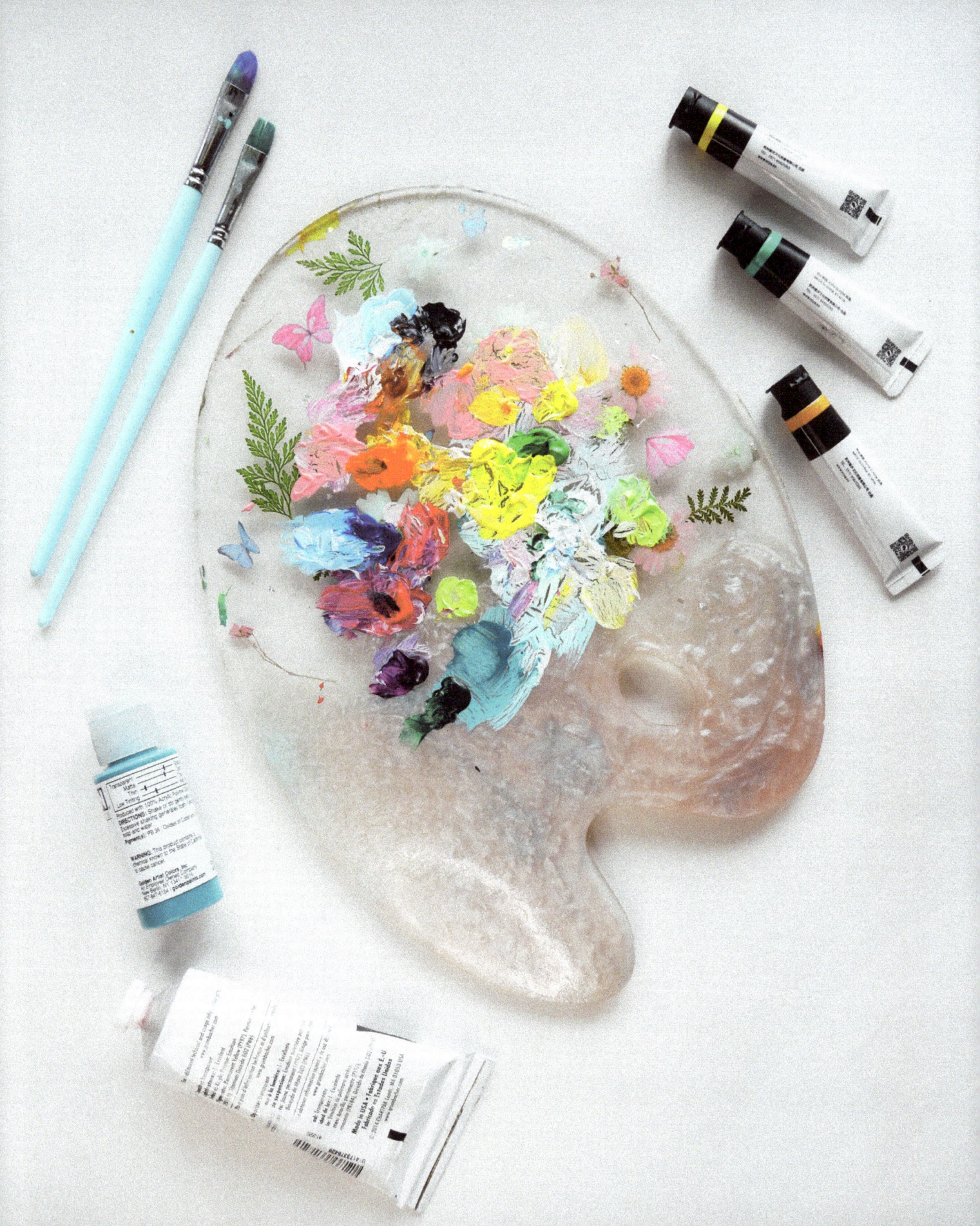

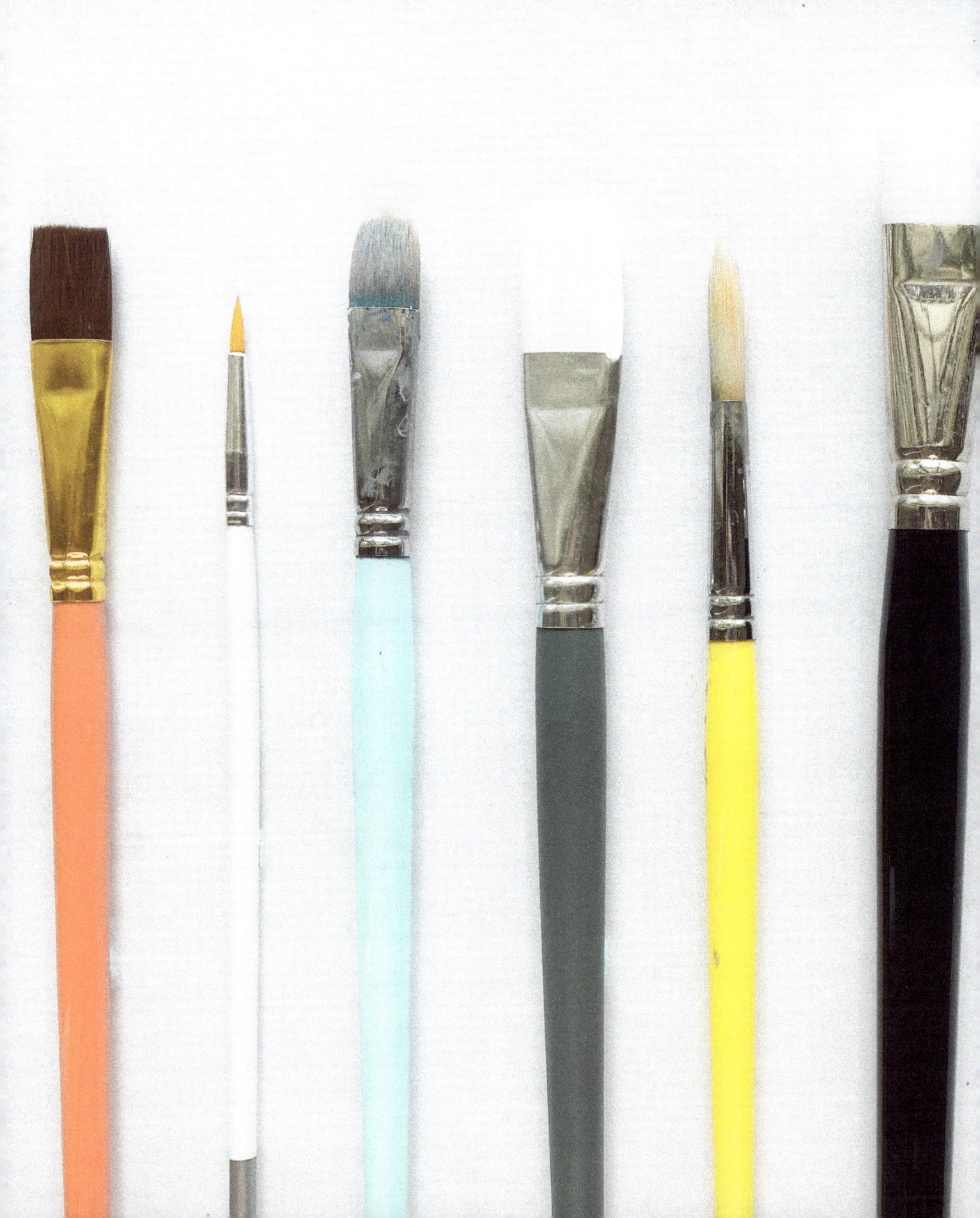

1

MATERIALS

- - - - - -

Walking into an art store and seeing the rows of paints, brushes, mediums, and all the miscellaneous tools and equipment can be both exciting and overwhelming. I love visiting arts and crafts shops to find interesting materials that will inspire me to sit down and create. Although you don't need a lot of tools to paint, it's best to learn which ones you need to get started and when and how to work with them. In this section, I'll give you an overview of the different kinds of materials used for acrylic painting.

ACRYLIC PAINTS

Acrylics are fast-drying, water-soluble paints made with pigment and acrylic polymer emulsion. Like most paints, acrylics come in student-grade and artist-grade quality. Student-grade paints contain more fillers, making them more budget friendly. Artist-grade (also known as professional) quality paints are more vibrant, with a higher concentration of pigment—meaning they also come with a steeper price tag. Here are the various types of acrylic paints and their properties.

Heavy-Body Acrylic Paint

As the name suggests, heavy-body acrylic paints are the thickest and heaviest of the lot. These paints are like butter when you spread them over your canvas. Heavy-body acrylics retain brush marks and textures well, and they can be thinned with water or a thinning medium. The versatility of heavy-body acrylics makes them popular among artists.

Soft-Body Acrylic Paint

Soft-body paints have the same creamy consistency and opacity as heavy-body acrylics but are smoother in application. These paints are more suited to fluid brushstrokes and can be used effectively to create even, watercolor-like layers. This type of paint won't retain brush marks as well as heavy-body acrylics, but you can create marks with a firmer brush if needed.

Fluid Acrylic Paint

If a project requires paint with more flow and evenness, fluid acrylics are your best option. Although they contain more water than thicker paints, fluid acrylics retain the opacity, vibrancy, and consistency of tube acrylic paint. They are often used for acrylic pour or drip paintings.

Acrylic Craft Paint

These paints have a lot of mediums and binders mixed in. Mediums may include fiber, sand, black lava paste, pastel ground, or molding pastes for texture. Craft paints usually come in a variety of colors and contain less pigment than more pricey acrylic paints. The paints are typically thinner and smoother than fluid, soft-body, and heavy-body paints.

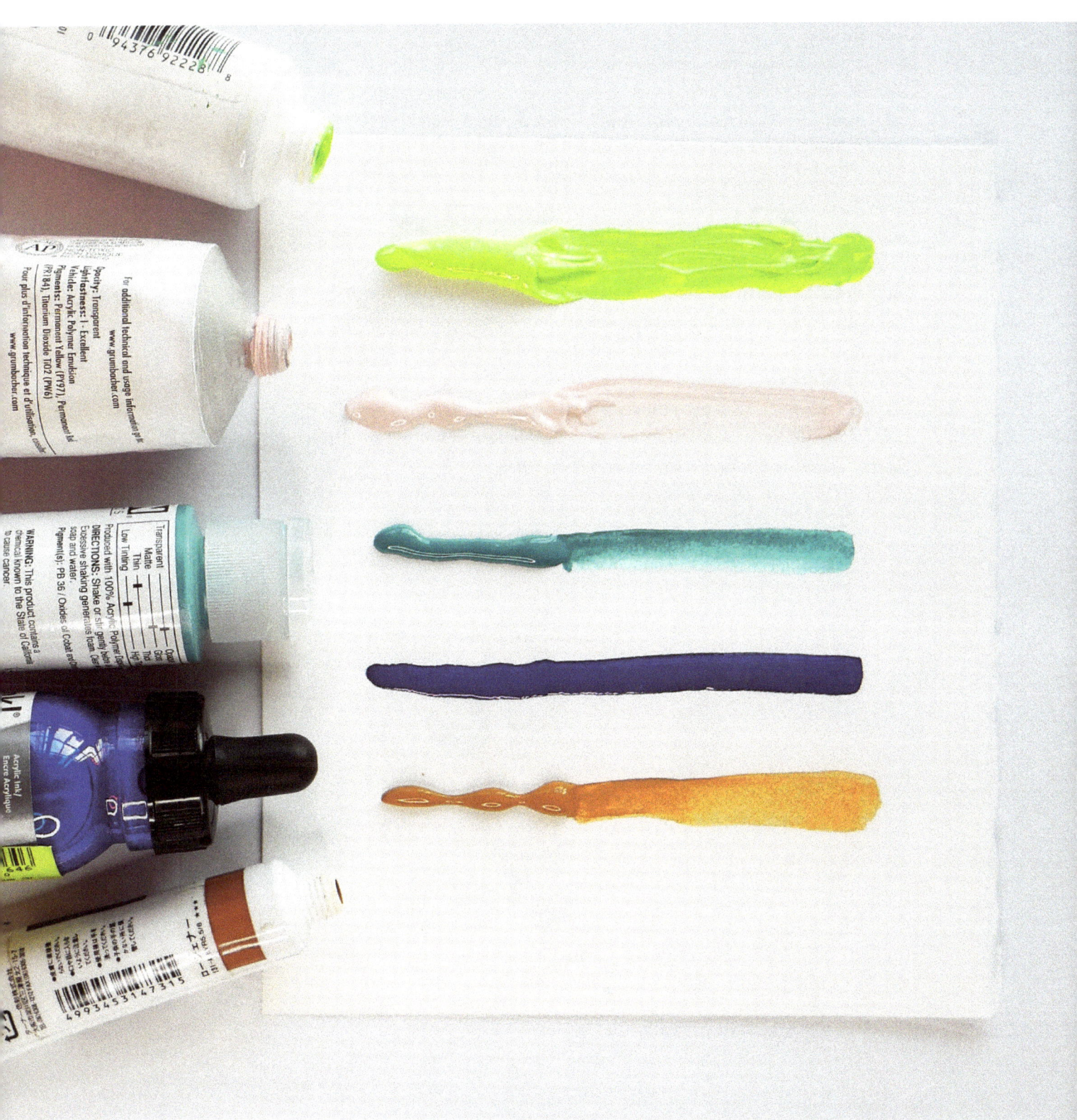

Acrylic Ink

Acrylic inks are made from finer pigments suspended in an acrylic emulsion and are even more fluid than thinner paints. They're ideal for creating translucent watercolor wash effects and airbrushing. Acrylic inks can also be combined with the other acrylic paints listed here.

Acrylic Gouache

Acrylic gouache is a hybrid paint, meaning it has properties of both acrylic and gouache mediums. Although pure acrylic tends to dry a bit glossy, acrylic gouache is more matte because it contains gum arabic as a binder. When completely dry, these paints are water-resistant like regular acrylics.

Acrylic Markers

Acrylics can also come in pen or marker form and are applied with pen nibs that range from thin to thick. Markers are particularly handy for writing on surfaces such as wood, glass, and stone, as they're permanent when dry.

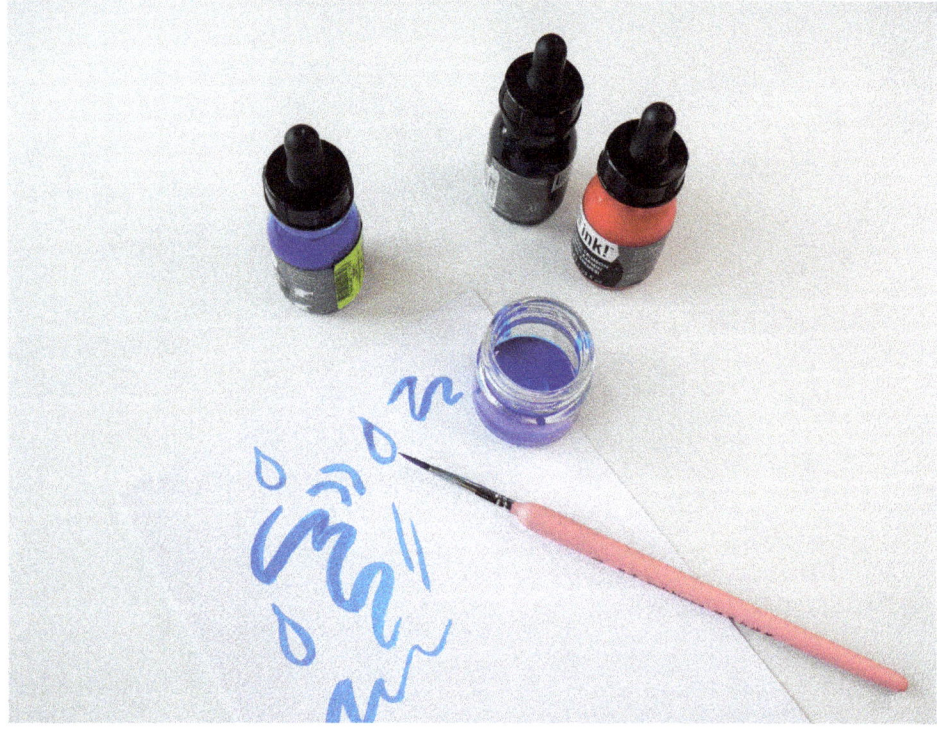

SUBSTRATES

Acrylics can be painted on many different surfaces or substrates, which is one reason why painting with acrylics is so fun and popular. Although most substrates require no prepping, some require a specialized kind of acrylic paint that allows the pigment to adhere better on the surface.

Canvas, Panels, and Pads

Canvas is the substrate most people associate with painting. Canvases are comprised of cotton or linen fabric stretched and fastened over wooden frames. These fabrics are absorbent and have a beautiful threadlike texture. Many commercial canvases are prepped with a primer that makes them ready for painting. Canvas panels are made of the same fabric but are backed with boards instead of wooden frames. Canvas fabrics are also bound together in pads that make them easier to store and use at home or on location.

Paper

Papers are easy to find and more cost-efficient than canvas. Paper especially made for acrylic painting stops paint from bleeding through and prevents buckling when layers of paint are applied. This paper is typically made of cotton or wood pulp, which makes it durable and long lasting. Watercolor paper can also be used for acrylic painting.

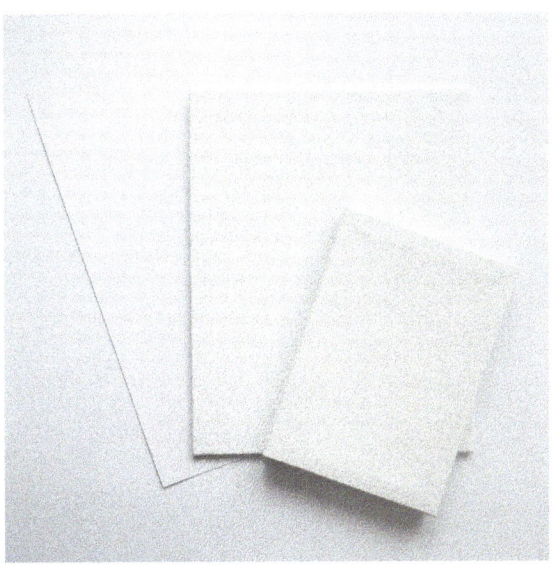

TIP

Heavyweight paper is recommended for acrylic painting. Look for the GSM rating on the package; GSM means "grams per square meter" and indicates the thickness or heaviness of the paper. Most papers for everyday use are about 80 to 90 GSM, and papers more suited for acrylic painting should be 300 GSM and above.

PREPPING PAPERS AND CANVAS
- - -

Most of the exercises in the book are painted on 300 GSM paper or on canvas. Here are some tips to prepare your chosen surface for painting.

Create Clean Borders

To create crisp, clean edges on your paintings, I highly recommend taping off the borders with low-tack craft tape, artist tape, or washi tape. This step is especially important if you're painting on paper, as it prevents the paper from warping when covered with paint. These tapes have enough adhesive to stick on paper but usually won't tear the paper when you pull it off after the painting dries. Test the tape on a piece of scrap paper to make sure the adhesive isn't too strong. Washi tape, common among crafters, is a lightweight decorative tape used for journaling and scrapbooking. These are my favorite tapes to use because they come in different sizes and designs and, most importantly, almost never tear the paper.

   Masking tape is another option, although I find that some types can tear paper. To help prevent this, remove some of the tape's adhesive by sticking the tape on a piece of cloth (your clothing will work) before taping it on the paper. Again, test the tape on a scrap piece of paper to make sure it isn't too sticky.

1 Mask off a ¼ inch (0.65 cm) border around the paper using low-tack or washi tape.

2 Go ahead and paint, working up to and over the taped edge.

3 After the painting is finished and dry, carefully remove the tape without tearing the paper to reveal a clean edge around your work.

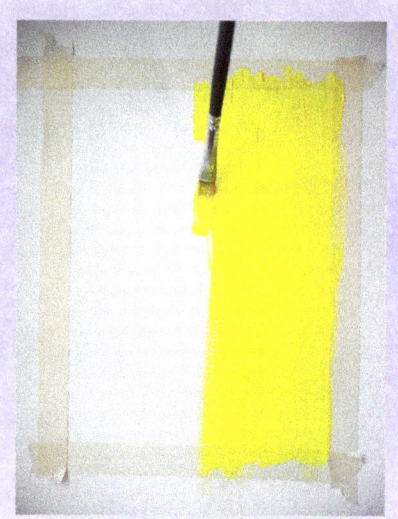

Priming Canvases

Many commercial canvases are pre-primed and ready for painting, but you can still opt to apply a layer or two of gesso. Gesso is a primer made up of an acrylic polymer binder, chalk, and pigment, and comes in white, clear (both can be tinted with acrylic paint), and a range of colors. To prepare a substrate such as paper, canvas, or wood, apply a thin layer of gesso with a flat brush. Another thin layer can be added after the first one is dry. Gesso acts as a barrier between the substrate and the paint, preventing the paint from soaking through.

Textiles

Most acrylic paints can be used on textiles as is, but it's best to use paint specially made for fabric. Another option is to add a fabric medium to acrylic paint, which makes it adhere better to the textile fibers. Since acrylic paint is hard when dry, painted fabrics can become stiff and rough after being painted. Always wash and dry the fabric before painting to stretch the fibers. After painting, most acrylic textile paints can be set by ironing, which prevents the design from bleeding after washing.

Wood and Clay

Wood and clay are great surfaces for acrylic paint. A bit of preparation may be needed, such as sanding to even the surface before applying the paint. Thick and opaque acrylic paints work best on these kinds of materials, as more transparent paints require several coats.

Glass and Stone

Glass can be tricky to paint because of its smooth surface, but it's not impossible. I've done quite a few works on glass with acrylics; it just takes more applications to get an opaque look. Paint adheres quite easily to stone with texture, and there are many shapes and sizes to choose from.

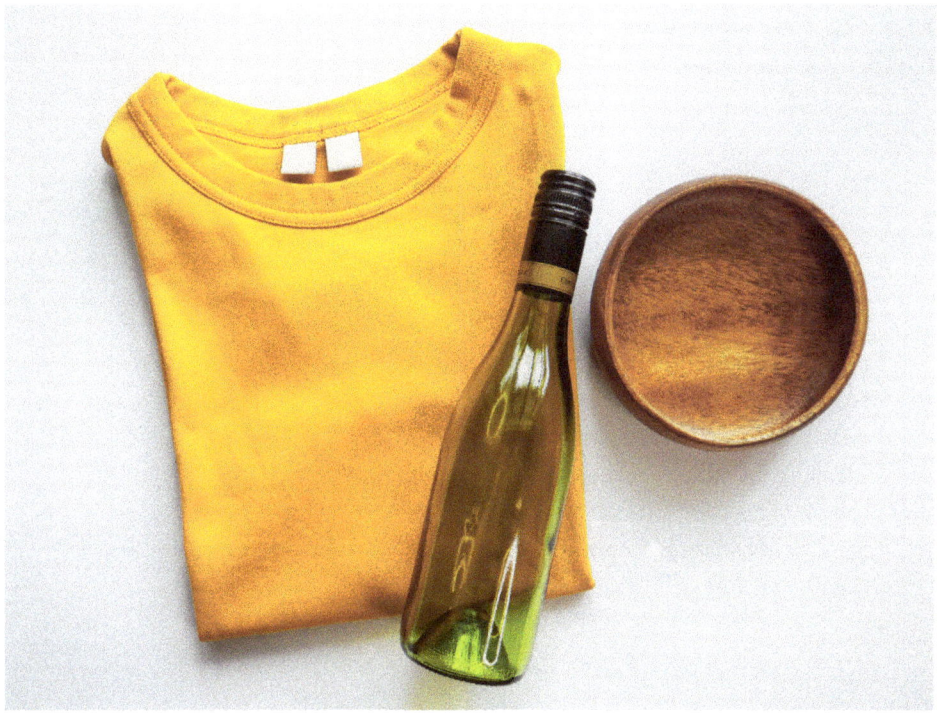

BRUSHES

Various types of brushes can be used to achieve different effects in paintings. Artists usually have preferences for certain brushes, just as writers may prefer specific pens because of the way they fit their hand or how the ink flows on paper. Here are some of my favorite types of brushes and examples of how I typically use them.

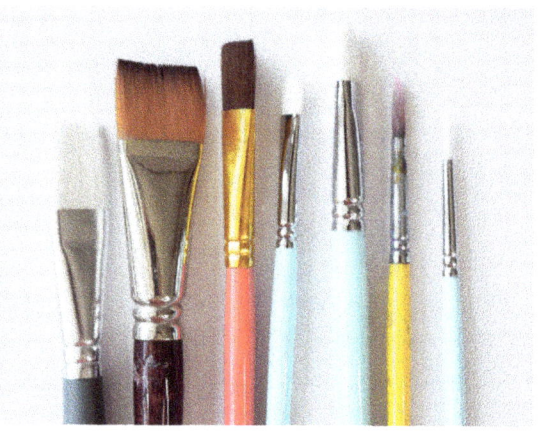

Round Brushes

Round brushes are my favorite because of their versatility. Big round brushes can hold a lot of paint and are great for painting larger areas. Because the brush hair can form a point, these brushes can also be used to paint finer details.

Flat Brushes

Flat brushes have rectangular or square ends that are handy for quickly filling an area with long, continuous strokes. The corner of the brush can also be used to create blunt edges and corners.

SYNTHETIC OR NATURAL?

- - -

Brushes are available with natural or synthetic hairs or bristles. I find synthetic brushes work best with acrylics. When acrylic dries, it hardens like plastic, which doesn't bode well for natural-hair brushes—especially if they're not cleaned thoroughly. Synthetic bristles are more durable and maintain their shape well even with constant application of heavy paints such as acrylics, making them great for experienced painters and beginners alike. I don't recommend using watercolor brushes for acrylic painting.

Filbert Brushes

Filbert brushes combine the best qualities of round and flat brushes. Most of the bristles are flat, but the end of the brush is rounded like an oval. These brushes are especially good for creating soft blends and painting large areas.

Angled Brushes

Angled brushes are similar to flat brushes but are slanted at the tip, making them ideal for painting corners and creating thin lines. These can also be used to paint leaves and branches.

Palette Knives

Palette knives are steel blades with a wooden handle that come in different shapes and sizes and are used to mix or apply paints. Artists typically use these tools to apply a thick layer of paint, similar to adding frosting to cupcakes. The knives can also be used to scrape off excess paint and create rigid and rough line details.

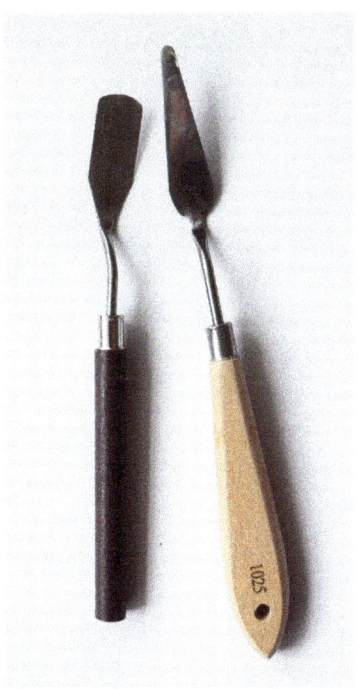

Palette knives

CARING FOR BRUSHES

Acrylic paints can easily destroy your brushes. Here are some tips for caring for and cleaning your brushes so they'll last a long time.

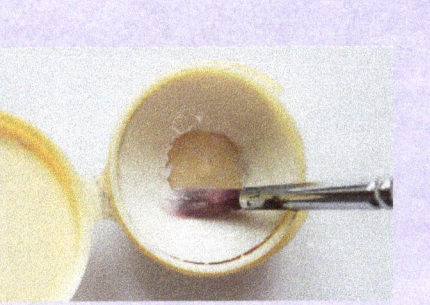

- Never let acrylic paint dry on your brush. Removing paint can be difficult (and sometimes impossible) once it has dried.
- Remove excess paint from the brush using a rag, which can be washed and reused.
- Soak the brush in warm water, then swish it around to help remove any paint residue. Don't leave the brush soaking in the water, as it will warp the bristles.
- Use a mild hand soap or specialized brush cleaner to wash the bristles, then rinse away the soap. Repeat this step until there is no longer any color coming from the brush when you submerge it in water.
- Squeeze out the excess water and place the brush horizontally on a surface to dry.

MEDIUMS

Mediums are acrylic-based substances that can be added to paint to change its properties. Mediums can extend the paint's drying time, make paint look glossier or more matte, add texture, make the consistency thicker or thinner, and more. Using mediums is optional, but they make painting more interesting. The lessons and projects in this book provide an opportunity to try some of these mediums. Here are some mediums that are fun to use.

Gloss and Matte Mediums

Mix these mediums with your paint to add a bit more sheen to your work or make paint more matte, mixing them well before applying the paint to your substrate. Both of these mediums can be mixed together, allowing you to customize the gloss/matte effect in your painting.

Glazing and Gel Mediums

Glazing mediums allow you to thin acrylic paint in preparation for glazing, a process that is covered in "Basic Painting Techniques" (see page 33). Gel mediums do the opposite, thickening paint so you can use acrylics more like a paste to produce noticeable textures.

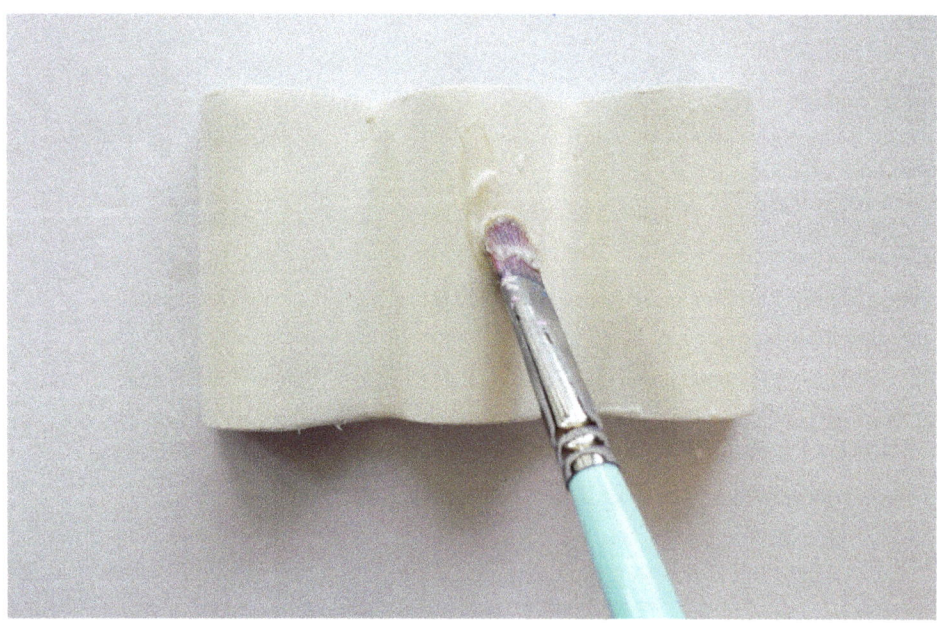

Modeling Paste or Texture Medium

This medium changes the consistency of acrylic paints, making them heavier and thicker, and is useful for adding texture to a painting. Mix the medium with paint or use it directly on the canvas on its own. Shape it however you like, and it will hold that form until it dries. You can then paint over the medium to add color.

Retarder

Retarders help slow down the drying time of acrylic paint, allowing you to have more time to blend colors and make changes to your work.

Varnish

Varnishes are applied after a painting is fully dry as a way to preserve the work. These mediums resist the damage of UV rays and dust, allowing paintings to last longer.

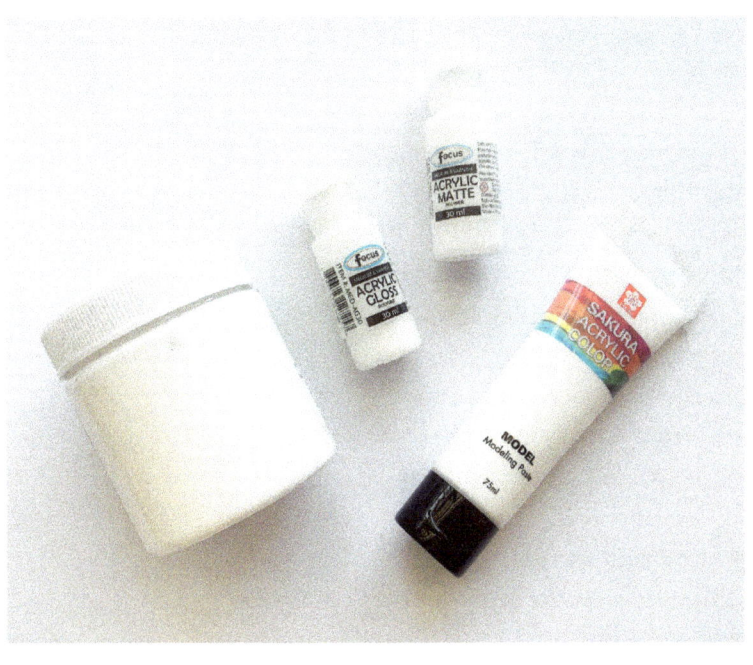

Modeling paste

USING MEDIUMS
— • • • —

Here are some tips for using mediums effectively in your painting.

- Add mediums after you've mixed colors. This prevents paints from becoming too runny.
- Avoid adding too many mediums because they thin the paint. Use mediums only when you need to achieve a certain effect.
- Experiment with ratios of medium to paint to achieve the effect you're looking for.
- Use only acrylic-based mediums with acrylic paint because other types (such as oil-based mediums) have different properties not suited for acrylics.

MISCELLANEOUS TOOLS AND MATERIALS

These materials will help you enjoy the painting process.

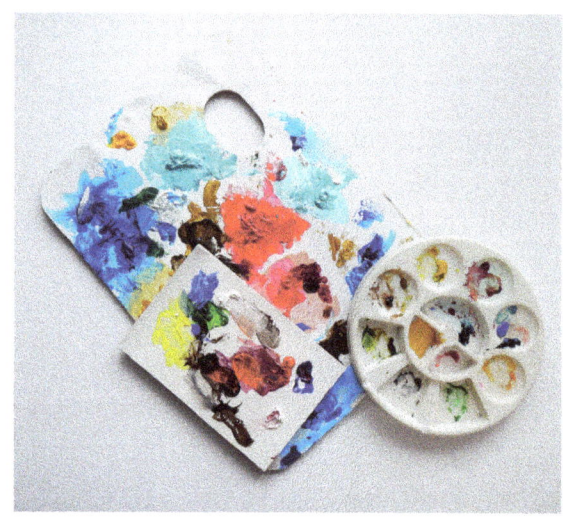

Mixing Palette

I find that plastic palettes work best with acrylics. Once the paint dries, you can peel the paint off. Wooden and ceramic palettes can't be cleaned this easily. Tear-off palette paper pads, however, are a great alternative.

Pencil and Eraser

These are easily the two materials I cannot live without! I like to sketch my ideas before starting to paint, so a pencil and eraser are the first things I reach for. I prefer using mechanical pencils with different colored leads, as they are consistently sharp, and dust-free erasers because I tend to erase a lot when drawing (which is completely fine).

MAKING A STAY-WET PALETTE
- - -

If you've mixed a large batch of acrylic paint and would like to store it for future use, you can keep it in a stay-wet palette. These are available at art supply stores, but you can also make one out of paper towels, wax paper, and a sandwich-size reusable plastic storage container with an airtight lid.

- Wet the paper towel and put it at the bottom of the plastic container. The paper towel doesn't have to be completely saturated.
- Place a piece of wax paper on top of the paper towel. For a large quantity of paint, double the wax paper so it doesn't tear.
- Transfer the leftover acrylic paint to the wax paper. Once the container is sealed, the paint will stay wet and be usable for a few days.
- Be sure to change and rewet the paper towels so they don't dry out. You should also occasionally mist the paints.

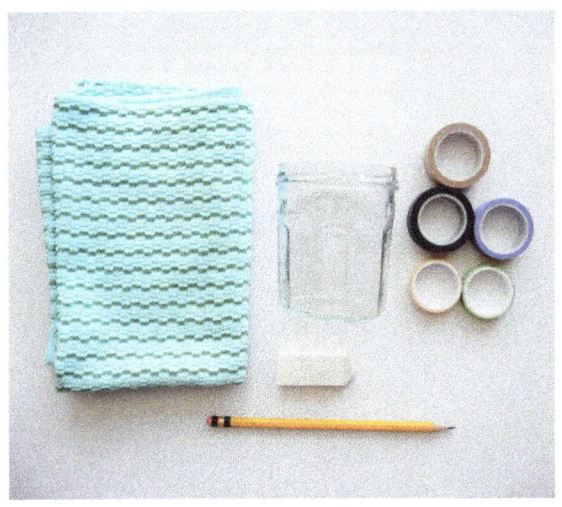 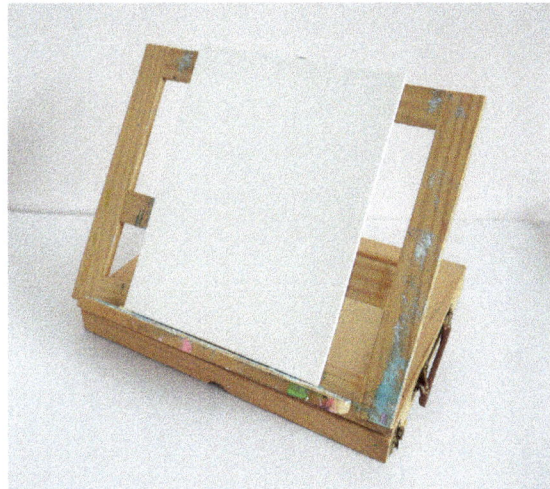

Water Container

Clean water in containers can be used for cleaning brushes and thinning paint. Some artists prefer having two separate containers, but I use one for everything. However, don't forget to refresh the water when it becomes dirty and murky.

Craft Tapes

Craft or washi tape can be used to create a clean border around your paper or to block off an area you don't want painted. These low-tack tapes allow you to safely peel them off without damaging the paper, but do a test first to make sure.

Easel

Tabletop or floor easels conveniently prop up your work, allowing you to be more comfortable while painting. Easels are especially useful if you're working on a large painting for longer periods. Painting on an easel also helps achieve better perspective, since you're viewing your work vertically, the way most paintings are shown.

Cloth Rag or Paper Towels

I keep a cloth rag beside me when I paint. Rags are handy for wiping excess water from brushes, cleaning brushes, and wiping up spills (which I'm prone to doing!). Cloth rags are also reusable; just wash them when they get dirty.

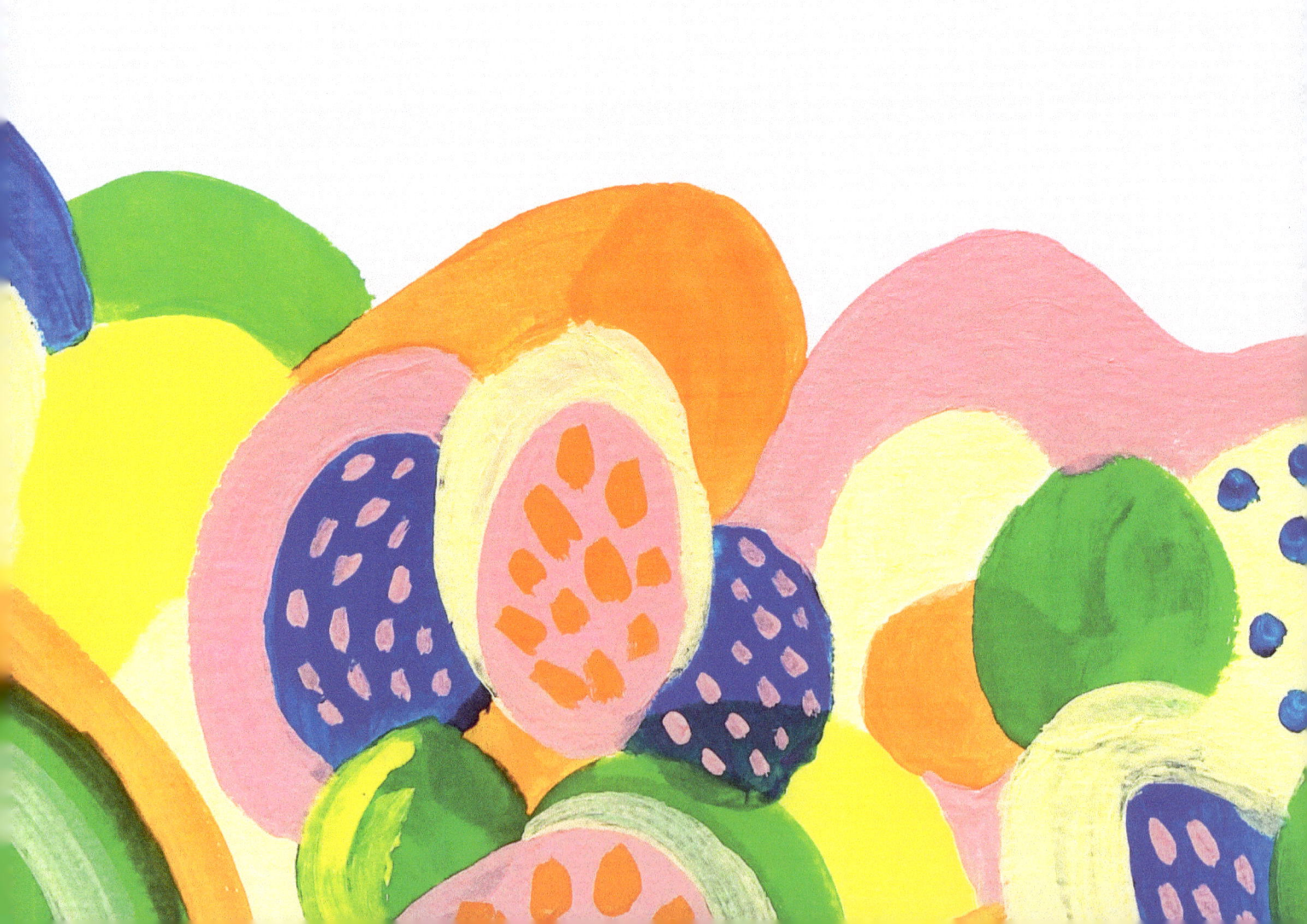

2

GETTING STARTED

- - - - - -

Beginning a painting is always the most challenging part, especially if the process is entirely new to you. Sitting in front of a blank canvas or paper, thinking about what you should paint, wondering whether the piece will turn out good or bad—these thoughts are enough to scare anyone out of starting. Know that these feelings are entirely normal. I've been painting for years, and there are days when I stare at a piece of paper hoping I can produce something. In my experience, planning and preparation help me move beyond this paralysis and toward painting. In this chapter, we'll go through preparations and initial lessons that will help ease you into painting with acrylics.

SETTING UP YOUR WORKSPACE

Think about the place where you'll paint and how you can make it a conducive learning environment. The spot could be a cozy corner in your home or a place where you feel energized to spend time lost in the creative process. I prefer to paint near a window for the natural light, but it's completely fine to use a lamp or any light source that will help you see your work clearly. Having a comfortable go-to place where you can practice painting is a wonderful way to keep the hobby going.

No matter where your workspace is located, acrylic paints should be stored in airtight containers and kept away from direct light, heat, and humidity. If you get paint stains on your table, use soap and hot water or a rubbing alcohol-soaked rag to remove the stain (make sure the table surface won't be damaged by the alcohol before using). You may have to hold the rag on the stain for a few minutes to fully remove it.

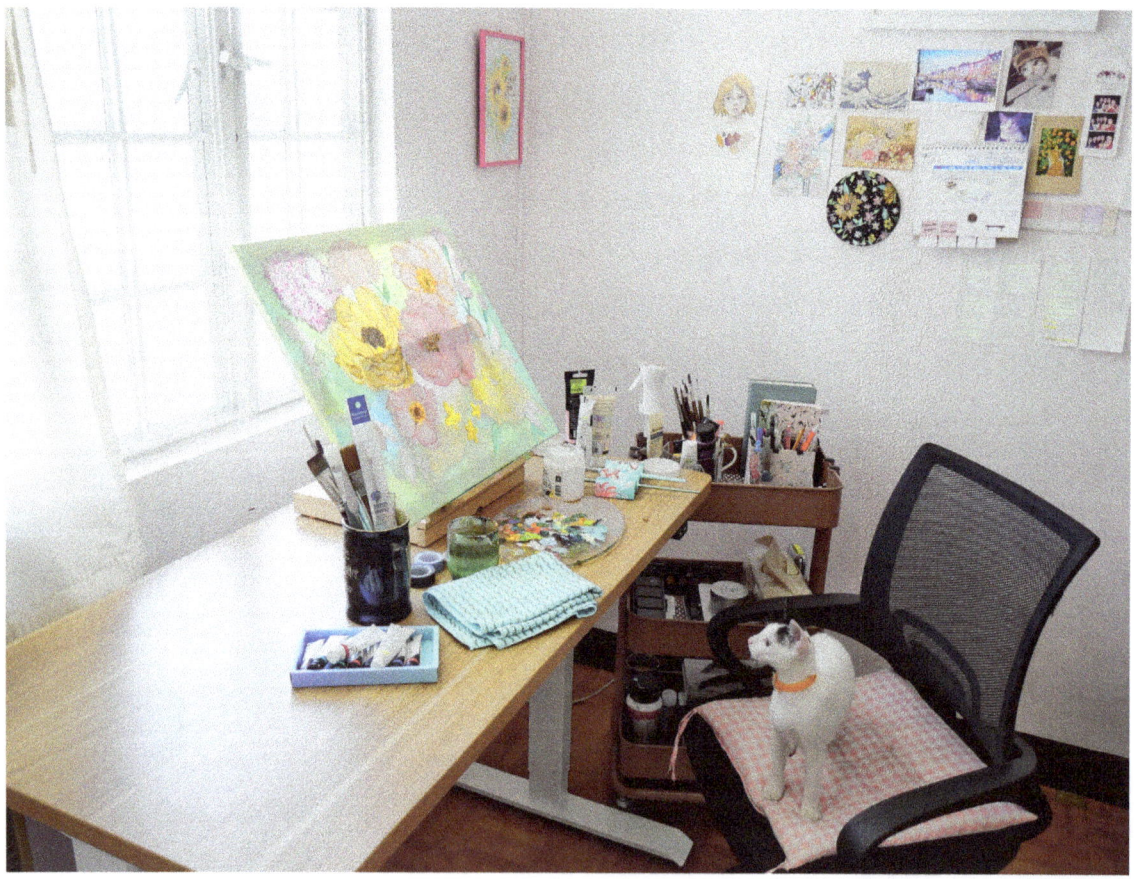

COLOR THEORY

Understanding color isn't just essential to painting—it also makes this activity so much fun to do. Everyone has a preference when it comes to selecting colors, as they're drawn to some and not a fan of others. This makes our artwork special and unique. This overview shows how we'll use colors effectively in our paintings.

The easiest visual guide to color is the color wheel. The wheel consists of the primary colors—red, yellow, and blue, which are the purest colors. Also included are the secondary colors—green, orange, and purple, which are produced by combining each of the primary colors with one another. The wheel also contains the tertiary colors—red-violet, red-orange, blue-violet, blue-green, yellow-green, and yellow-orange, which are created by combining primary and secondary colors.

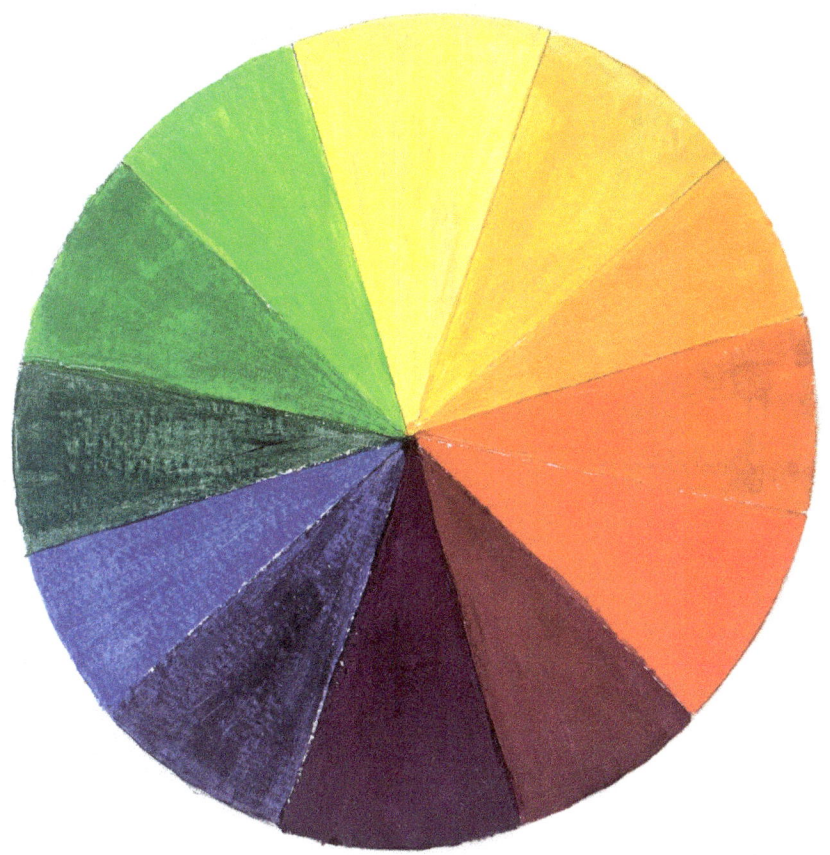

By using the color wheel, we can select colors that go well together, making a painting look balanced and harmonious. Here are some suggestions for finding colors that work well together.

- Complementary colors are opposite each other on the color wheel.
- Analogous colors are adjacent to one another.
- Triadic colors form an equal triangle with one another on the color wheel.
- Red, orange, and yellow are warm colors, while green, blue, and purple are cool colors. Warm colors tend to pop while cool ones recede. Most paintings usually consist of both warm and cool colors.

COLOR MIXING METHODS

- - -

When two complementary colors are mixed together (such as green and red) they produce a neutral color, sometimes referred to as mud. This blend is useful if you need to neutralize a color. To create it, find a color's opposite on the color wheel. Mix them, and you've dulled the original color. I often use this technique to create shadow colors. If I don't have black or gray paint, I can easily mix two complementary colors to create a neutral shade. Try mixing complementary colors in different ratios to see the effects.

These color mixing methods are only a few of the ways you can use color blends in your paintings, but there are many more ways to select and mix colors using the color wheel. I always encourage my students to experiment and discover the techniques that work best for them.

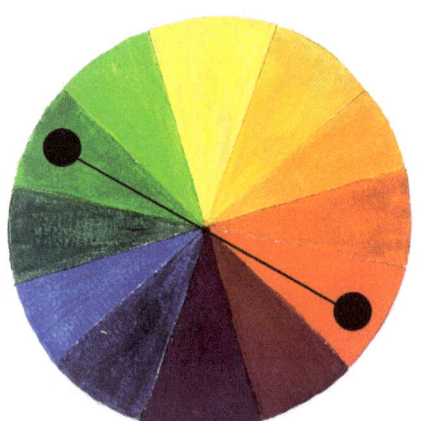

Complementary colors

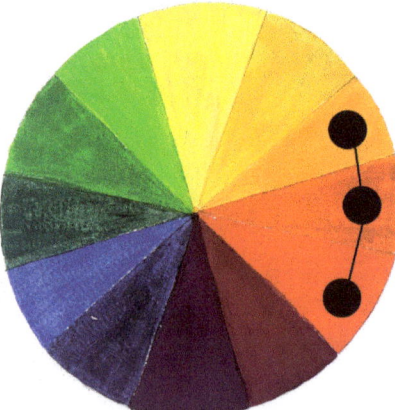

Analogous colors

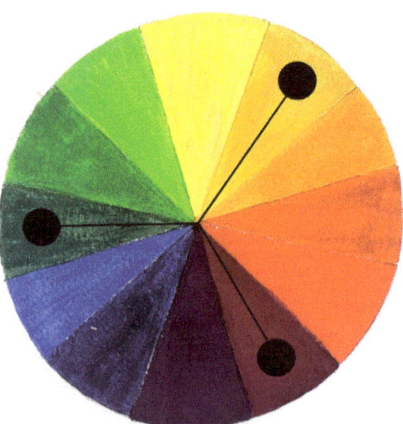

Triadic colors

My Acrylic Color Palette

In the lessons and projects throughout this book, you'll see straightforward paint colors in the materials list, such as red, blue, yellow, and so on. I usually have two types of each basic color, as they can make a difference in achieving the right color mix: one warm and one cool. For example, one shade of red may have more orange or pink tones, and a shade of blue may have more purple or green tones. (See below.) I also use other colors that add interest to my palette and complement many different subjects. These colors are also listed on page 30, along with the subjects for which I usually use them. I highly recommend starting with the basic palette and then slowly introducing new colors once you have become comfortable mixing these basic shades. Too many color choices can be overwhelming; I've seen many students who are new to painting freeze up when confronted with too many options.

BASIC PALETTE

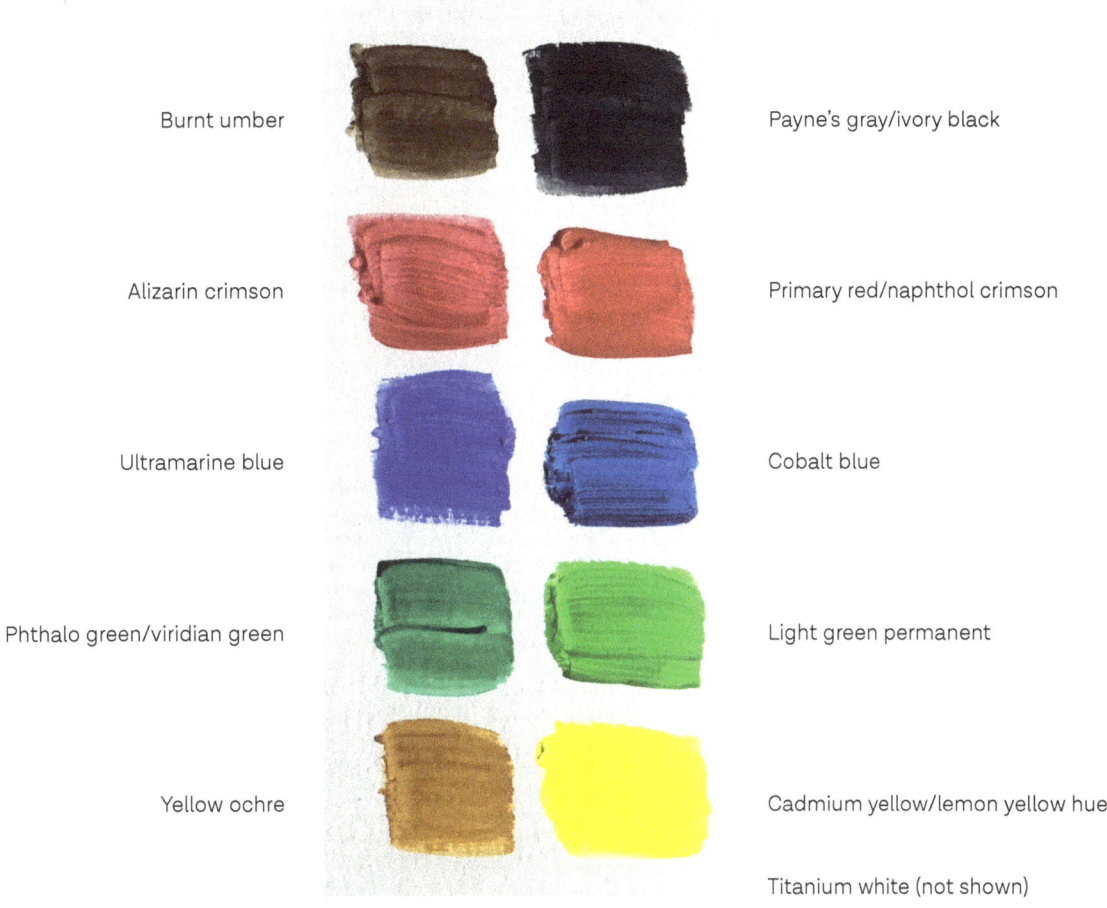

Burnt umber

Payne's gray/ivory black

Alizarin crimson

Primary red/naphthol crimson

Ultramarine blue

Cobalt blue

Phthalo green/viridian green

Light green permanent

Yellow ochre

Cadmium yellow/lemon yellow hue

Titanium white (not shown)

OTHER COLORS

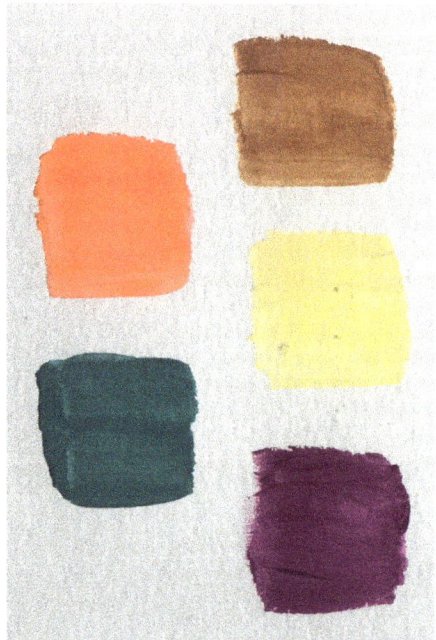

Cadmium orange hue: for florals and landscapes and for creating a neutral color when mixed with ultramarine blue.

Turquoise blue: for skies, seascapes, bright backgrounds, and adding interest to floral paintings

Raw sienna: for florals, landscapes, portraits, and still lifes

Naples yellow hue: for florals and skin tones

Deep violet/dioxazine purple: for creating a neutral color when mixed with burnt umber

COLOR INSPIRATIONS

— — —

The color wheel is a great source for color inspiration, but there are countless other ways to find beautiful color combinations. Nature is one. Skies, fields, and flowers provide so many ideas for choosing colors. I live in a city and often take photographs during my travels. I compile photos of interesting subjects on my phone or computer so they're ready to pull up whenever I need a boost of inspiration. You can also create color swatches to use as a guide when painting. Swatches allow you to place colors side by side and see how one shade complements another. Creating a color palette before working on a painting enables you to plan ahead and makes your work look more cohesive.

Color Exercise

This fun color exercise will help you become acquainted with mixing colors. You'll need acrylic paints in primary colors (red, blue, and yellow), plus black and white; a mixing palette; acrylic paper, canvas paper, or watercolor paper; and a size 6 flat brush. *Optional:* Section the paper into rectangular color swatches using low-tack craft tape or washi tape.

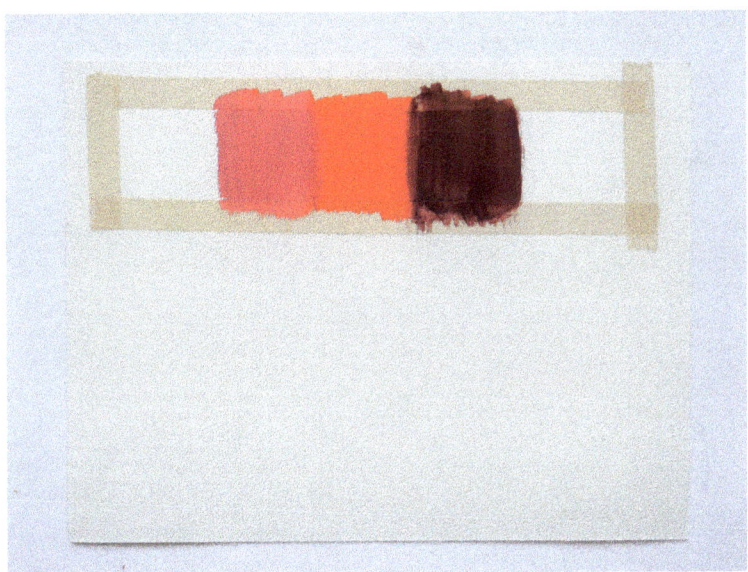

1 When a color is mixed with black, it's called a shade, and when it's mixed with white, it's called a tint. Add a swatch of plain red to the middle of the box. Mix red paint with black to produce a reddish-black shade and add it to the rectangle to the right of the plain red. Mix red and white to produce a tint and add that to the rectangle to the left of the plain red. This is one of the most-used techniques for color mixing and will play a huge role in the lessons in this book.

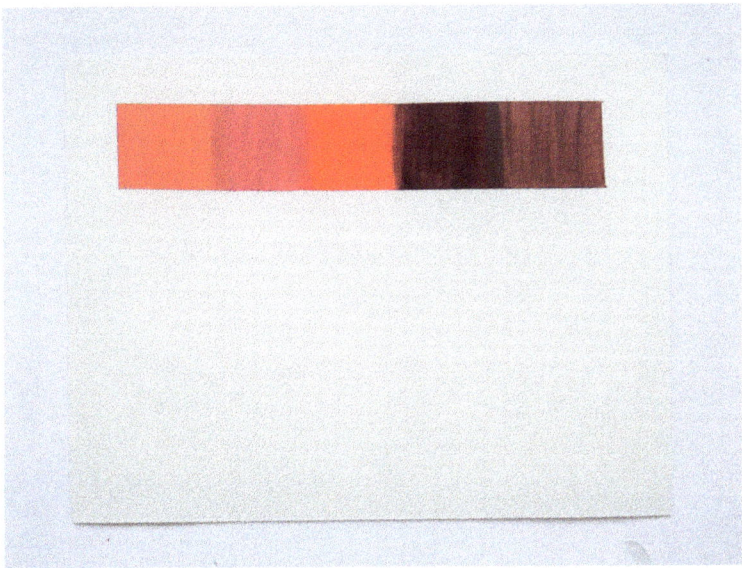

2 You can also mix any other color with a shade or a tint. See what colors you create when you add yellow to the red shade and tint. The far left swatch is red + white + yellow, and the far right is red + black + yellow. Allow the paint to dry and remove the tape if you used it.

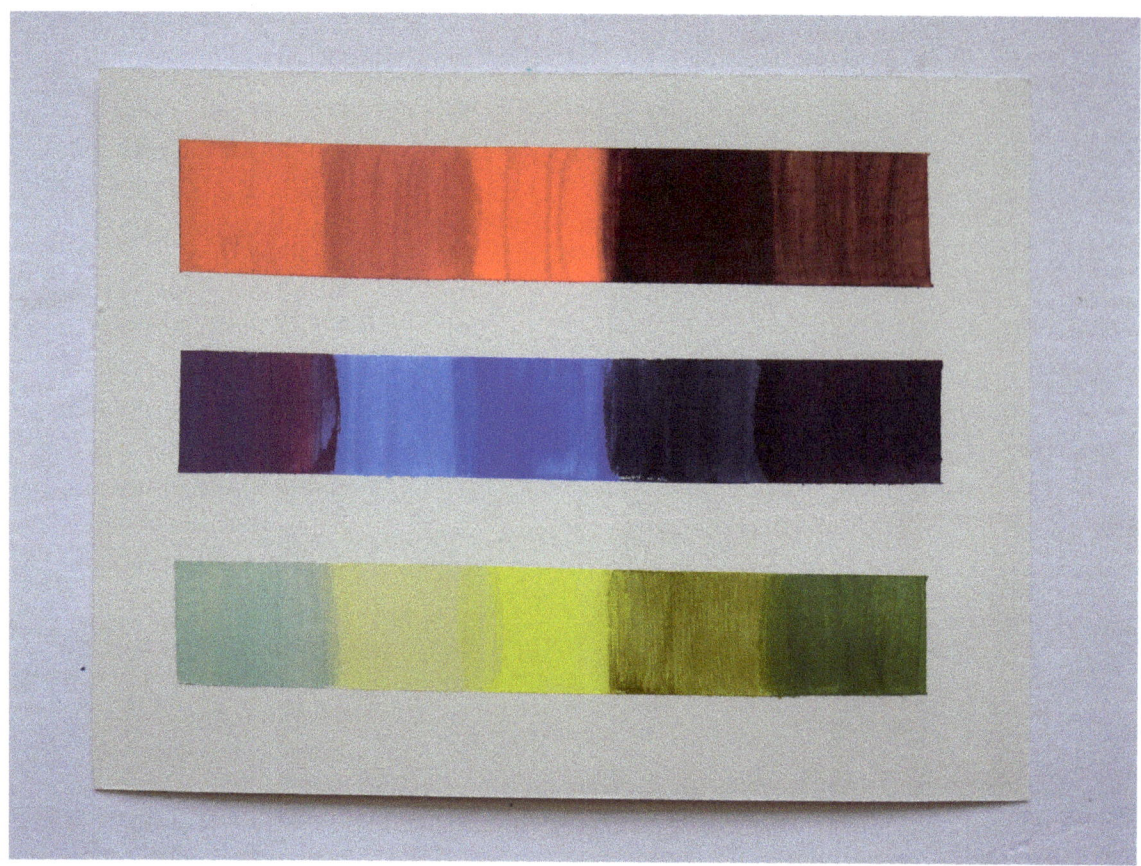

3 Use blue and yellow for the next two exercises. Mix the main color with black and white before mixing it with another primary color. For the middle swatch, I mixed blue with red, and for the bottom swatch, I blended yellow with blue.

Isn't this color palette satisfying to look at? This simple exercise is a fun way to learn how to create multiple hues using basic primary colors, plus black and white. Experiment on your own to see what colors you can create.

PAYNE'S GRAY

– – –

Payne's gray is my go-to color when it comes to darkening any basic color. Payne's gray is a beautiful dark bluish-gray shade used by many artists as an alternative to black. I prefer Payne's gray (or any other dark neutral shade) over black because incorporating black in a painting can make it look harsh. Look closely at shadows and you'll often see that they're not solid black, but more of a dark blue or purplish shade. Payne's gray also blends well with other colors in a painting, whereas black can sometimes draw attention away from other colors. When choosing colors for your paint arsenal, give Payne's gray a try. I'm sure you'll fall in love with this shade, as I have.

BASIC PAINTING TECHNIQUES

Acrylics are easy to work with, but to get the most out of this medium, we'll first explore some popular painting methods. These brush techniques will enable you to build the basic skills you need, and you'll be able to apply them in the lessons later in the book.

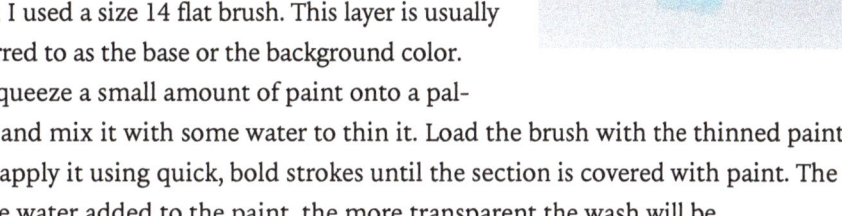

Flat Wash

This brush technique allows you to apply a block of color to a surface. This is usually done with a broader and bigger brush to quickly cover the surface; I used a size 14 flat brush. This layer is usually referred to as the base or the background color.

Squeeze a small amount of paint onto a palette and mix it with some water to thin it. Load the brush with the thinned paint and apply it using quick, bold strokes until the section is covered with paint. The more water added to the paint, the more transparent the wash will be.

Glazing

A glaze is similar to a wash, but a glaze sits on top of a base layer, allowing the color underneath to shine through. To apply a glaze correctly, the paint layer underneath must be completely dry to prevent it from being lifted as more layers are added. An acrylic glazing medium added to the paint makes it more translucent and also extends its drying time.

To create a glaze, paint a flat wash and let it dry. Add a little paint to your palette and then combine it with the acrylic medium using a flat brush. The glaze can be a different color from the wash, and there should be more medium in the mixture than paint. The number of glazes you can apply is limitless, so this technique is something you can use frequently to add interest to your paintings.

Differences exist between glazes and washes. A wash sinks into paper or flows over it, depending on the substrate. Because a glaze uses an acrylic medium to thin the paint, it has more body, allowing the paint mixture to appear as though it's floating on top of the layer underneath. The bottom right image shows the difference between a glaze (left) and a wash (right).

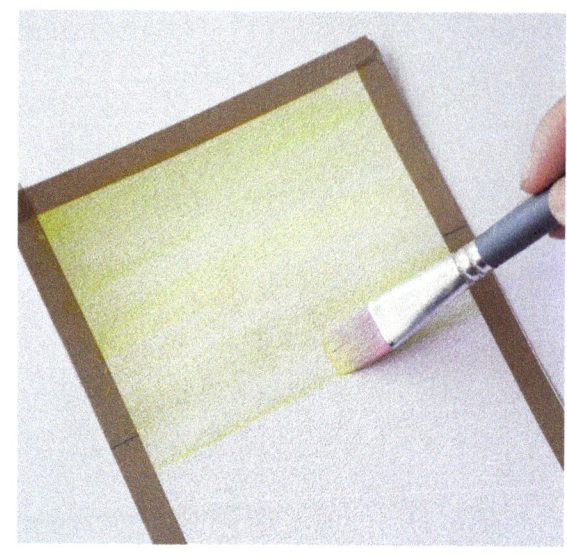

TIP

Acrylics are quick to dry, so keep a spray bottle filled with water nearby and lightly mist your palette from time to time. Once acrylic paint dries, you will not be able to reactivate it using water, so be cautious with it as we don't want to waste our precious paints.

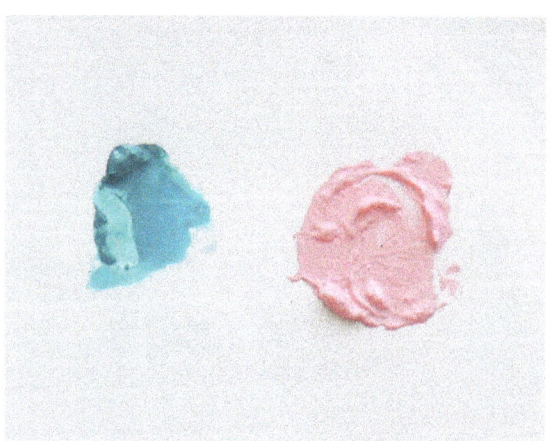

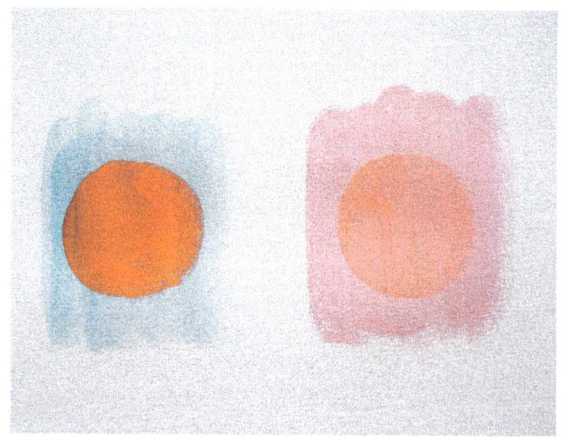

Dry-Brush Technique

Dry brushing is a great way to add interest to a painting. Use a relatively dry brush—I recommend a stiff brush such as hog hair—load the brush tip with paint, and dab the brush on a paper towel to remove any extra paint before painting. Use quick, light strokes so the marks appear as if they were scribbled with colored pencil or crayon. This technique is particularly helpful when adding effects to woods, trees, animal fur, and grass.

Adding Texture

Acrylic paints can be thickly layered on surfaces and acrylic mediums, such as modeling paste or texture gel, can add even more body to regular acrylic paint. By painting this simple tree you'll learn how adding texture gives dimension to the leaves.

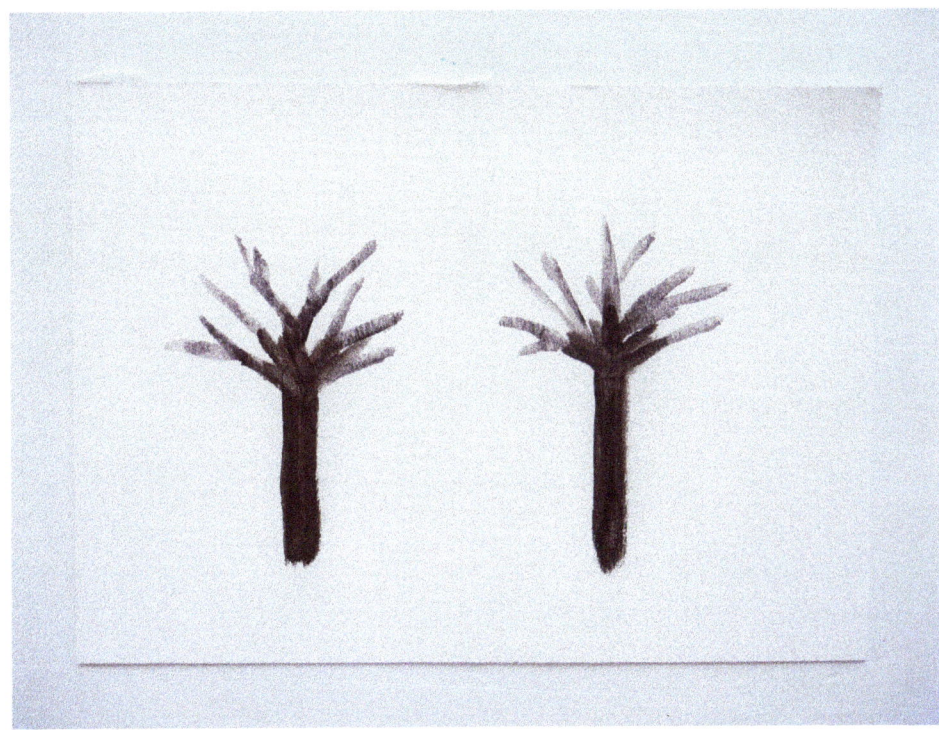

1 Paint two simple tree trunks and branches using brown acrylic paint and a flat brush. To create the trunk, paint a vertical wash of brown about ½ inch (1.25 cm) thick. Add short branches around the top, extending them in different directions.

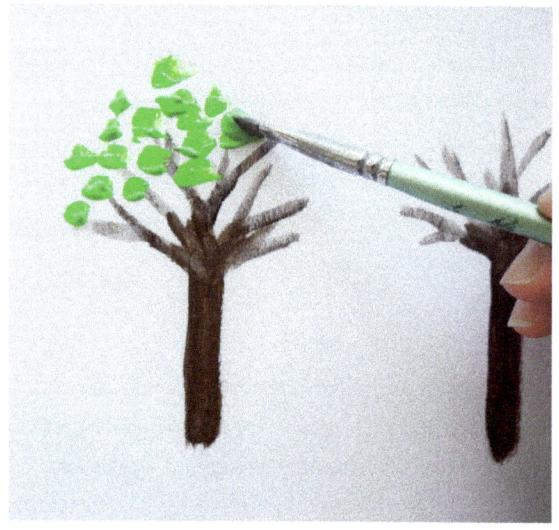

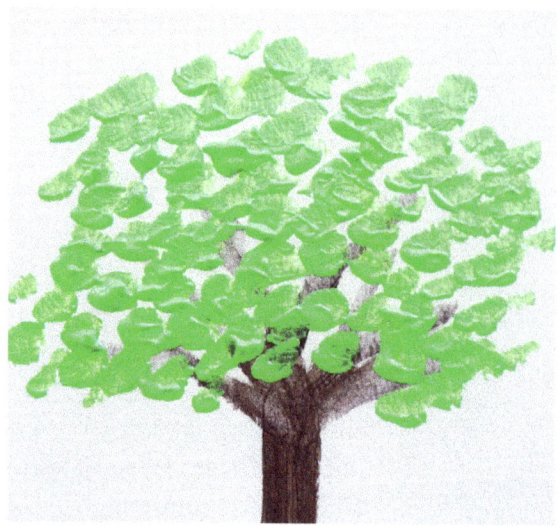

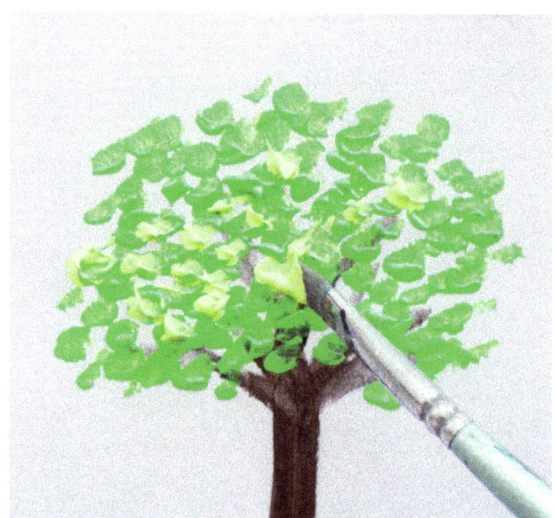

2 Texture effects require a lot of paint, so make sure you have enough on your palette. Scoop up a pea-size amount of primary green from the palette with a flat brush and touch just the tip of the brush onto the branches of the tree on the left. The paint should form a small, thick blob and slowly release from the brush. The more paint on the brush, the thicker the texture will be. Allow the first leaf to dry and then add more leaves with the same technique, using a mix of two parts green paint with one part yellow.

TIP

Thick applications of acrylic paint and mediums tend to dry slowly. Depending on the thickness of the paint and weather conditions, it may take several days for a painting to dry thoroughly.

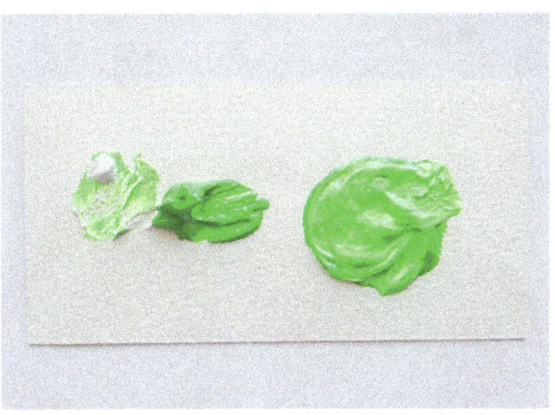 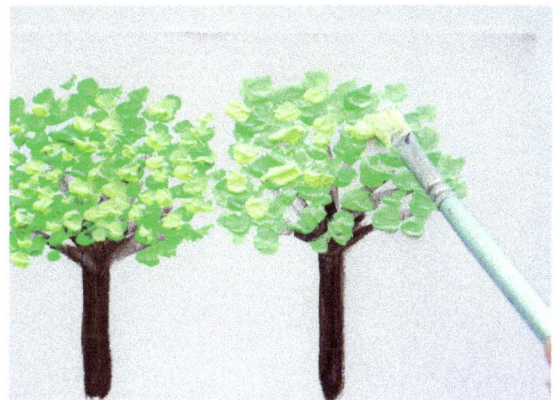

3 Mix a bit of modeling paste with primary green to create a thick, paste-like mixture. Use your flat brush to apply this mixture to the tree on the right the same way you applied paint in step 2. Do you notice a difference? By adding the modeling paste (or a texture gel medium), the acrylic paint is nearly the thickness of plaster, a consistency you can mold into shapes. Mix two parts green paint to one part yellow and add a bit of modeling paste. Use this mixture to add more leaves to the tree.

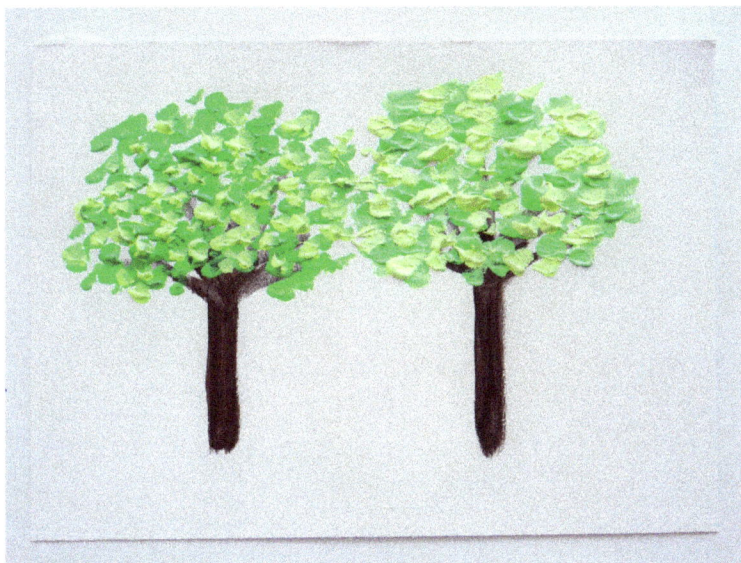

In this side-by-side comparison, you can see that the modeling paste leaves on the right have more dimension than the leaves on the left. Keep in mind that the leaves made with paint alone may flatten a bit as they dry, while the modeling paste leaves will retain their form better.

Some of the lessons in the book include texture effects, and you'll find more ways to use texture in your paintings.

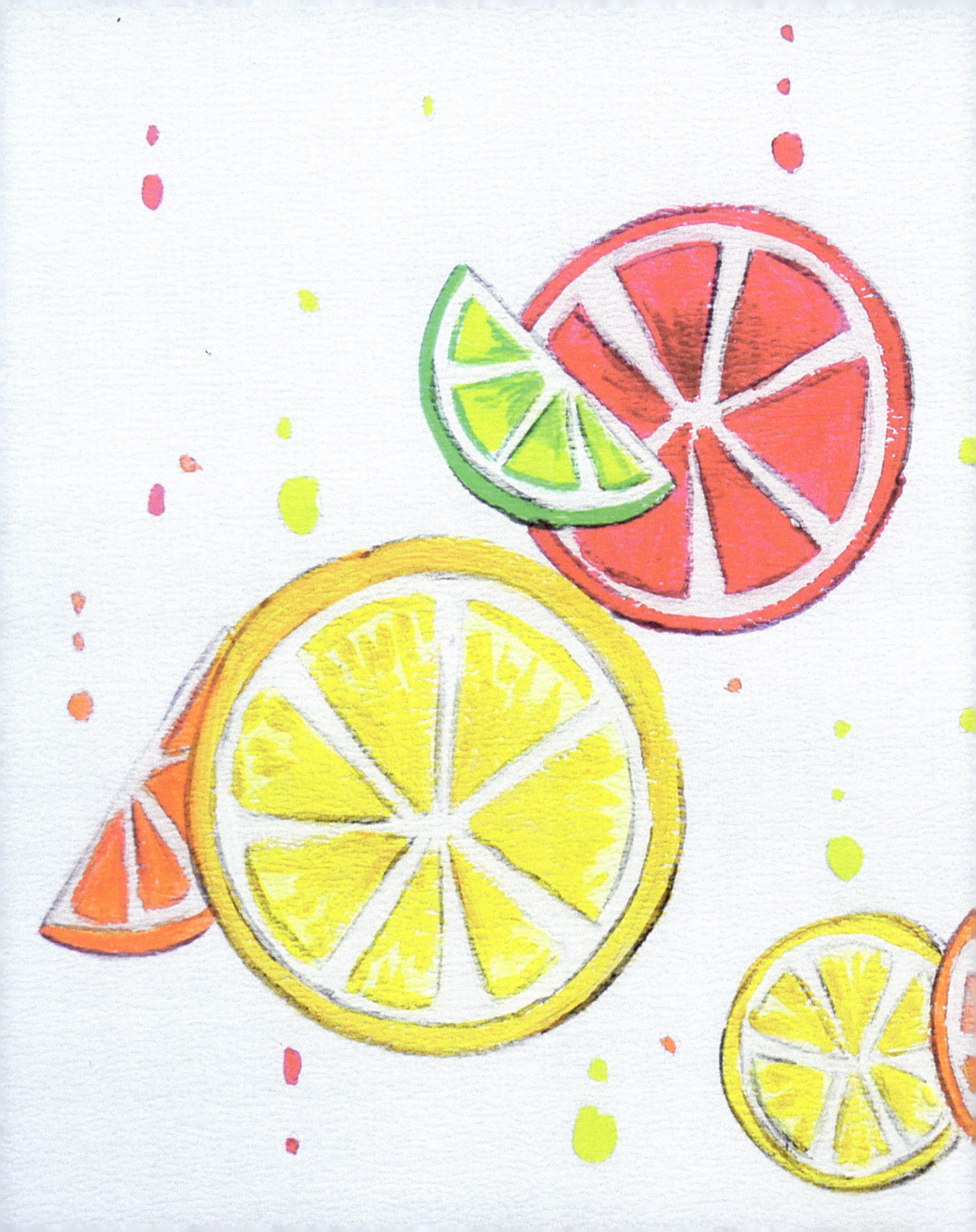

3

STILL LIFE

- - - - - -

The very first subject I painted as a kid was a huge watermelon on an equally huge canvas. During that painting session, I focused solely on making the fruit appear somewhat realistic. The fact that it was essentially a solid round shape on canvas made it less difficult to paint. This helped train my mind to look at real-life objects as they appear and try my best to capture them in a painting. Still life paintings can be made of different inanimate objects in various compositions. You can work from a photo or set up your own array of still life subjects at home. In this chapter, I'll walk you through how to make simple objects come alive using the concepts of light and shadow.

A SIMPLE ORANGE

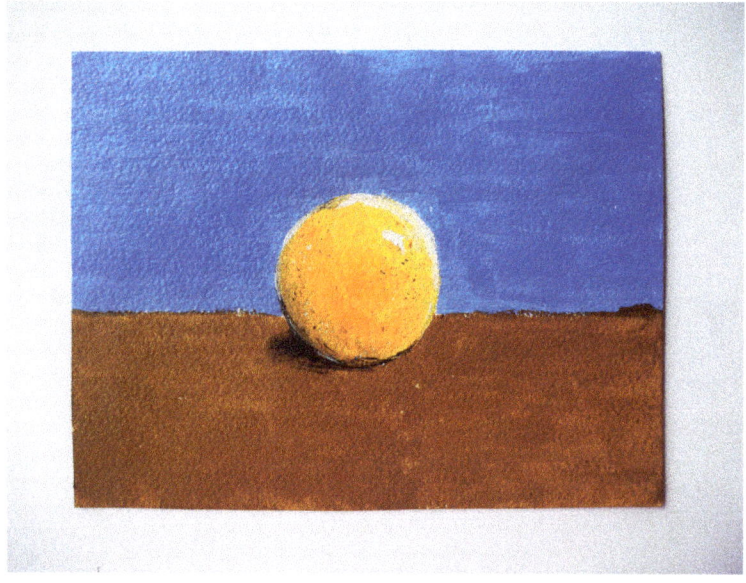

MATERIALS

- - -

Acrylic paints in orange,
   brown, blue, white,
   yellow, and black
   or Payne's gray

Canvas paper
   (I used a 5" × 6"
   [12.5 × 15.25 cm]
   piece.)

Pencil

Flat brush, size 4 or 6

Round brush, size 4 or 6

Mixing palette

In this lesson, you'll learn how to paint a simple subject—an orange—with a foreground and background to give it dimension. You'll build the depth of the painting gradually with these easy steps.

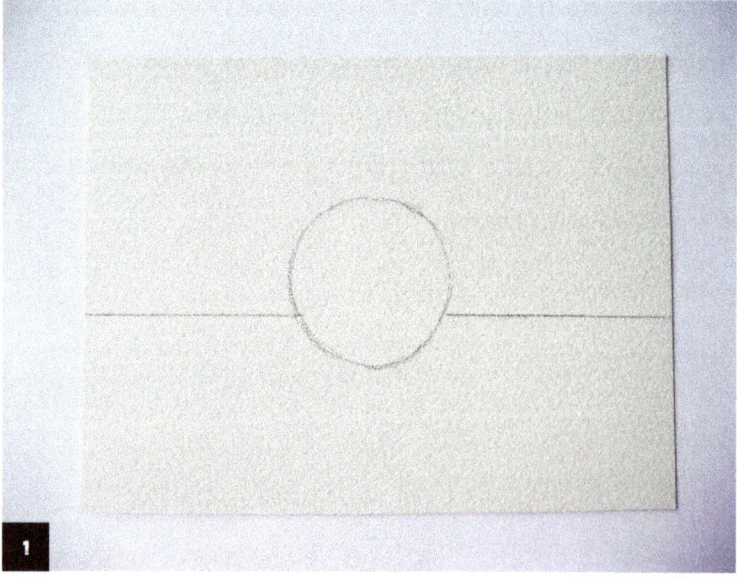

1 Sketch a horizontal line on the paper with a pencil to act as a guide for where to place the orange. I created a line a little less than halfway up the page. As a reference, you can use a real orange or a photo or conjure up an orange with your imagination.

2 Sketch a circle in the center of the paper; this will be your orange.

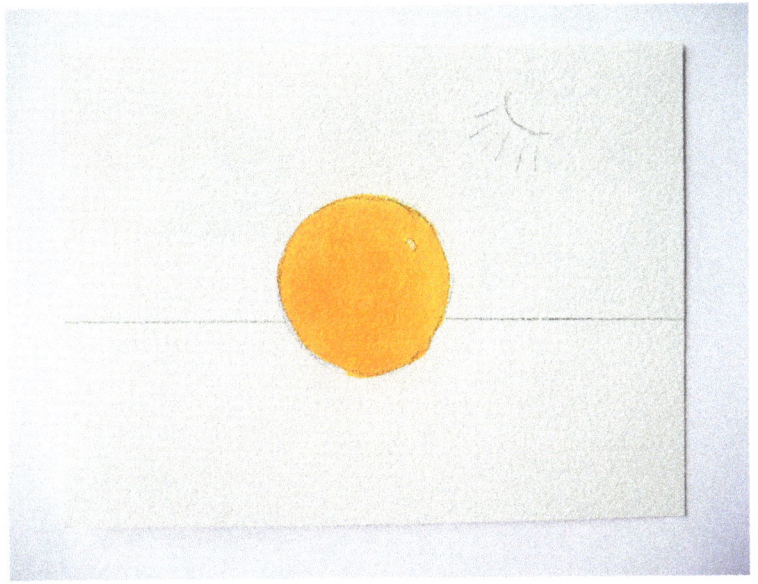

3 Block out the colors of the painting, beginning with the orange. Blocking is painting the initial colors in areas of the painting. Paint the circle with orange and allow it to dry.

(continued)

A PAINTED SKETCH

— — —

Sketching with paint is an alternative to sketching with a pencil. You can create a rough painted sketch, called an underpainting, using burnt umber or light earth tones. Many artists prefer creating an initial monochromatic layer before adding colors and more layers to their work. This simplifies the painting because the placement of light and shadow can be determined before more color is added.

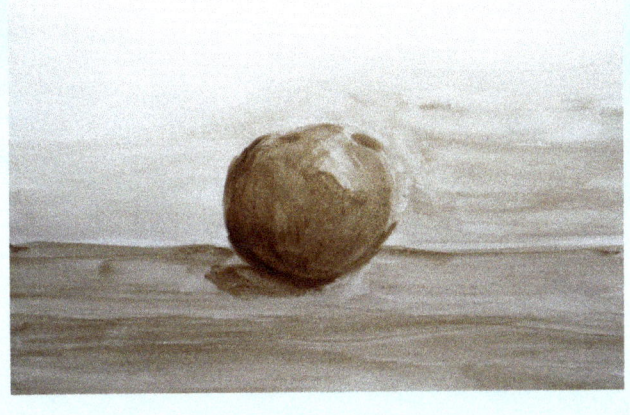

TIP

If you don't have orange paint, remember the color wheel (see page 27) and mix red and yellow to produce orange. Because acrylic paint dries a little darker, start with lighter mixes and gradually build deeper shades. To darken orange, add a brown hue such as raw umber.

4 Now that the base color of the subject has been established, move on to adding values. Values are the lights and darks of a painting, and they're important because they create a focal point as well as a dimensional effect. Make sure your paintings have a variation of light and dark tones.

5 Imagine a light source; I placed it at the top right of the painting. Add a lighter orange or yellow paint to the side of the orange facing the light. Dab a bit of white paint where the light would directly hit, making it the lightest part of the subject. Mix a small amount of brown paint with orange and apply it opposite the light source, to the underside of the orange, to create a shadow. Paint the background blue. Adding this darker color will make the warmer one—orange—look brighter.

6 Paint the foreground. I chose brown. By adding color to the foreground and background you can assess what the painting may lack or what can be enhanced.

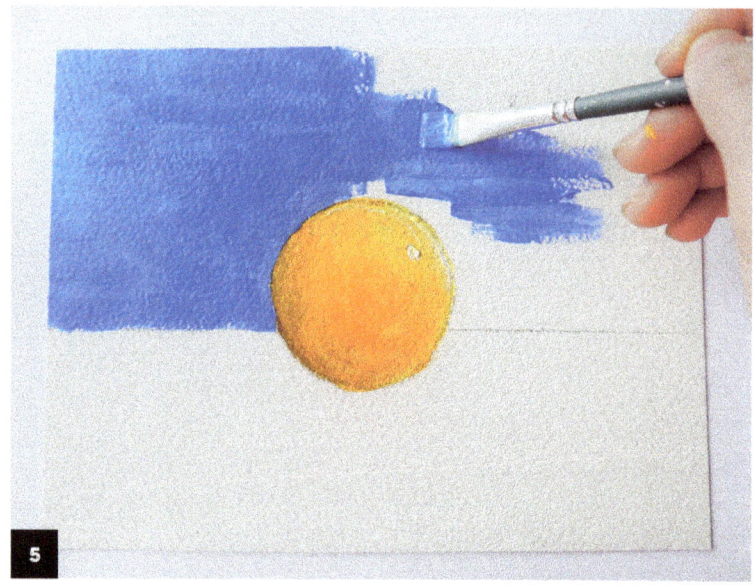

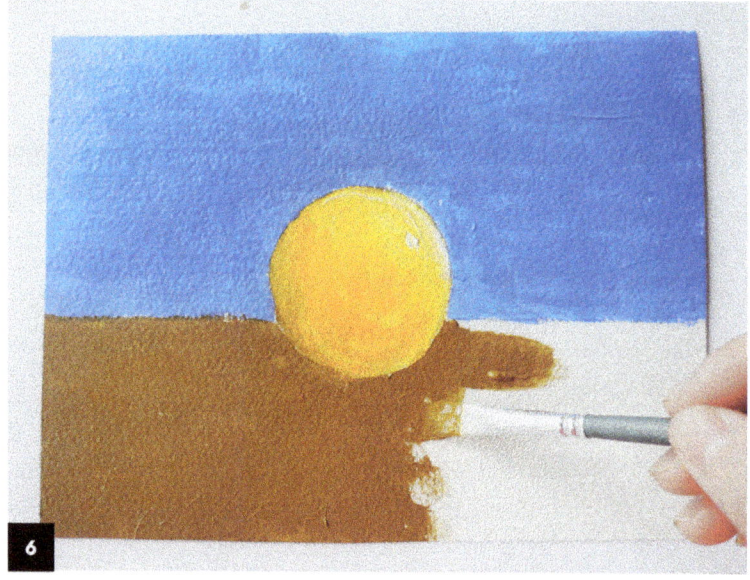

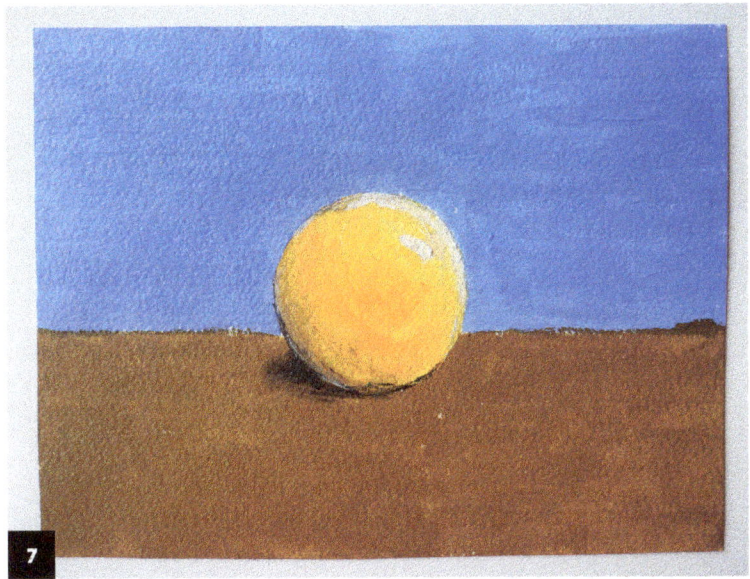

7 Add darker colors beneath the orange to create a shadow—this should be opposite the light source, where light is at a minimum. Mixing two complementary colors (in this case blue and orange) produces a dark neutral color that works well when creating shadows. You can also opt to use black or Payne's gray. Add a touch of white to the top part of the orange to show how the fruit reflects the light. I also added a tiny bit of white to the shadow underneath. A hint of reflected light often appears at the top of a shadow.

8 Add some tiny dots to the orange with the tip of a paintbrush. I added bits of brown and white to simulate the texture of the fruit.

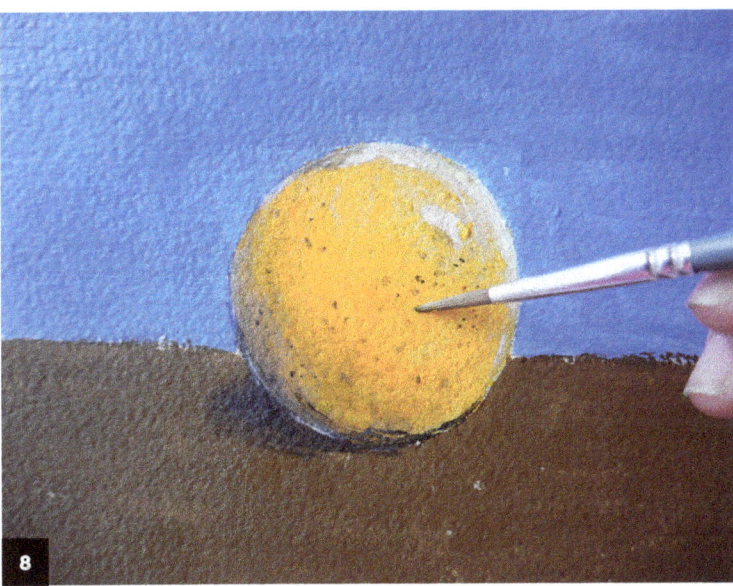

PURPLE GRAPES

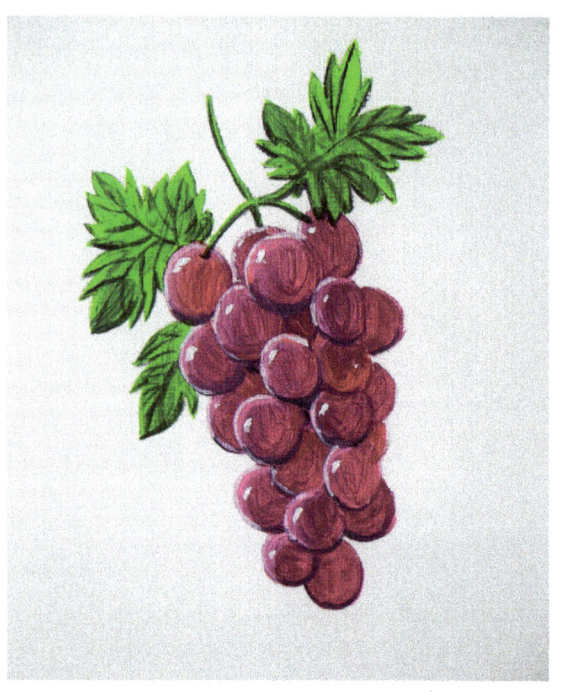

MATERIALS

Inspiration photo, a real cluster of grapes, or a template (see page 139)

Acrylic paints in purple (or mix red and blue), yellow, green, white, and black or Payne's gray

Canvas paper (I used a 5" × 6" [12.5 × 15.25 cm] piece.)

Pencil

Round brushes, sizes 2 and 6

Mixing palette

Now that you've painted one simple shape to create an orange, try painting a more complex subject. In this exercise, you'll paint a cluster of grapes, learning how to convey lightness and darkness with several shapes arranged closely together.

1 Use the template or sketch an oblong cluster of grapes. The general shape is like an inverted triangle, so draw more packed circles at the top and then gradually make them more spread out as you move toward the bottom, overlapping the individual grapes. I added a stem on top and star-shaped leaves.

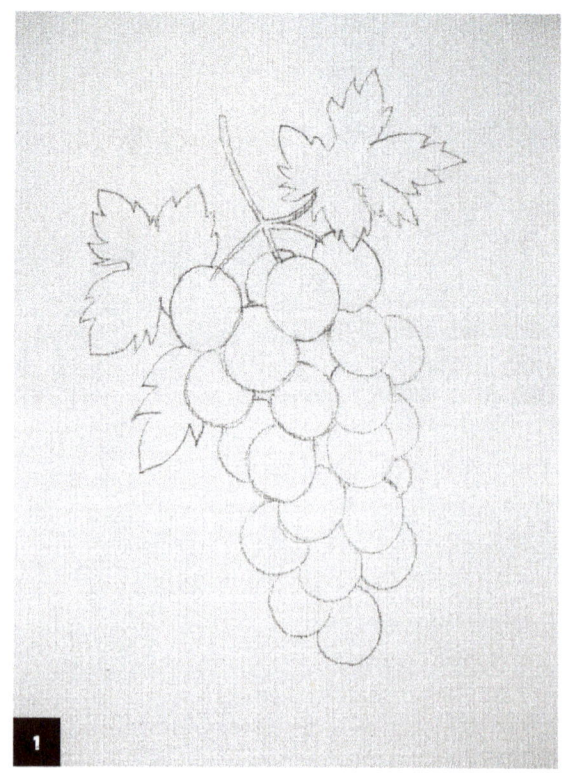

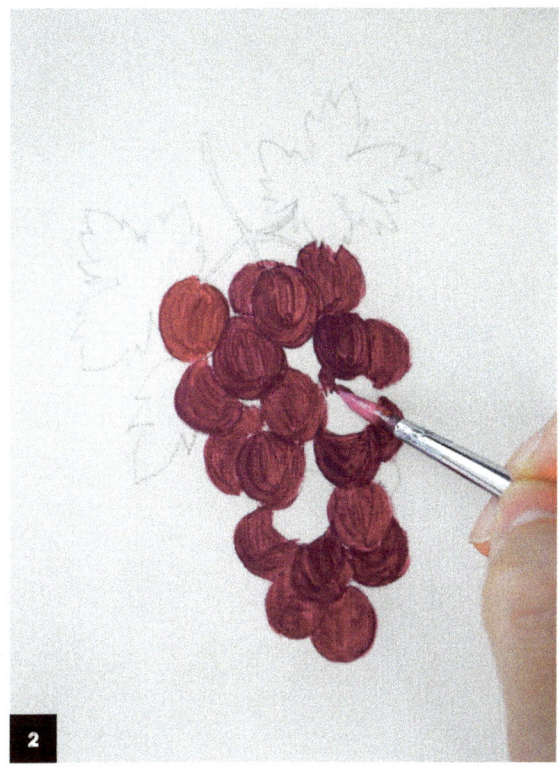

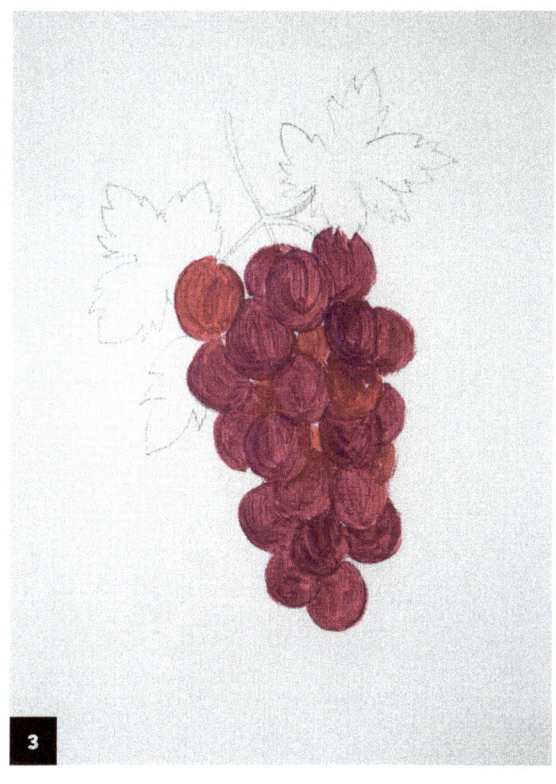

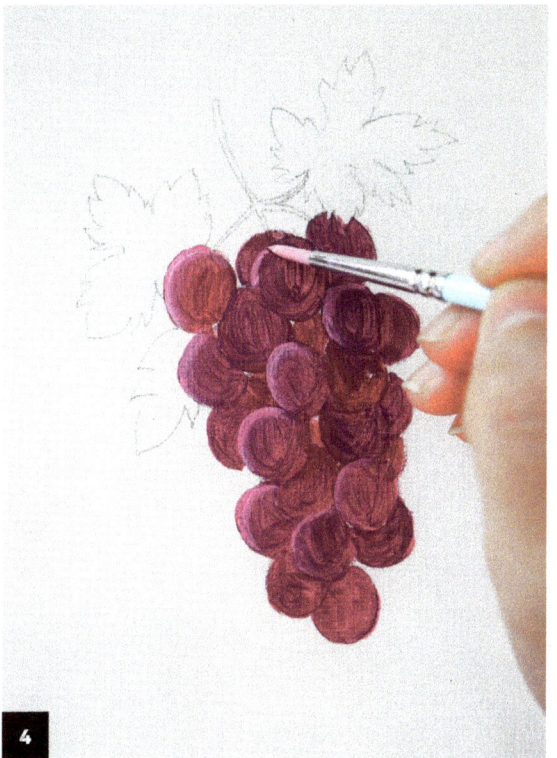

2 Using the size 6 round brush, fill in the individual grapes with purple acrylic paint, or mix blue and red to create violet. You can make the violet shade redder by adding more red to the mix.

3 Use the paint you mixed in step 2 to paint each circle individually so that each grape stands out; this will be important in the next steps. Allow the paint to dry.

4 Add a bit of white to the purple paint to produce a light purple/pink color to highlight the grapes. Imagine where the light may be coming from and apply this light purple color with the size 2 round brush on the top part of one grape, where the light would be hitting it. Paint the highlight by making an arc on top of the circle.

(continued)

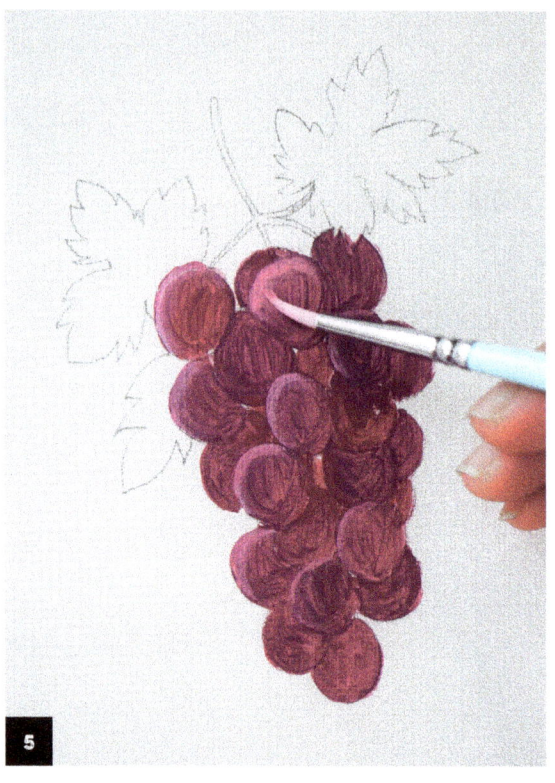

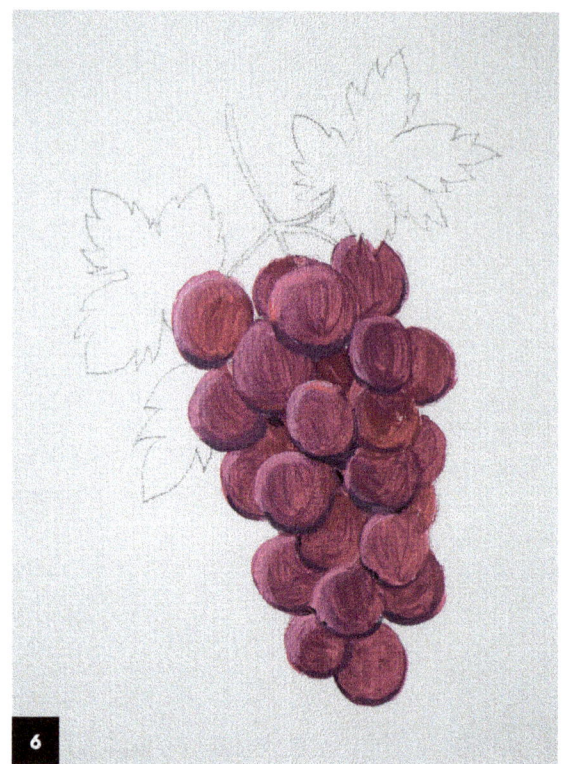

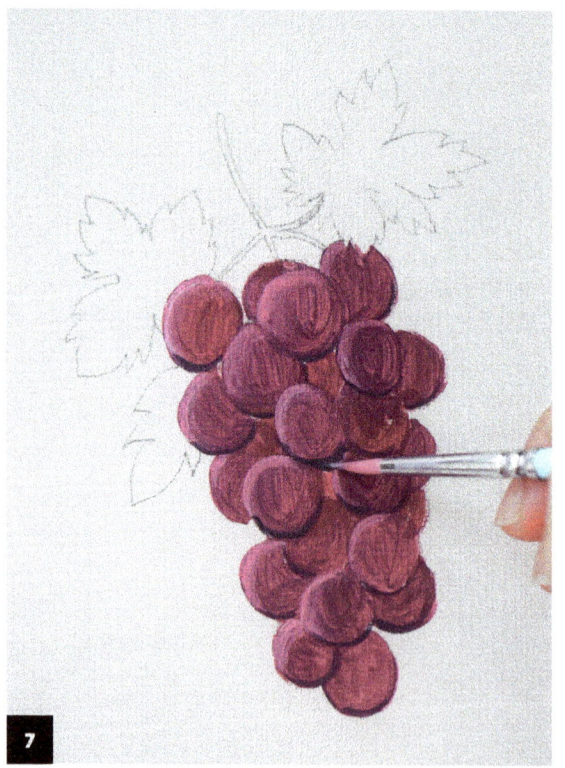

5 Quickly wash the brush, and while the highlight is still wet, gently soften the edge of the light purple color so it blends with the purple grape. The top of the grape should look lighter than the rest of it. Repeat this step for the topmost grapes that are not hidden by other grapes.

6 Paint a thin dark arc at the bottom of each grape using a bit of black or Payne's gray and the size 2 round brush. This further emphasizes the shadows underneath the fruit.

7 For grapes nested behind other grapes, add a little of the dark color to the gaps in between. Those dark areas help emphasize the roundness of each grape, giving life to the cluster of grapes.

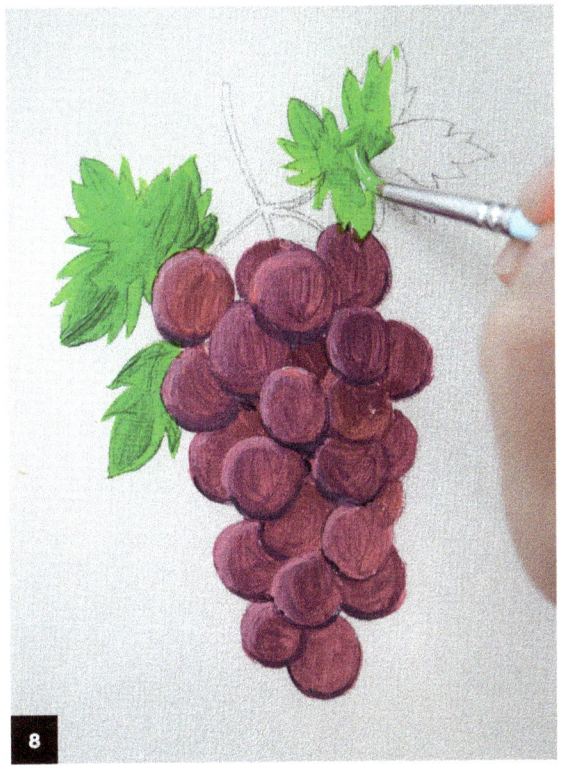

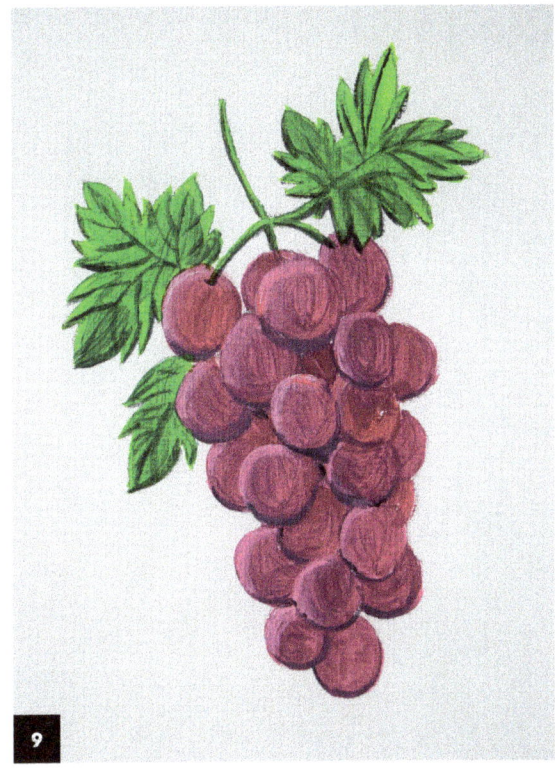

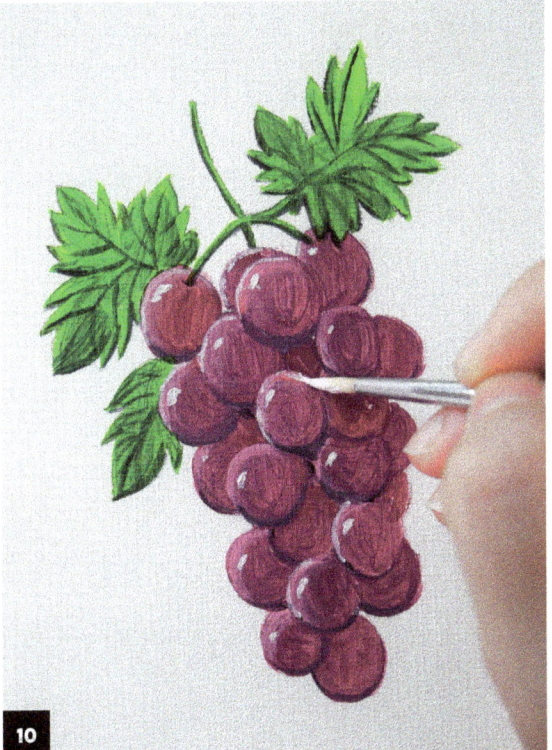

8 Combine green and yellow paint to create a bright shade for the leaves and stem and paint them using the size 6 round brush. Allow the paint to dry.

9 Add the leaf veins with a bit of black paint and the size 2 round brush. Creating veins is easy: Paint a thin line at the tip of the leaf and continue until you reach the stem. Add evenly spaced diagonal lines starting from the center line to the edge of each leaf.

10 Use the size 2 brush to add a small dot of white to some of the more prominent grapes and skip the grapes that are covered or hidden by the others. Add the white highlight near the corner where you applied the light purple arc in step 4. You can also add a thin white line to that same light purple arc, but this time don't blend it with the purple; this will make it more prominent.

COFFEE MUG

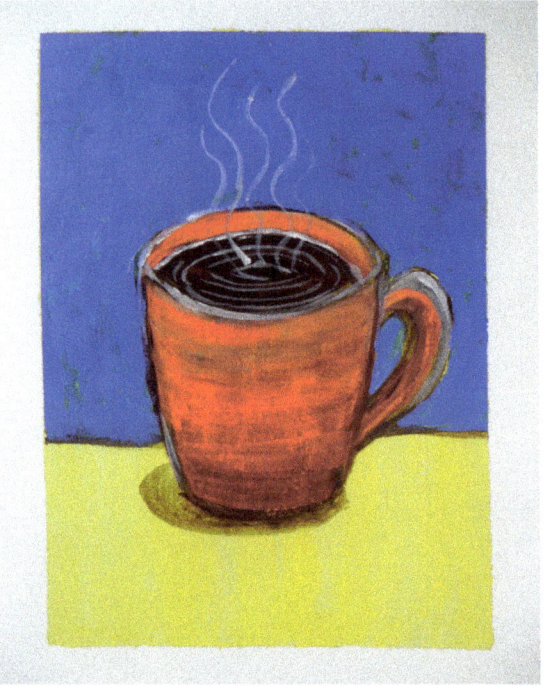

MATERIALS

— — —

Acrylic paints in yellow, brown or burnt umber, blue, white, and black or Payne's gray

Canvas paper (I used a 5" × 6" [12.5 × 15.25 cm] piece.)

Round brush, size 2

Flat brush, size 6

Mixing palette

Everyday objects are a convenient source of inspiration for painting. By learning to paint different objects we quickly train our brain where to add the lightest and darkest colors, understand what kind of shapes these items produce, and become more comfortable with acrylic paints. In this exercise, you'll paint a common household object—a mug—without doing an initial sketch. Instead, you'll allow your imagination to guide your painting, allowing you to use more loose and expressive brushstrokes. Painting items around your home is a wonderful exercise. I encourage you to find more items that inspire you to paint.

1 Follow the directions to "Create Clean Borders" on page 16.

TIP

Try holding the brush farther up, away from the center of the handle. This enables you to move your arm more freely as you make light brushstrokes. This technique is also useful when painting background washes quickly or if you want your brushstrokes to appear loose and expressive. When painting details or smaller areas, move your hand closer to the brush ferrule (the part of the brush where the bristles attach to the handle) for more control.

2 Paint the entire background with a yellow wash using the flat brush (to create a wash, see page 33). Add a brushful of water to the yellow to make it easier to spread across the paper. This light color will give the subsequent layers of color a brighter appearance. Allow the paint to dry.

Imagine your favorite mug, or place one in front of you for you for inspiration. (Avoid accidentally setting your paintbrush in your mug like I did!) Using the flat brush and brown paint, lightly paint an oval in the center of the paper. This will be the rim of the mug and the starting point of the painting.

3 Paint a concave line on each side of the oval and a smaller arc at the bottom to complete the shape of the mug.

4 Paint another arc inside the rim of the mug; this will become the coffee or tea or whatever drink you have in mind. Lightly paint two arcs

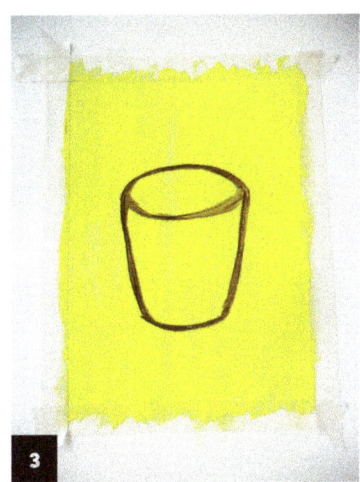

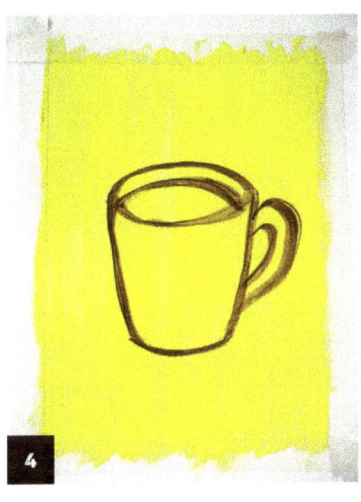

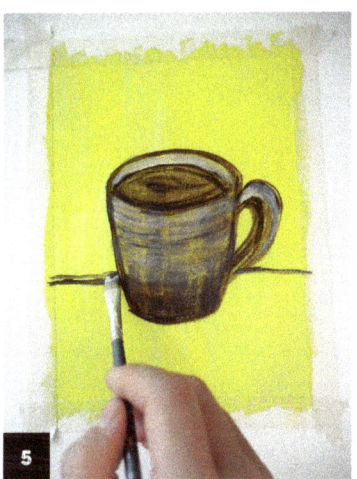

on one side of the mug for the handle. The painting doesn't have to perfectly represent a mug, it just has to loosely resemble one. You'll continue to build up the image in the next steps.

5 Now that the painted sketch is complete, lay down the light and dark tones of the mug to serve as a guide in the next steps. Mix a bit of white into the brown paint and apply this to the top part of the mug. Add more brown to the mix and continue to paint the mug, making it darker toward the bottom. At the very bottom, use even more brown to emphasize the shadows. Color the liquid inside the mug; I used brown paint. Seeing the yellow color peek through is fine, as this adds warmth and brightness to the painting. Allow the paint to dry.

Using the same flat brush and a bit of brown paint, draw a thin horizontal line behind the mug, a little below its center, but be careful not to paint a line over the mug. This indicates where our mug is resting (below the line) and provides a background (above the line). Clean the brush for the next step.

(continued)

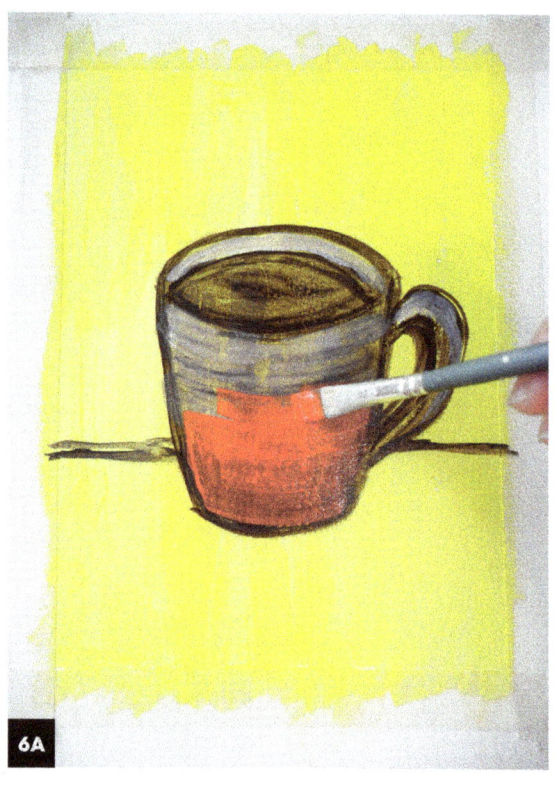

6A

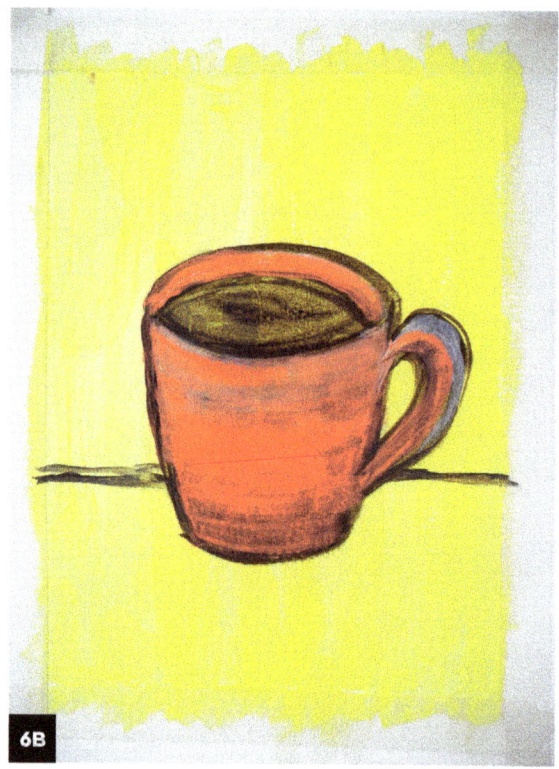

6B

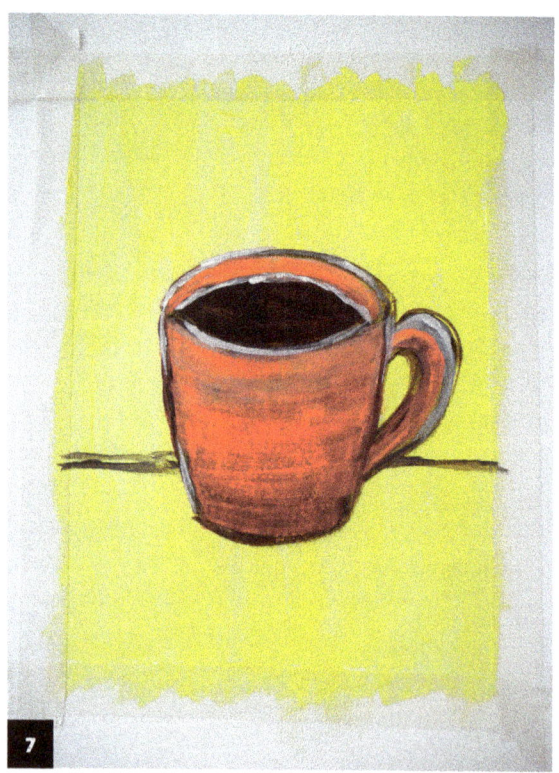

7

6 Choose another color of paint for the mug and mix it with a little water to thin it (I used red) **(A)**. Using the clean flat brush, apply this wash to the mug except for the center, where the contents will be. Notice how some of the browns and whites added in the previous steps can be seen, accentuating the light and dark values **(B)**. Clean your brush.

7 Finish painting the liquid in the mug. I chose a dark brown color for my drink of choice, my homemade cappuccino. Block out the area inside the mug with the flat brush. Using the tip of the brush and white paint, add a highlight along the rim of the mug, the top of the handle, and a bit on one side of the mug where the light source would be. Also add white around the liquid in the mug. Adding subtle highlights such as these adds interest.

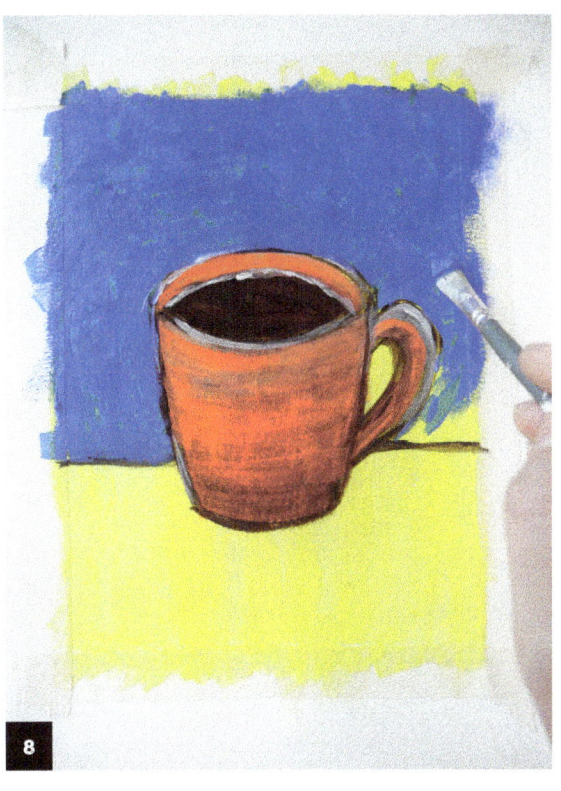

8 Another way to maintain interest is by adding a complementary background color. I used a bright blue. The color doesn't have to completely cover the yellow; the brushstrokes underneath can show through, allowing the painting to be more of an expression rather than perfectly finished.

9 Use the round brush and white paint to add little swirls in the liquid **(A)** and steam rising **(B)**. Steam can be drawn as a thin, continuous S shape that begins on the surface of the drink and floats up. This detail adds that realistic feel of a nice, hot drink.

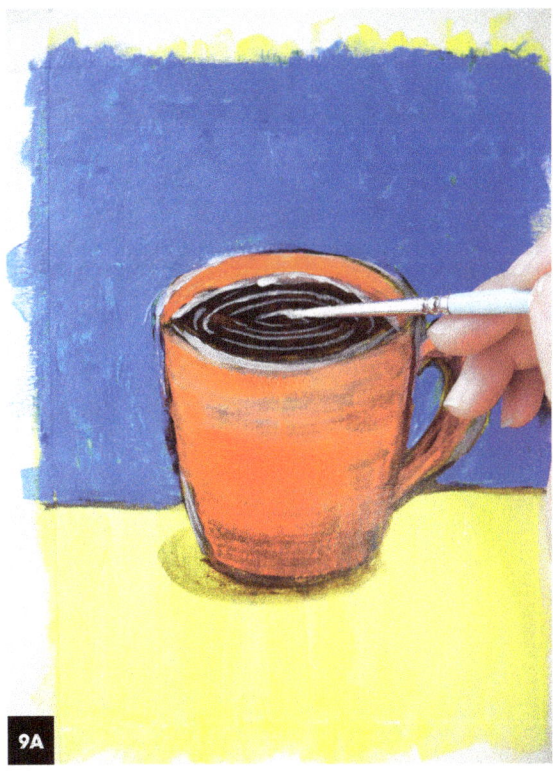

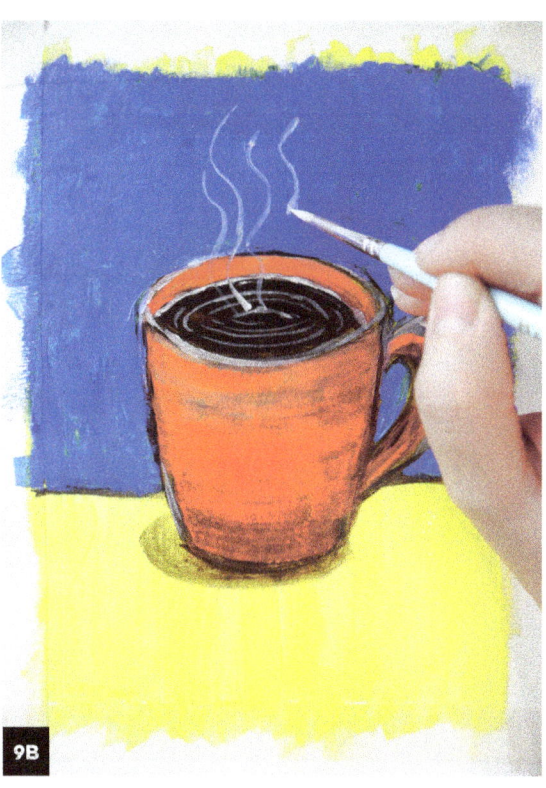

COLORFUL DONUTS

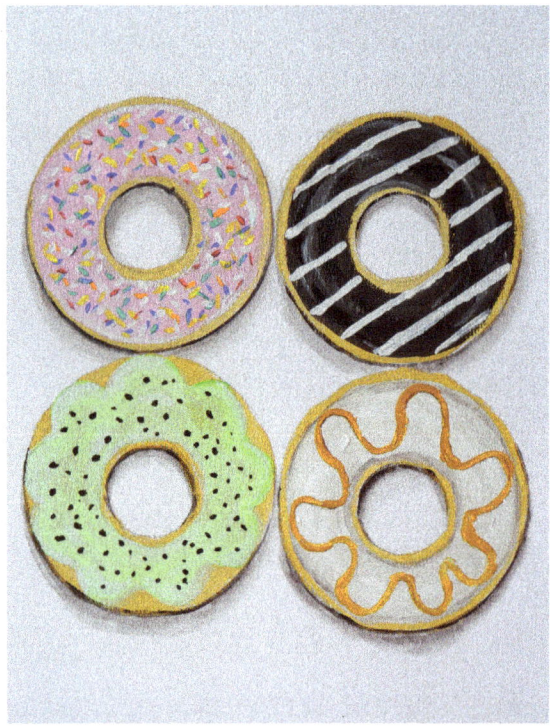

MATERIALS
- - -

Acrylic paints in red, yellow ocher, green, brown, white, and black

Canvas paper (I used a 9" × 12" [22.75 × 30.5 cm] piece.)

Two circular objects to use as a template for the donuts, one larger for the donut and one smaller for the hole

Pencil

Ruler

Round brushes, sizes 2 and 6

Flat brush, size 5

Mixing palette

Would you care for some donuts? In this lesson, you'll paint multiple objects, each with its own unique details, in a single painting. You'll incorporate what you've learned about light and shadow to paint delicious donuts that appear so real you'll want to grab one and eat it!

1 Sketch the circles to create the donuts. Trace two circles each in two rows using the larger circular object and a pencil for a total of four donuts. In the center of each of the larger circles, trace the donut hole using the smaller circular template.

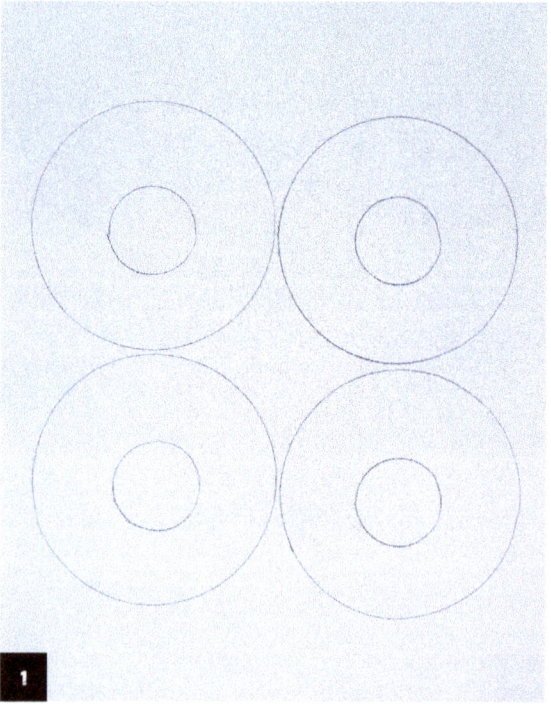

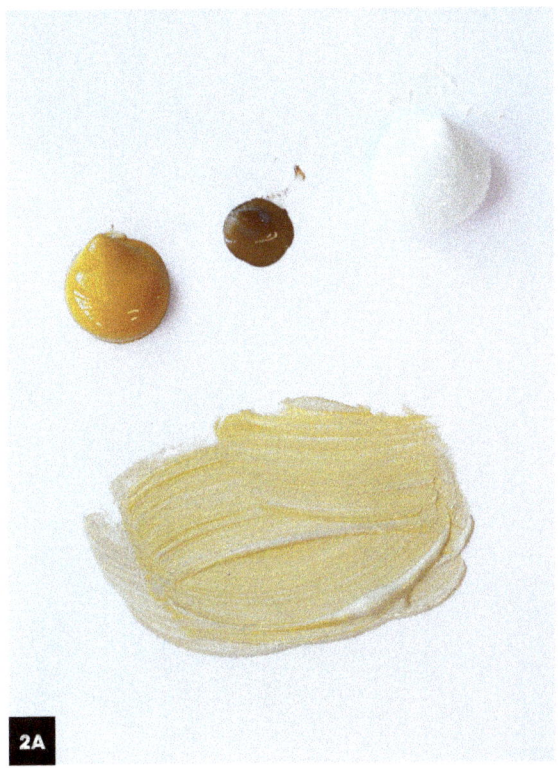

2A

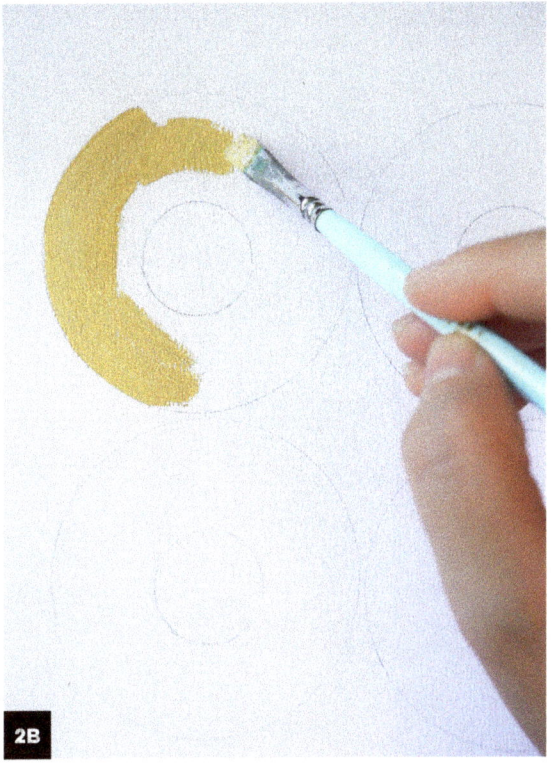

2B

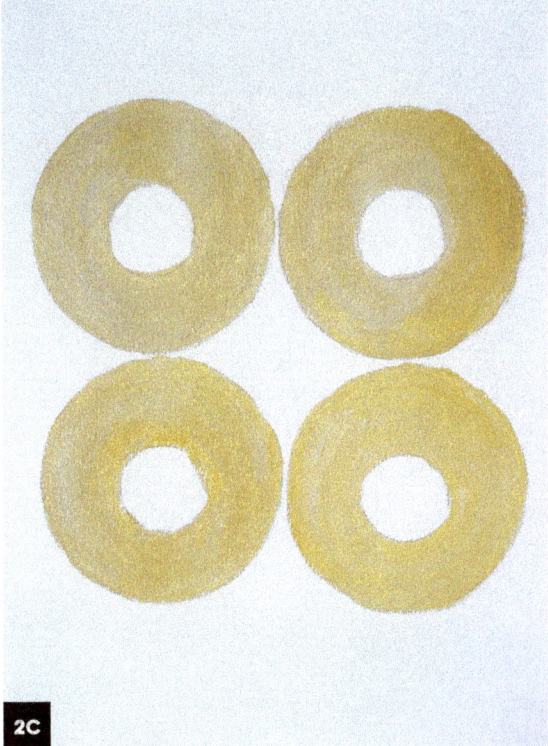

2C

2 Mix yellow ocher and a bit of brown on the palette to create a nice bread-like color for the donuts **(A)**. Add a dab of white to lighten the color and then load the flat brush with this mixture and paint the donuts **(B)**. Allow the paint to dry before adding the toppings **(C)**.

You can create several different types of donut toppings with acrylic paint. Let's start with the top left donut and paint sprinkles.

(continued)

Sprinkle Donut

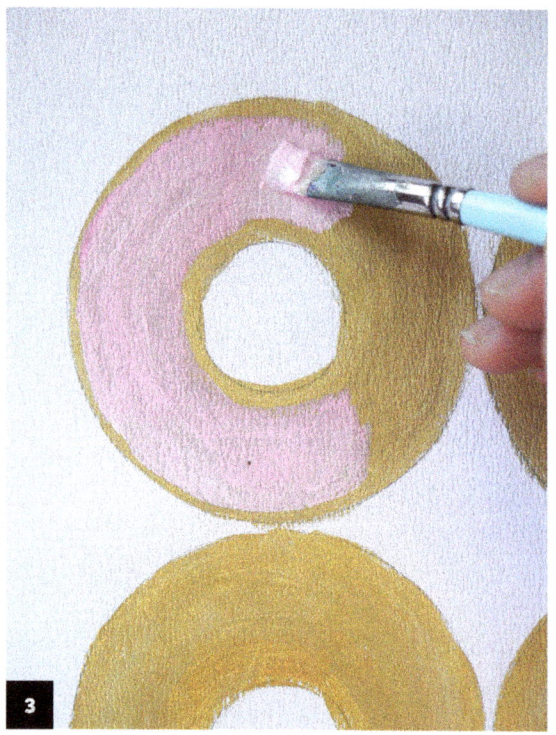

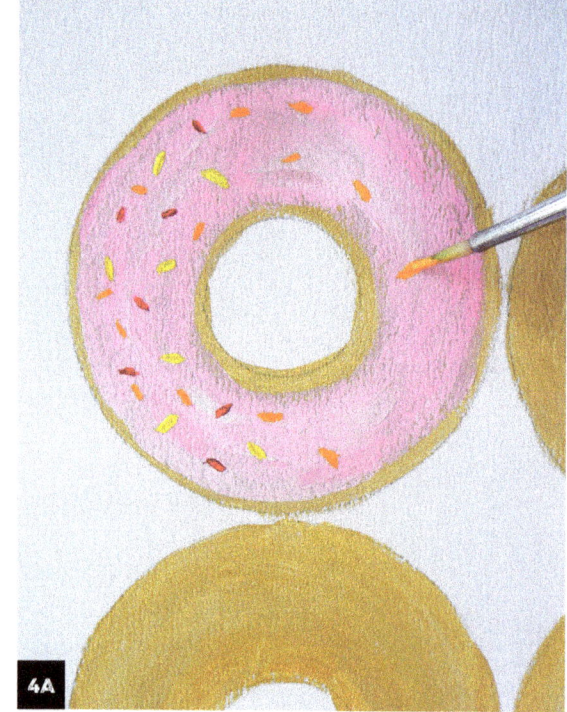

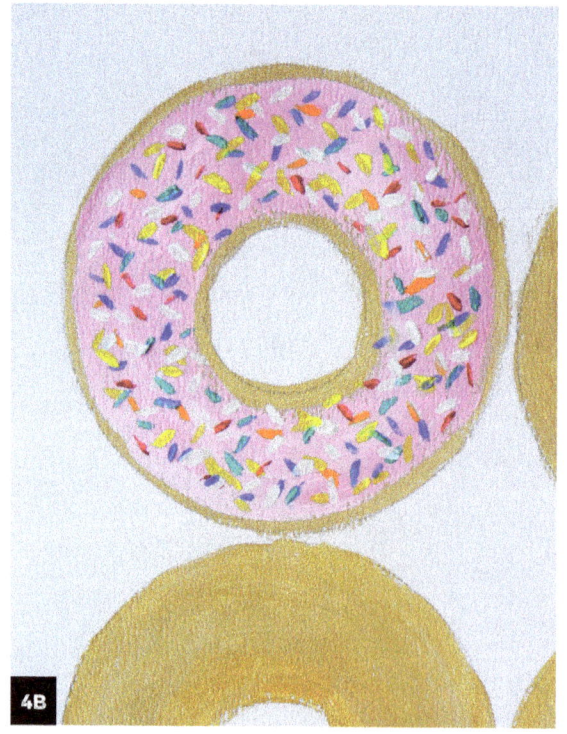

3 Mix a little red with white acrylic paint to make pink, which will be the donut glaze. Using the flat brush, paint the glaze on the top left donut, leaving a small border on the sides and taking care not to paint over the hole. Let this pink glaze dry.

4 Add bits of red, green, yellow, blue, white, and orange paint to the palette for the sprinkles **(A)**. Paint thin, short strokes using each of the colors all over the pink glaze **(B)**.

Chocolate Glazed Donut

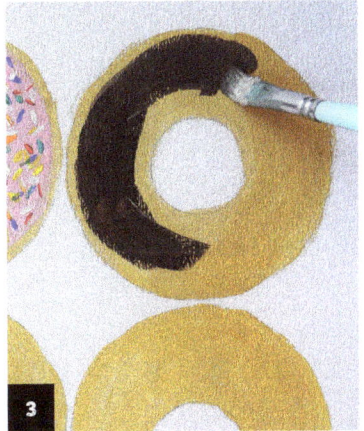
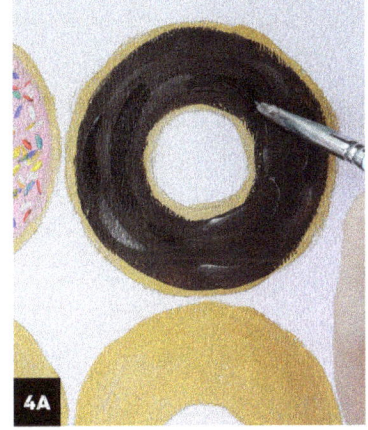
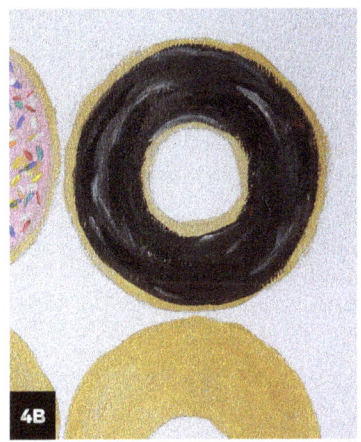

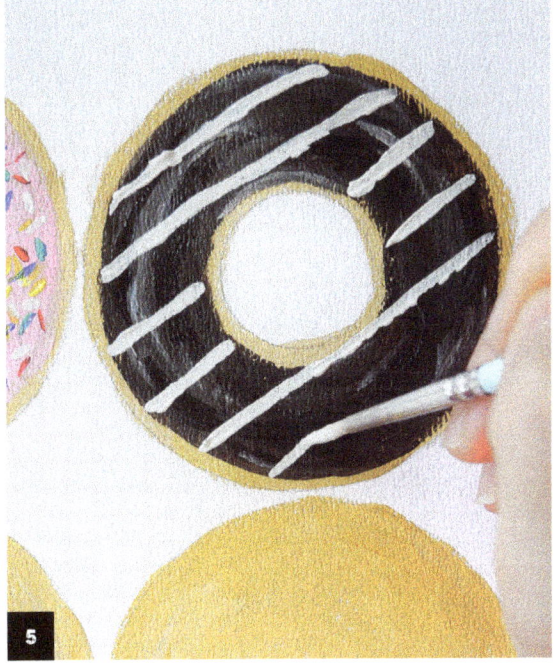
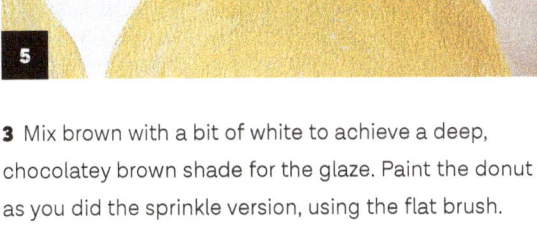
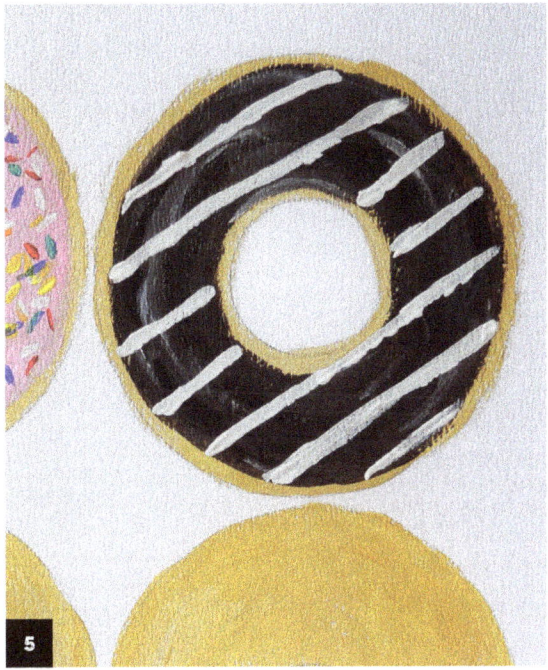

3 Mix brown with a bit of white to achieve a deep, chocolatey brown shade for the glaze. Paint the donut as you did the sprinkle version, using the flat brush.

4 Add some dimension to the donut using the flat brush and brown paint straight from the tube. Make small arcs of brown paint with the brush, leaving a nice thick texture that looks like chocolate syrup **(A)**.

Clean the brush, wipe it dry, and dip it in white paint and make similar arcs to create highlights. After adding the white paint, blend it into the brown to create the appearance of a highlight on the glaze **(B)**.

5 Make a thin zigzag pattern over the glaze using the size 2 round brush and white paint.

(continued)

Green Tea Glazed Donut

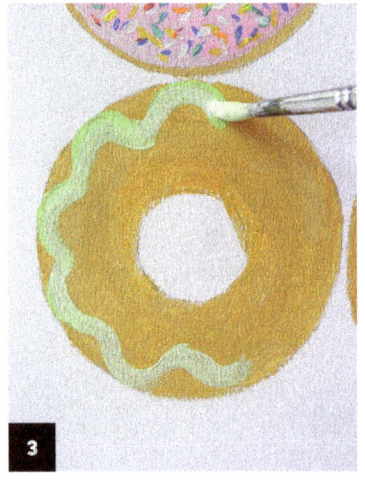 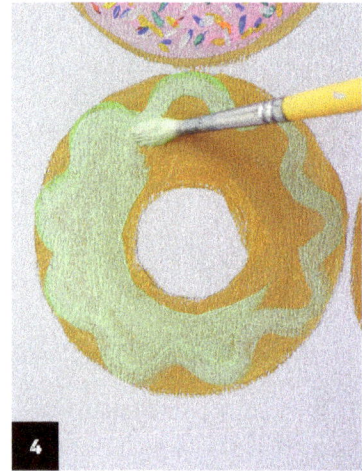 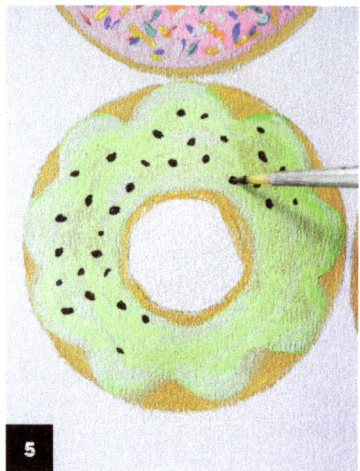

3 Create a green tea glaze by mixing a small amount of green with white acrylic paint. Trace a flower-shaped outline on the donut using the size 6 round brush.

4 Block in the outline with the green-colored paint. Add subtle highlights on the curves and center of the glaze with white paint. Be sure to blend the white into the green.

5 To create the chocolate sprinkles, add short, thin lines over the green glaze, working in short strokes of brown paint with the size 2 round brush.

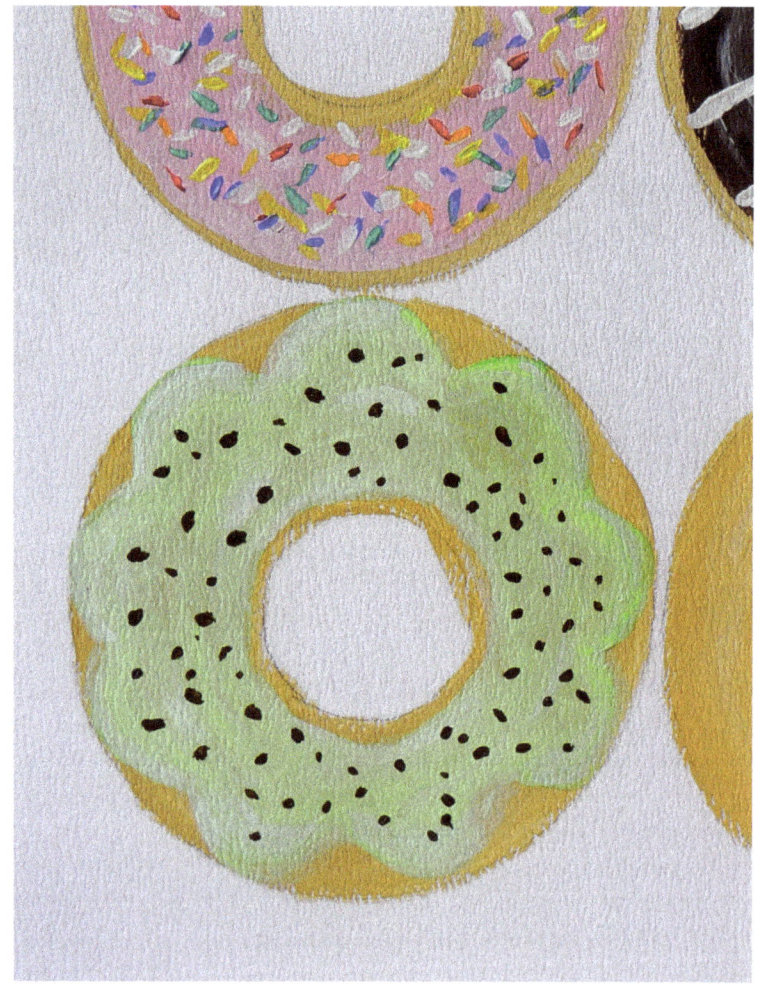

Iced Donut

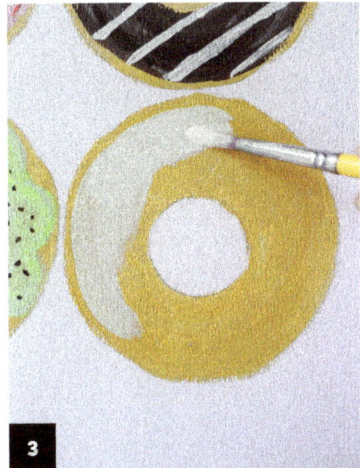

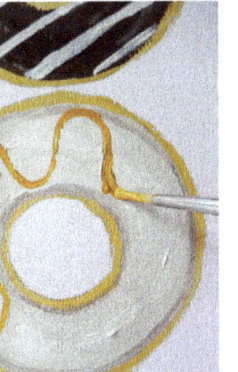

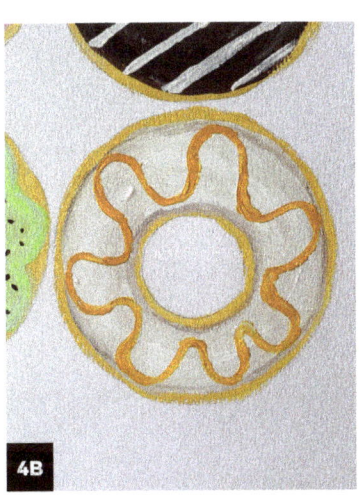

3 Create a white glaze by mixing white paint with a tiny hint of yellow ocher and then paint it on the donut, remembering to leave a border on the sides. Add some texture to the glaze with white paint straight from the tube, using the size 6 round brush to make small arcs of thick white paint on the donut.

4 Mix water and a small amount of brown paint to create a wash. Paint the wash on the top and bottom part of the glaze to make it look more lifelike. Paint a flower-shaped outline over the white glaze, using the size 2 round brush and yellow ocher paint **(A)**. Paint thick lines to make it look like icing on the donut **(B)**.

ADDING SHADOWS AND HIGHLIGHTS

Now that the donuts are decorated, move on to painting the shadows and highlights that will make them look extra delicious. Imagine a light source at the top of the painting and create a shadow underneath the bottom of each donut with a wash consisting of a little Payne's gray and water. This gives the illusion that the donuts are sitting on the foreground. Add the wash under the top of the inner donut hole, which also has a shadow.

Using white acrylic paint and the size 2 round brush, add highlights on the glazes along the top ridge of the donuts, where the light would hit them.

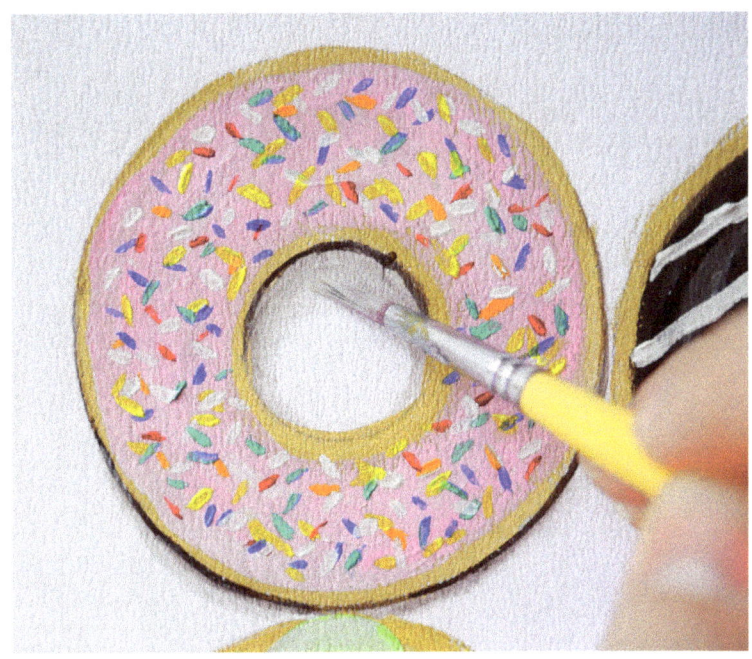

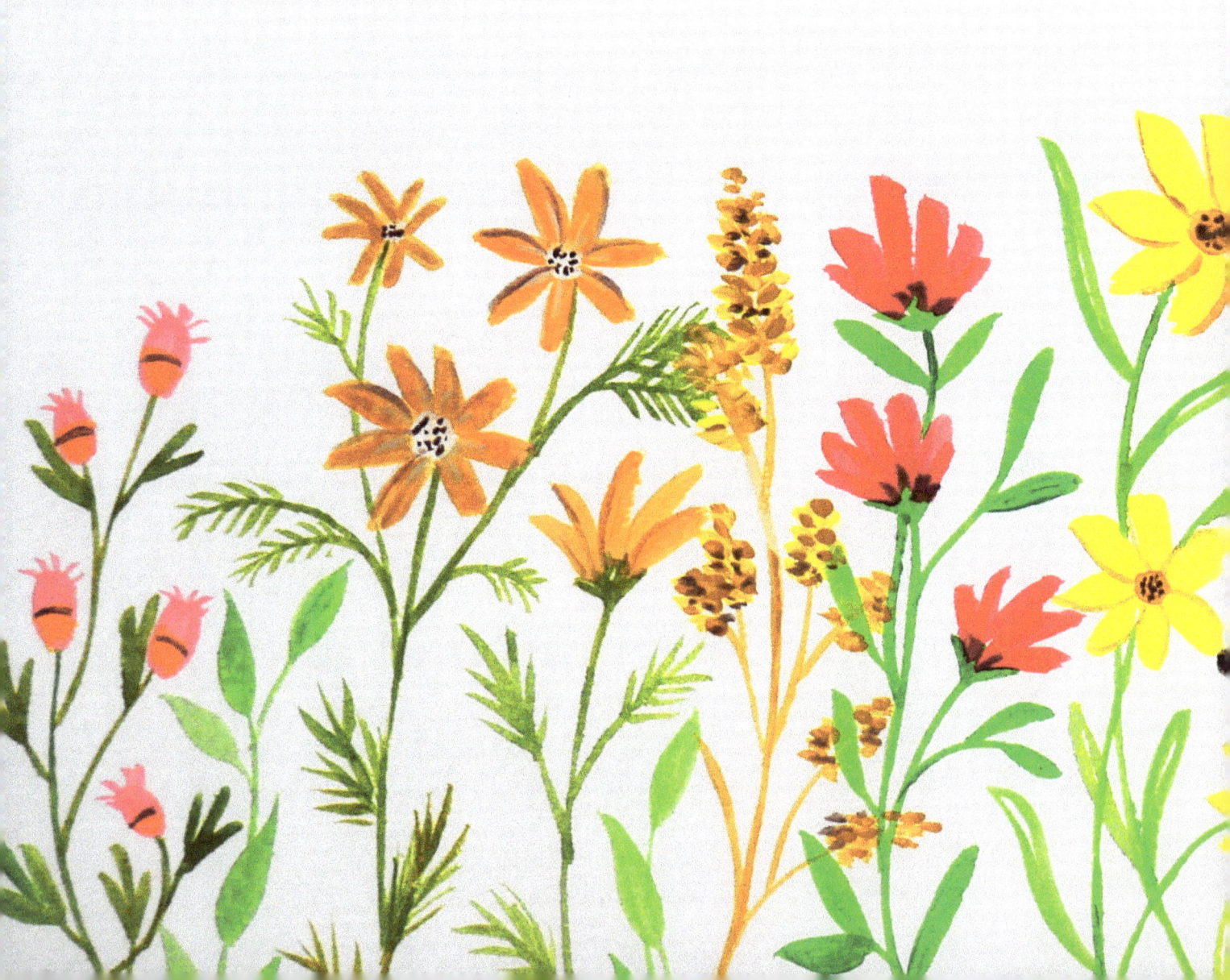

4

FLOWERS

- - - - - - -

Flowers are among my favorite subjects to paint. They can be rendered loosely as an expression of their form or painted in intricate detail. Floral designs are popular motifs on notebooks, wrapping paper, wallpaper, decorative tape, and countless other items. I love that there are so many different kinds of flowers that inspire me. In this chapter, I chose some of my favorite flowers to paint, and I'll show you a variety of techniques you can use to create them. You'll learn how to paint loose and realistic florals and find the most harmonious compositions and color palettes for your artwork.

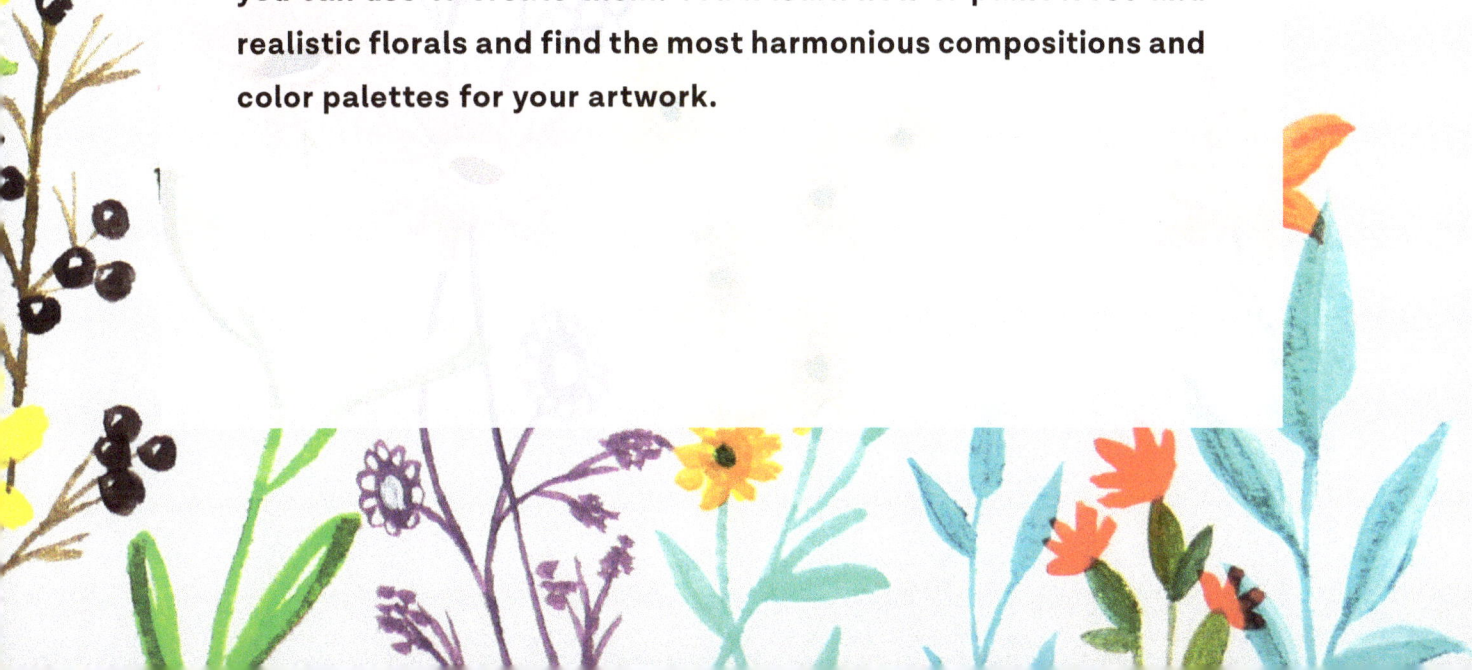

HYDRANGEA

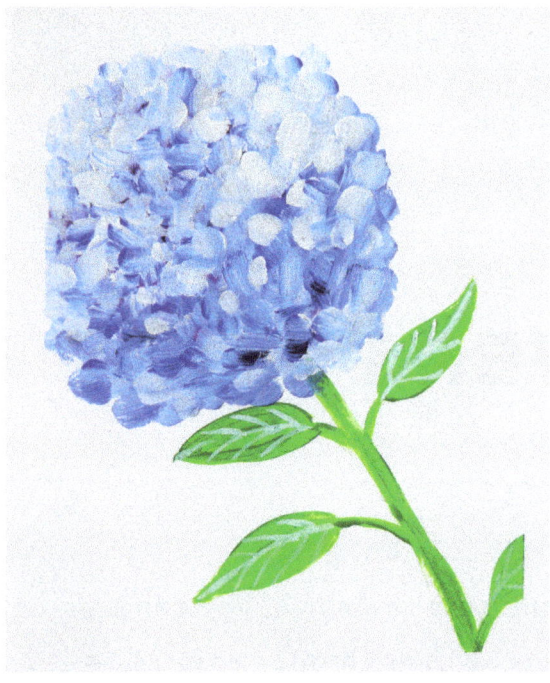

MATERIALS

- - -

Acrylic paint in blue, dark violet, green, white, and black or Payne's gray

Canvas panel, 8" × 10" (20.25 × 25.5 cm)

Low-tack craft tape or washi tape

Round brush, size 6

Filbert brush, size 4

Mixing palette

Hydrangeas come in beautiful round clusters that are easy to recreate using acrylics. Painting the individual tiny petals is easy when you learn how to load the brush with two colors.

1 Follow the directions to "Create Clean Borders" on page 16.

2 Begin by painting the stems and leaves. With the round brush and green acrylic paint, add a long, slightly curved vertical line on the canvas. Angle the line a bit to the side so the flower will be in the center of the paper.

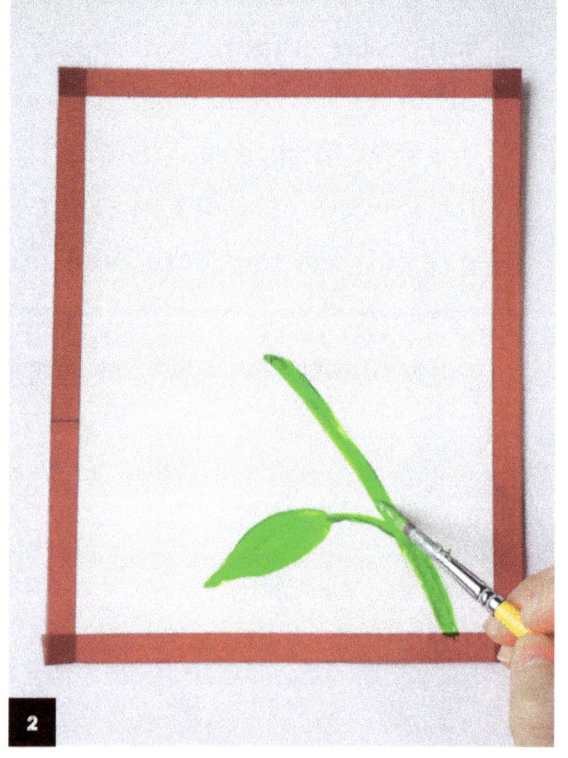

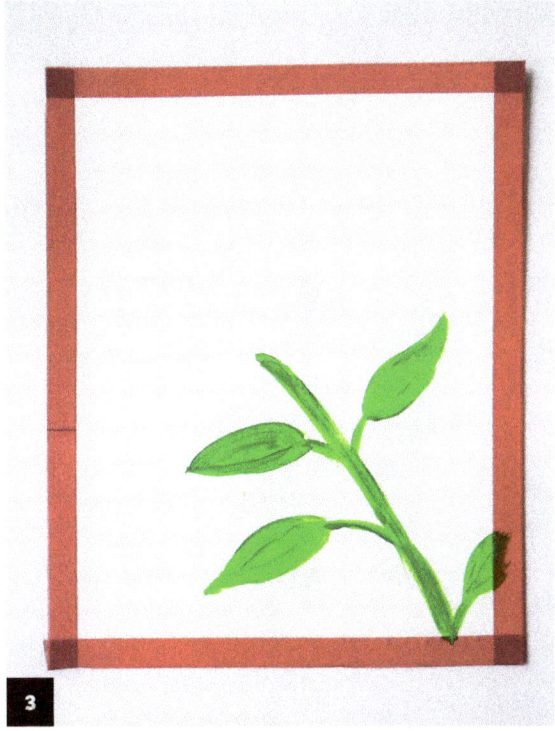

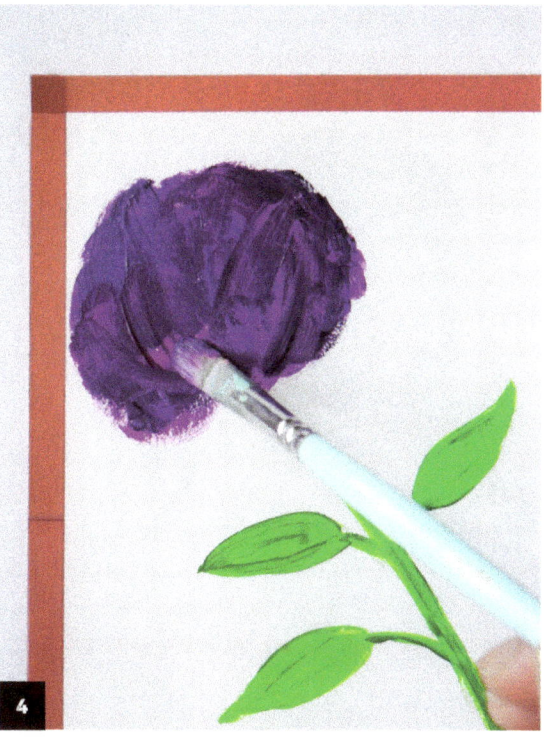

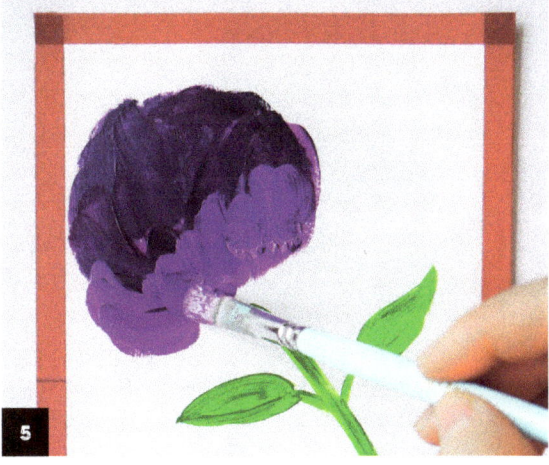

3 Paint two oval-shaped leaves on each side of the stem, staggering them a bit so they're not perfectly symmetrical. Allow the paint to dry completely.

4 Paint the base layer of the hydrangea flower. Add dark violet paint to the palette and begin painting the top part of the flower using the Filbert brush. Hydrangeas are quite round, but the shape doesn't have to be a perfect circle. Allow the paint to dry.

5 Mix some white with the violet on the mixing palette to create a lighter purple shade. Begin painting this color near the stem, slightly overlapping the dark violet.

(continued)

TIP

Starting with a darker base color allows the lighter petals to stand out.

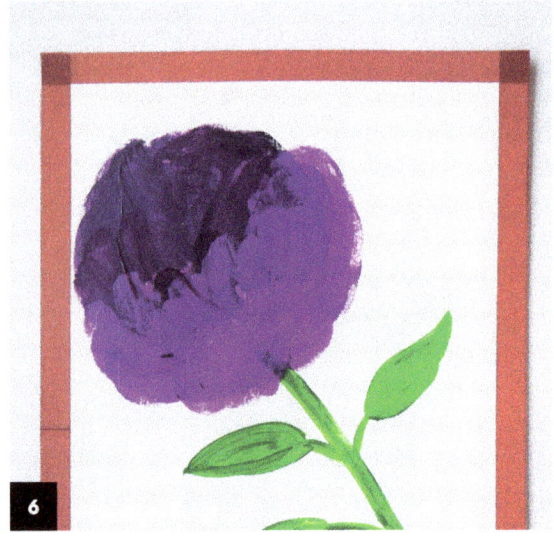

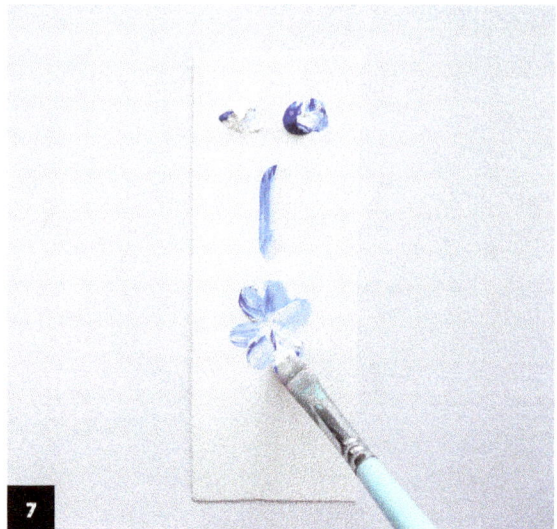

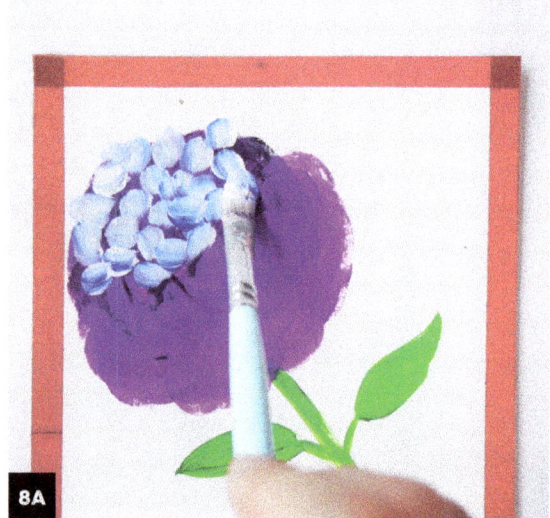

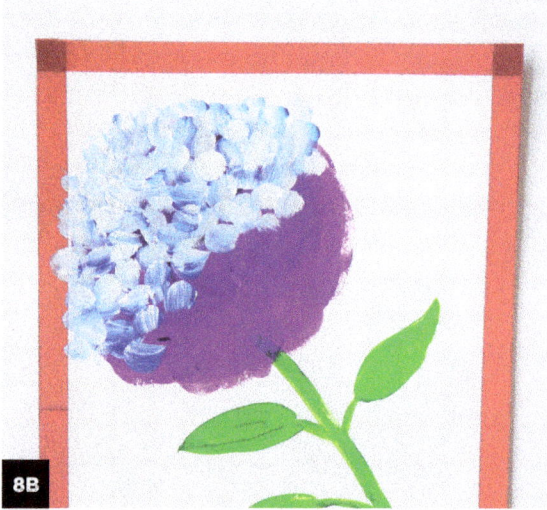

6 Continue painting the lighter purple about halfway up the flower. This will contrast with the tiny flowers you'll paint in the next step. Let dry.

7 Before painting the rest of the flower, prepare the paint mixes for the petals. Add blue and white paint to the palette and pick up a little bit of both colors on the Filbert brush. Check the brush hairs to make sure the two colors are there, but not fully mixed—this is the key to the painting. The images show how the brush should look and how the paint should look on paper.

8 Now that the brush is prepared, paint the tiny flowers. Make a short stroke with the brush on the dark violet area. You should see that the brushstroke created a blue-white streak **(A)**. Apply this short blue-white streak at different angles, reloading the brush with blue and white paint when it runs out **(B)**.

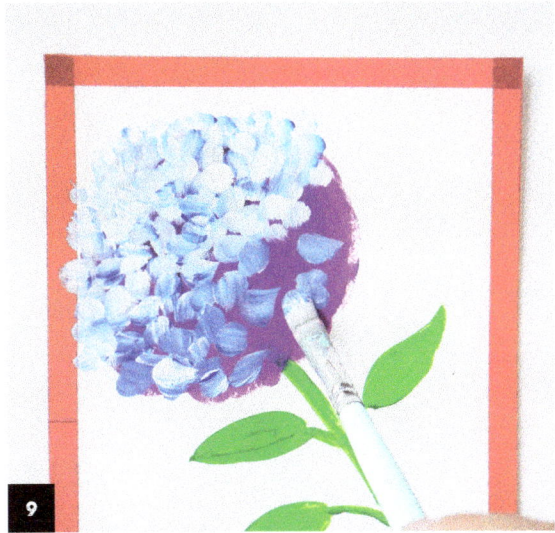

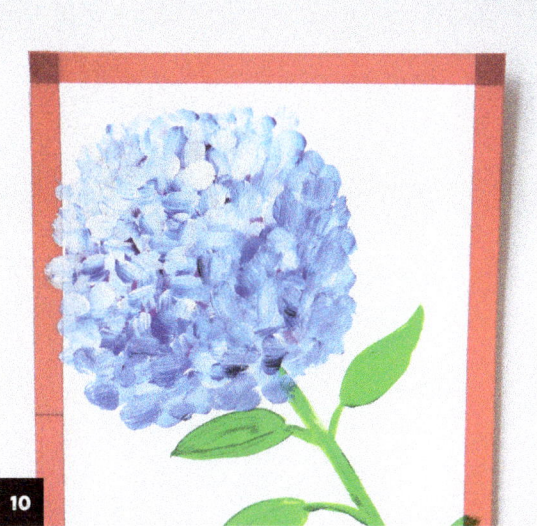

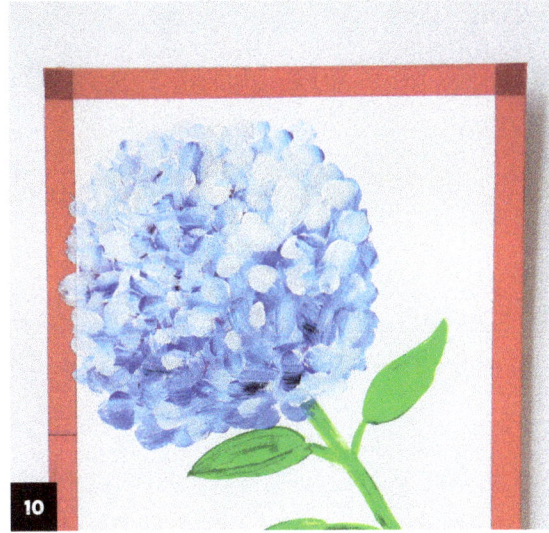

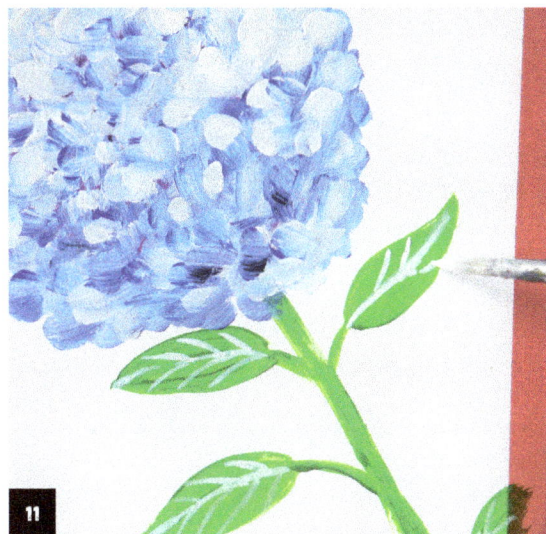

9 As you move toward the lighter purple area of the flower, load more blue onto the brush, still including a tiny bit of white. The petals here are darker because they're at the bottom of the hydrangea. Continue adding short brushstrokes to cover the remainder of the base color. You can also paint petals slightly outside the edge of the circle to make the flower look more natural.

10 After filling the entire shape, you should have a light-to-dark gradient of petals. If needed, add more white petals on the top part of the hydrangeas.

11 Add veins to the leaves you painted in step 2, using white paint and the round brush. Once the paint is dry, carefully remove the low-tack tape and admire your beautiful hydrangea acrylic painting.

ROSE

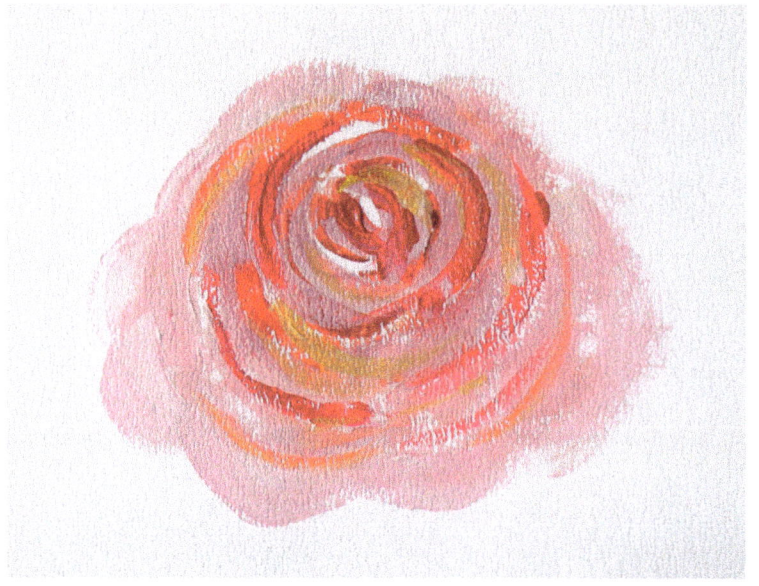

MATERIALS
- - -

Acrylic paint in red, yellow, green, white, and black or Payne's gray

Canvas paper (I used a 5" × 7" [12.5 × 17.75 cm] piece.)

Round brush, size 6

Flat brush, size 4

In this exercise, you'll paint a simple and elegant pink rose. What I like about this technique is that you don't need to sketch each rose petal, which can be challenging. Instead, you'll use varying tones of red, pink, and white to express the rose's multitude of layers.

1 Mix a bit of red and yellow acrylic paint on the palette; this color will be used for the rose centers. Paint two close parentheses shapes in the center of the paper using the flat brush.

2 Use a light touch to make the curved petals on the sides of the rose.

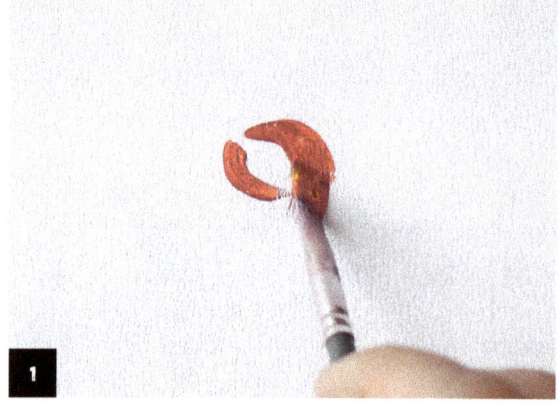

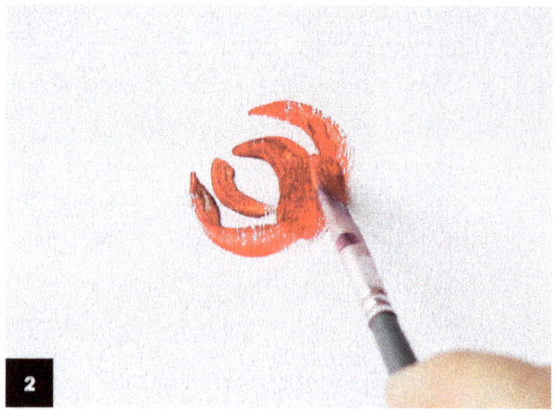

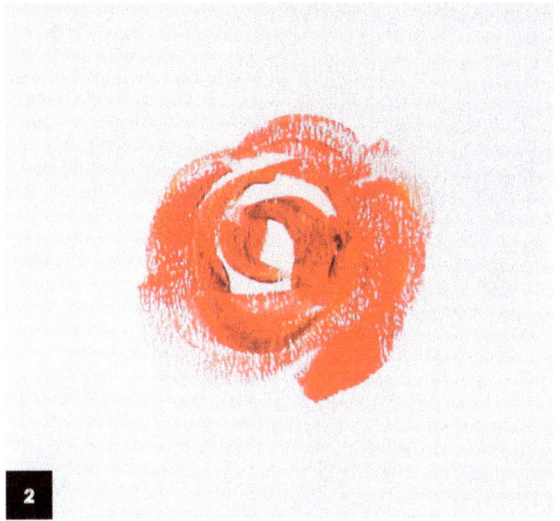

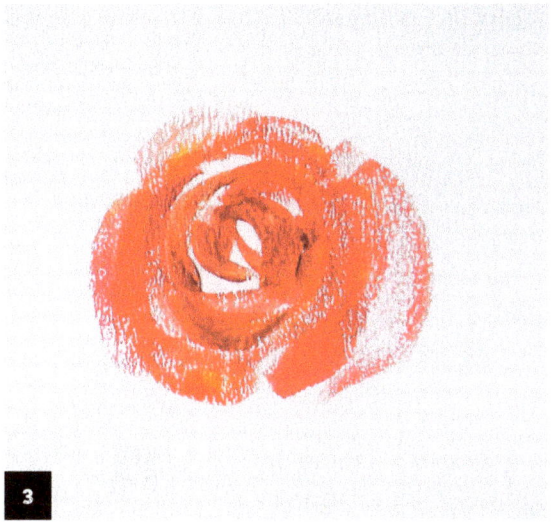

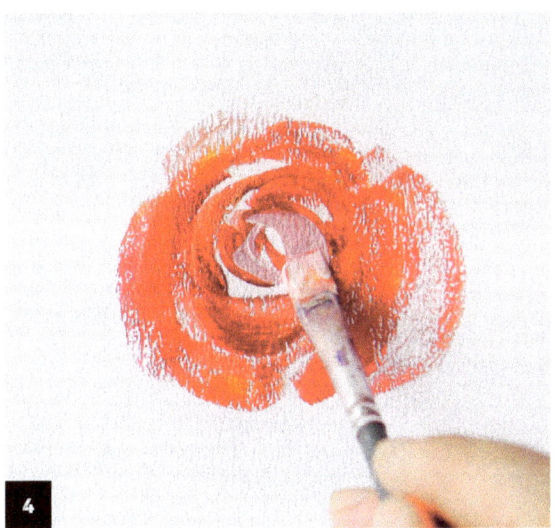

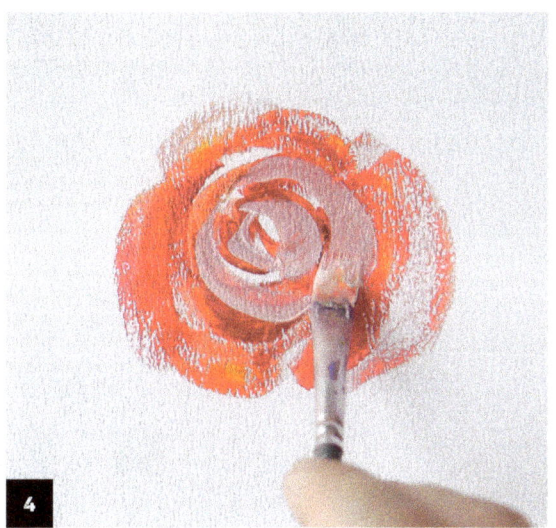

3 Add a bit more white to the red and yellow mixture as you paint the third layer of petals, as these outer layers are lighter compared to those in the center. Allow the paint to dry.

4 Blend white and red paint on the palette to make a pink shade. Use the flat brush to make an incomplete spiral on the base layer you created in step 1. Begin the spiral slightly off center, making sure you don't paint over the center color.

(continued)

TIP

I like using a flat brush to create these rose petals because I can paint a thin line with the edge of the brush and a broader stroke when I press the brush more firmly against the paper.

5 Paint the inner part of the spiral with a thin stroke and then press down on the brush a little more to paint the outer part of the spiral. Painting this pink layer over the darker layer creates outer petals that are more spread out than the compact petals in the middle of the rose. This layer doesn't have to be completely dry before going on to the next step.

6 To give the flower more depth, mix red with a bit of Payne's gray. Lightly add a thin spiral starting at the center of the rose, using the round brush. This makes it look as though the center of the rose has tightly packed petals.

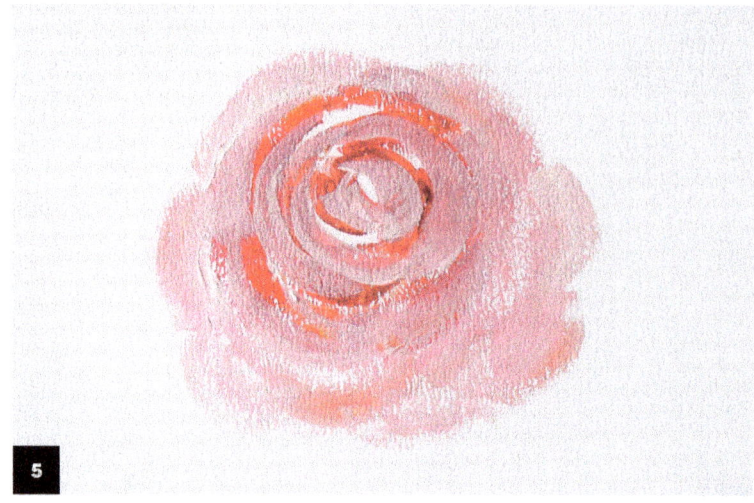

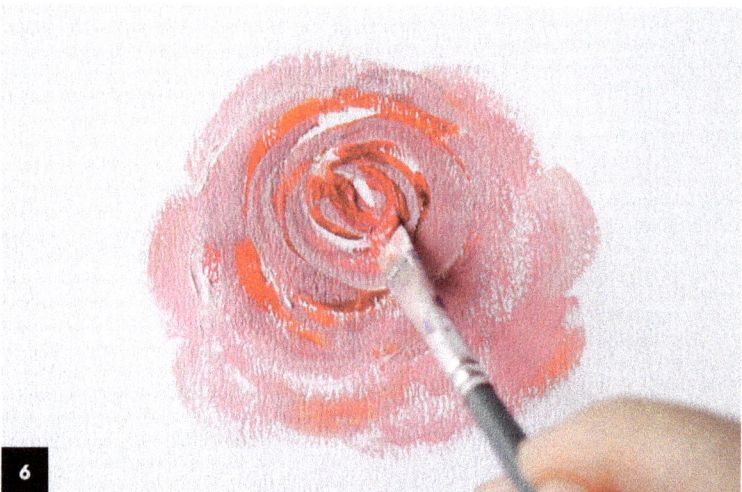

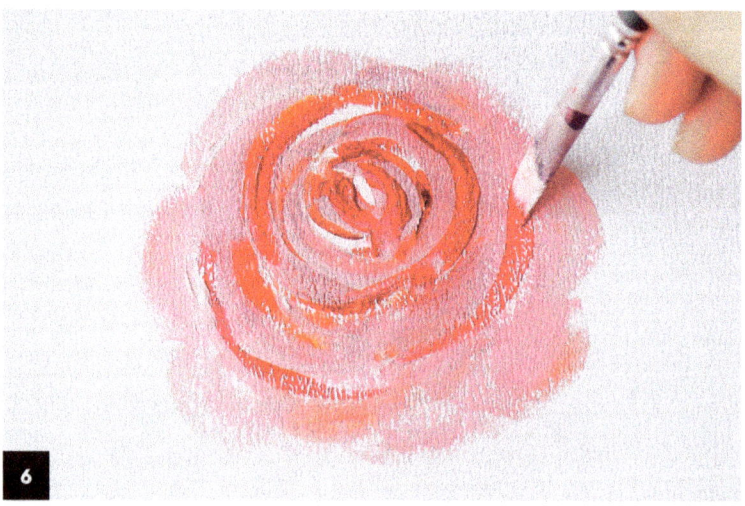

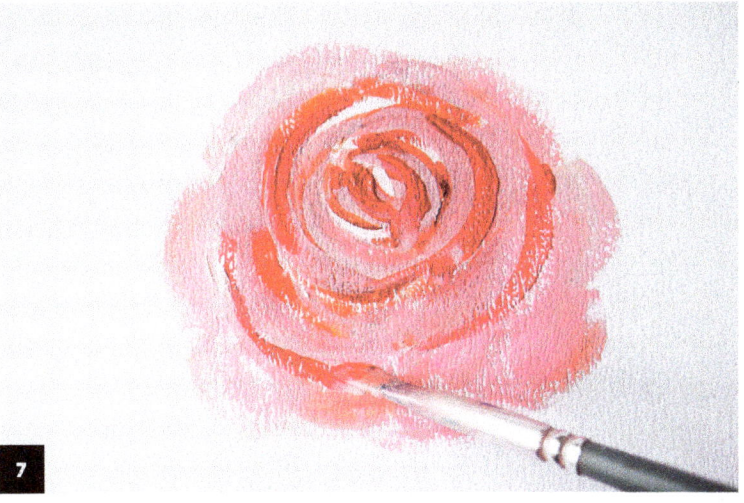

7 Add a bit of white to the dark red mix to soften it a bit and use this paint to make some of the outer petal layers pop.

8 Add more white to the pink shade for the outer petals to better define the final shape to the rose. Create bold spiral strokes near the outer edge of the rose, pressing down with the flat brush. You don't have to create a neat spiral; continue layering the spiral strokes until you're satisfied with the shape of the rose. Painting a triangular-shaped corner on both sides of the rose creates large, loose petals.

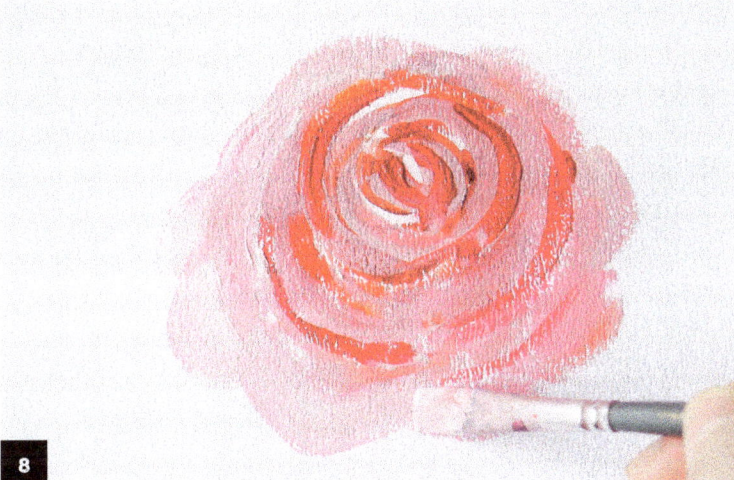

9 Add highlights to the rose using white or yellow for a warmer accent. Add thin curved strokes to the center of the rose with the round brush, then gradually add fewer highlights as you move toward the outer petals.

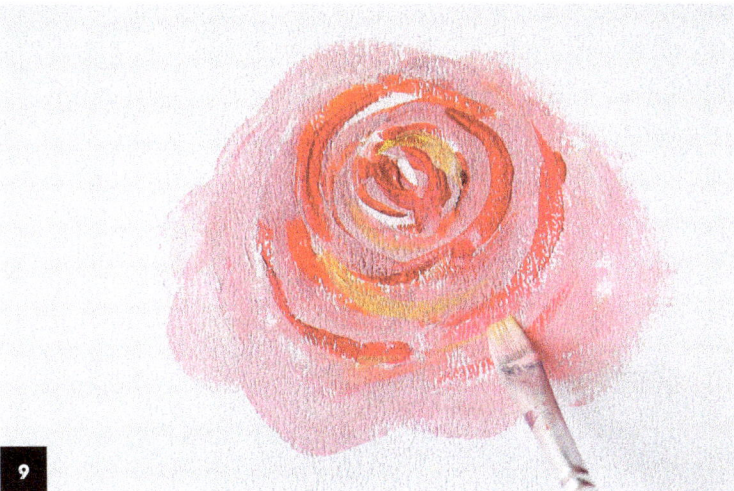

SUNFLOWER

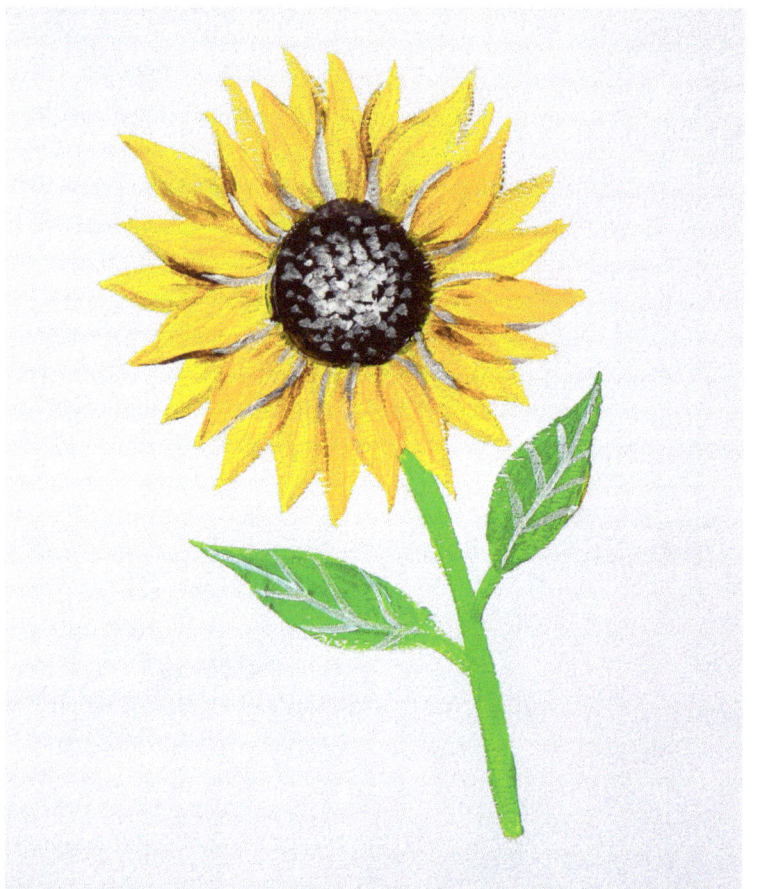

MATERIALS
— — —

Acrylic paints in red, yellow, orange, green, white, brown, and black or Payne's gray

Canvas paper (I used an 8" × 10" [20.25 × 25.5 cm] panel.)

Round brushes, sizes 6 and 8

Sunflowers give such a positive vibe to any garden or bouquet, making them some of my favorite flowers to paint. Many people don't realize how easy they are to create. In this lesson, you'll learn brushstroke techniques that make beautiful petals instantly.

1 Start painting the flower from the center. Mix yellow and brown to create a medium brown. Paint a circle 3 inches (7.5 cm) in diameter in the center of the paper using the size 6 round brush. Allow the paint to dry.

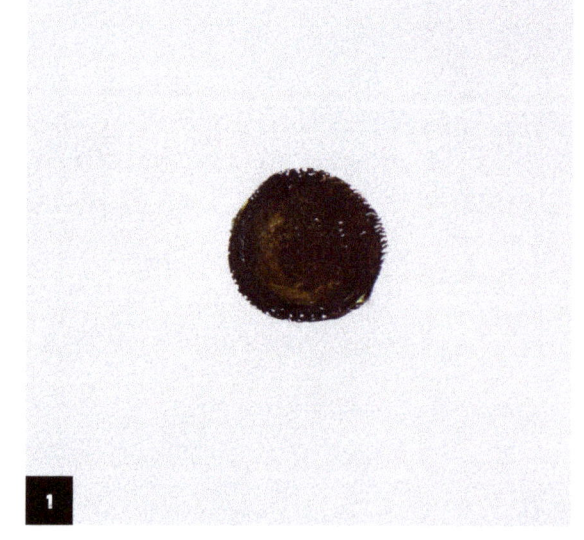

1

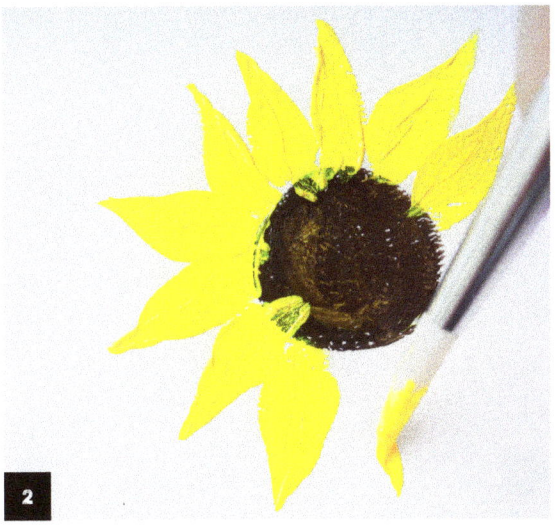

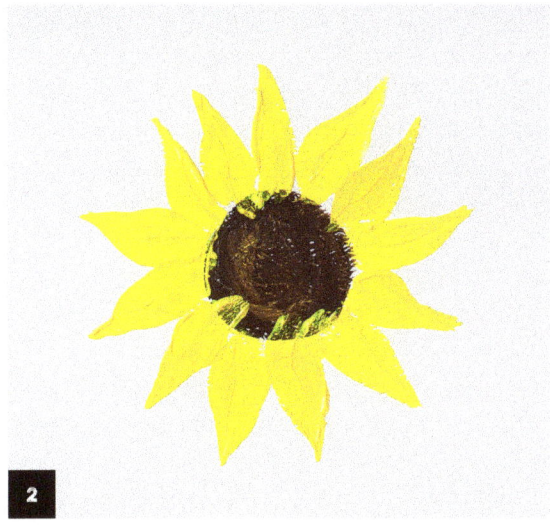

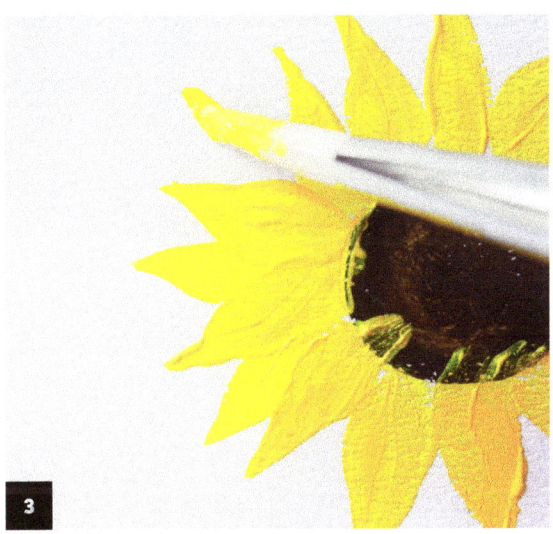

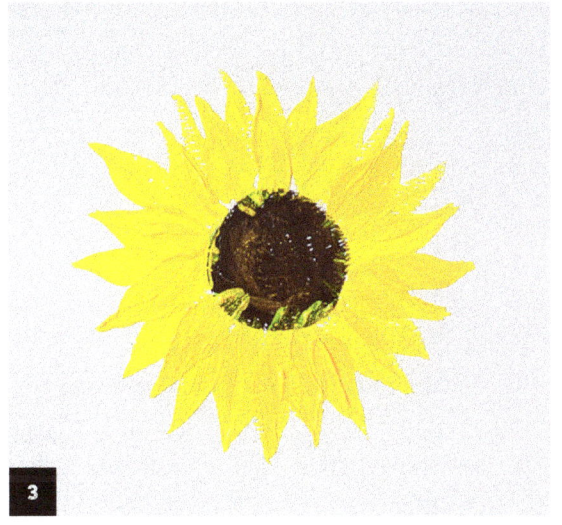

2 To mix the shade for the petals, add a generous amount of yellow paint to the palette and blend it with a bit of orange to create a deep, vibrant yellow. Position your brush about 1 inch (2.5 cm) out from the flower center and begin painting the petals from the tip. Make a short, thin line with the tip of the size 8 round brush, and, without pausing, gently press down and lift the brush as you reach the edge of the brown circle. Add a thin line of paint along the brown center and fill in the petal with yellow. Continue adding each petal in this manner, working your way around the center until you complete the circle.

3 Create a second layer of petals, using the same method in step 2. Place each petal between the *V* of two petals in the first layer. Allow the paint to dry.

(continued)

4 Add shadows to the petals to give them depth, using yellow and a hint of brown to create a color slightly darker than the petals. Starting with the first layer of petals, begin at the center of the petal and move outward, creating a gradient so the color fades as you reach the tip. Use a dry-brush technique for the shadows.

5 Add shadows to the petals in the outer layer using the size 6 round brush and brown paint mixed with a little water. If one petal overlaps another, add a shadow to the area where they meet. After painting the shadow, remember to wipe off the brush and soften the edges of the shadow.

6 Add highlights to the center of the flower. Paint tiny dots in the center of the flower using the tip of the size 6 round brush loaded with white acrylic paint. Pick up some brown and white acrylic paint and continue adding tiny dots around the flower's center.

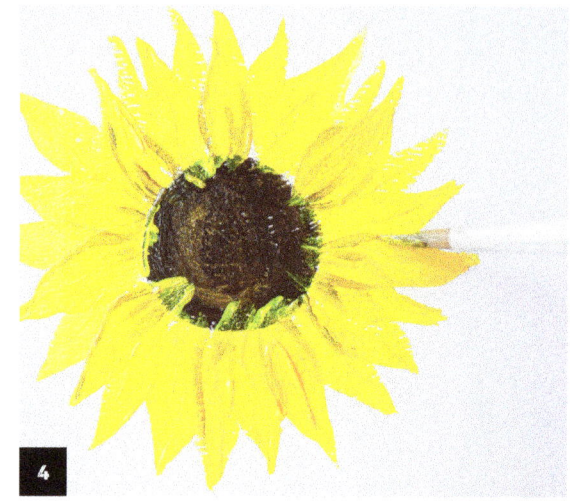

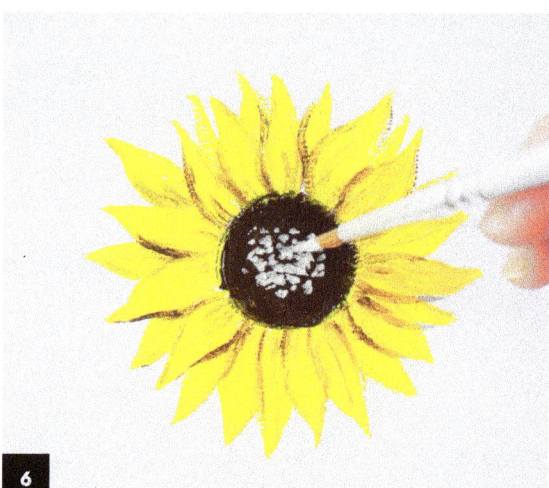

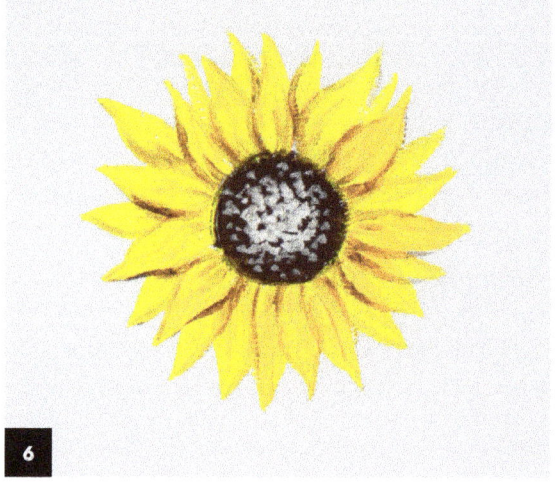

DRY-BRUSH TECHNIQUE

- - -

The dry-brush technique is often used to enhance part of a painting, giving it a textured, scratched up, worn out look that adds interest to an otherwise flat layer. Choose a brush with stiffer bristles instead of softer bristles, which are used for blending. Before using the brush, make sure it's completely clean and dry. Now paint in short, quick strokes. You'll use this fun technique to add shadows to the petals. (For more information on this technique, see page 35.)

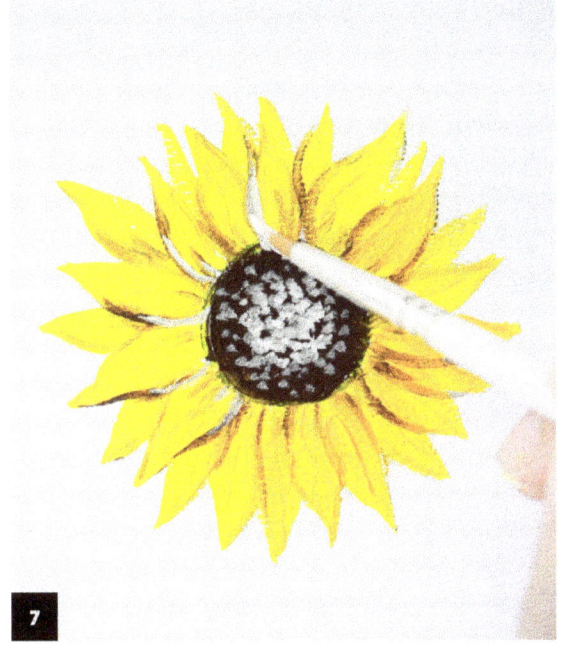

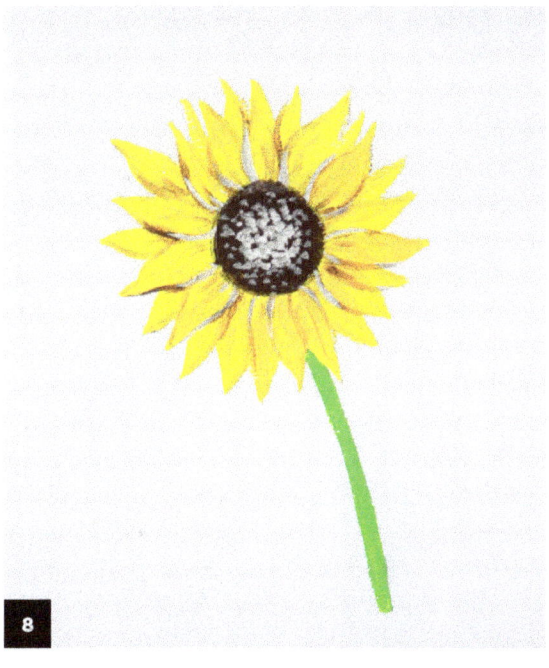

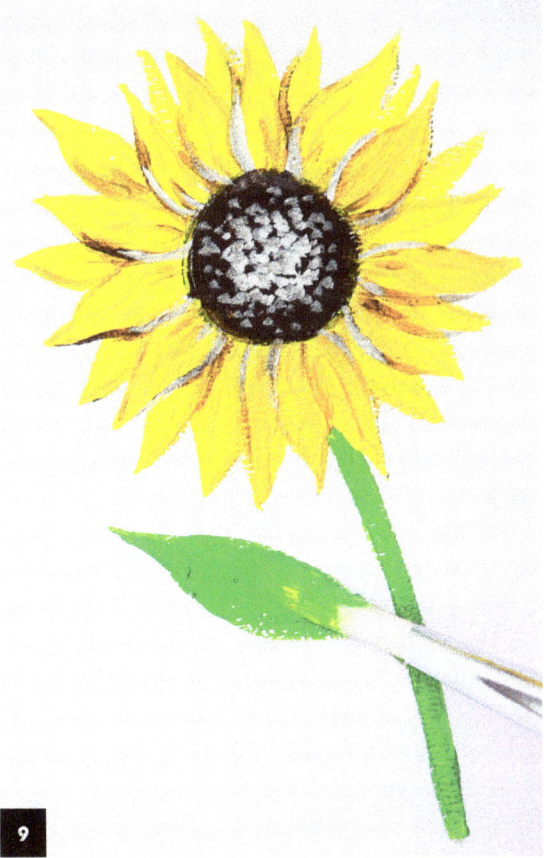

7 Add highlights to the petals and the center of the flower. On the side of each petal opposite the shadow, trace an outline of the highlight using the size 6 round brush loaded with white paint. This brightens up the petals and also separates them from each other.

8 Paint the flower stem. Mix green with a little yellow on the palette to create a spring green. Load the size 6 round brush with the paint and, beginning at the bottom right of the flower, create a slightly diagonal line about 3 inches (7.5 cm) long.

9 Paint a leaf. Using the same technique as with the petals, begin painting a thin line with the tip of the brush 1 to 1½ inches (2.5 to 3.75 cm) away from the stem and then press down to broaden the stroke, creating the leaf and connecting to the stem.

10 Paint another leaf on the other side of the stem. Use white acrylic paint and the size 6 round brush to add veins to the leaves to complete the sunflower (see finished image, page 68).

FLORAL BOUQUET

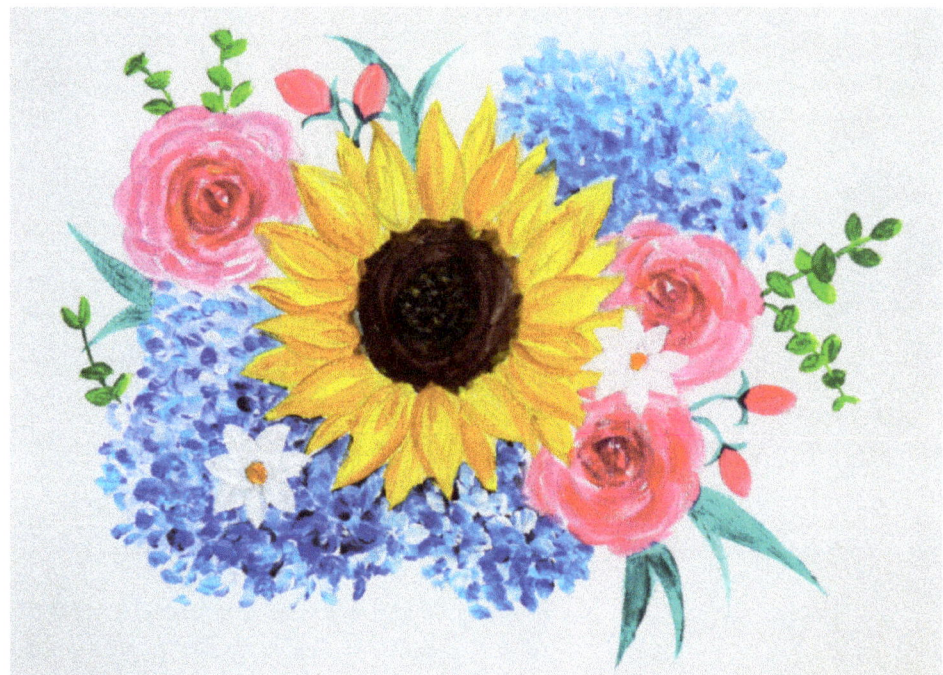

Let's combine all the flowers you've painted so far into a harmonious composition. You'll learn how to choose colors, how to position the flowers, and how to create different kinds of floral and greenery fillers that will make the final arrangement look like it's in full bloom.

The instructions for the individual flowers will refer back to the original lessons, allowing you to focus on the techniques that make the flower arrangement cohesive as you combine the different elements.

1 When painting a floral cluster, think about the flowers you want to include. For this lesson, we'll paint hydrangeas, roses, and sunflowers. Next, choose one flower that will be the highlight of the entire piece; the others will be supporting and complementing that flower. Let's make the sunflower the focus.

Draw an outline of a sunflower in the center of the paper, then draw three roses surrounding the sunflower. Odd numbers in groupings look more interesting because the composition isn't too symmetrical. When adding the roses, situate the blooms so they face the viewer. Hydrangeas are perfect additions because their large blooms can fill gaps in the arrangement. As you add flowers, have some petals and leaves overlap others slightly to make the arrangement look more realistic.

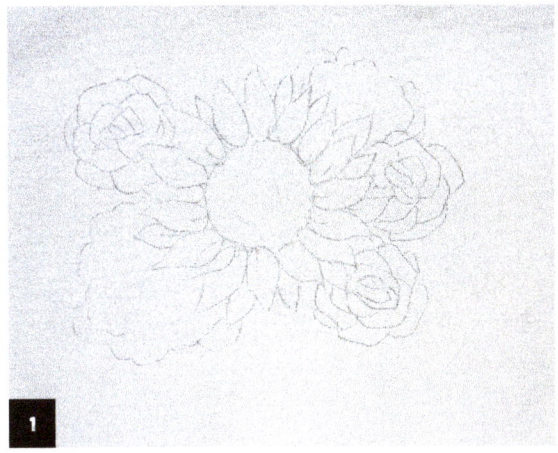

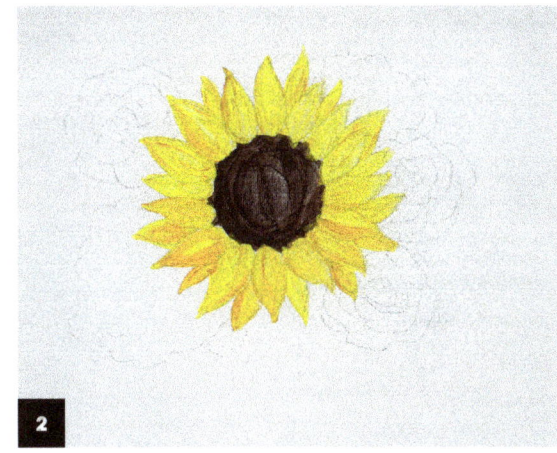

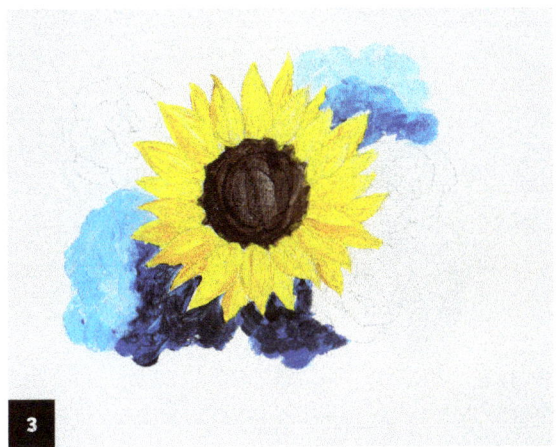

2 Choose a flower as a starting point. I prefer painting the main flower first, as it makes it easier to choose complementary colors and elements as I progress in the painting. Paint the center of the sunflower in a warm brown, allow it to dry, and then paint the petals in a rich yellow using the round brush (see pages 68–71).

3 Add dark blue paint to the palette, load some onto the flat brush, and paint the lower, dark area of the hydrangea (see pages 60–63). The dark blue provides great contrast to the yellow. Mix some white with the blue to create a lighter shade, then paint the top part of the flower.

4 Wait for the base layer to dry. Then dab on the tiny hydrangea petals, using the two-color technique with blue and white paint on the flat brush.

(continued)

TIP

Pay attention to areas where a flower or leaf is beneath or beside another one; make these areas a bit darker because they are in shadow.

5 Paint the roses that adorn the sunflower. Begin by painting the dark red center of the flowers first using the round brush and then adding lighter red shades as you paint the outer petals (see pages 64–67). As some of the roses are underneath the petals of the sunflower, be careful not to paint over the sunflower petals. If you do, simply paint the sunflower petal after the rose has dried. Let this layer dry before adding more elements to complete the flower cluster.

6 Add a variety of small elements to the painting to make it look more complete. Imagine you're buying a bouquet from a florist, and you're in charge of creating the arrangement. Tiny, pretty flower buds are great to include because their shape is different from the blooming flowers. You can select a similar color to the other flowers or a complementary shade. I chose light pink, in keeping with the roses. By choosing a shade that complements the other flowers, the elements in the arrangement add to the overall pleasing look of the flower cluster.

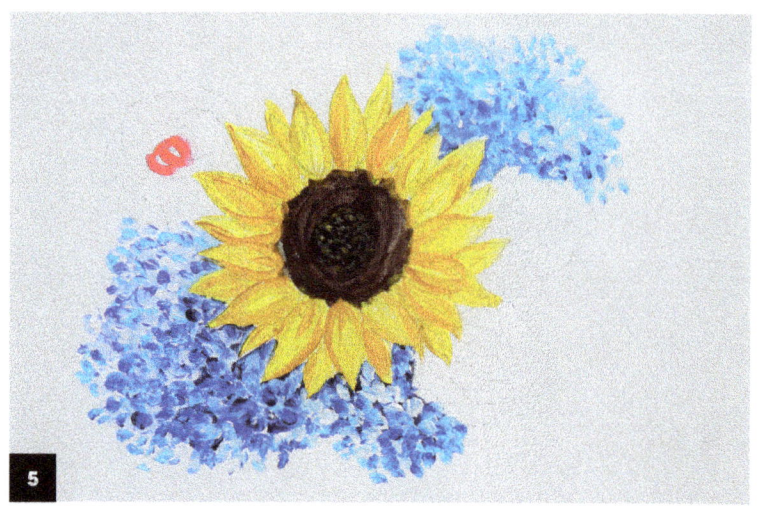

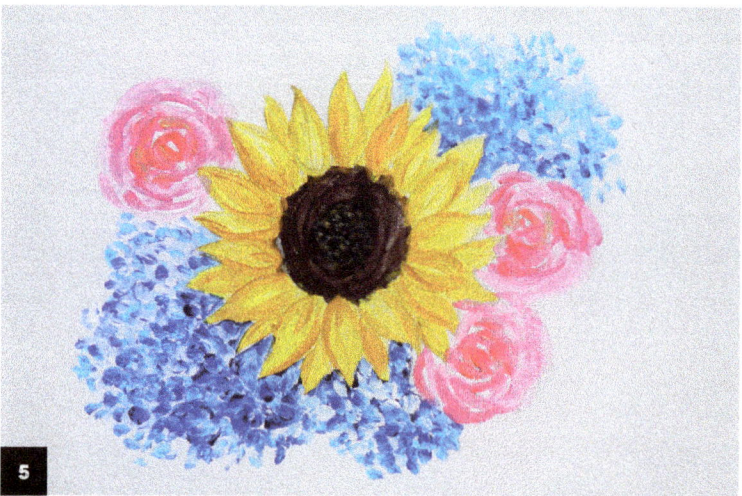

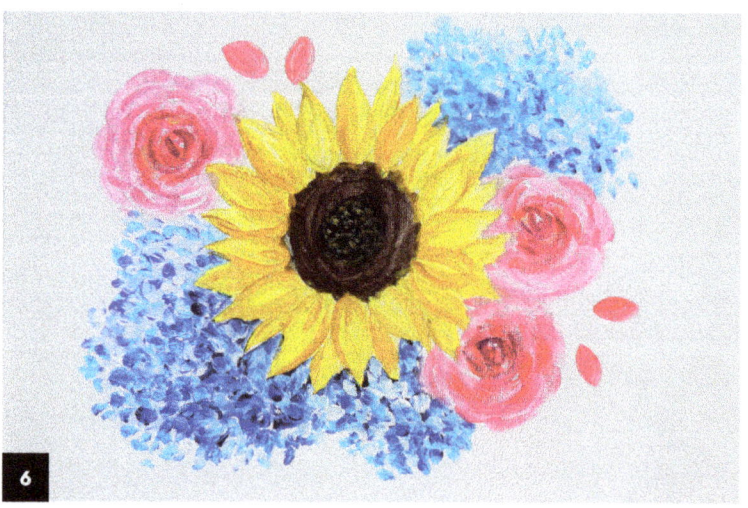

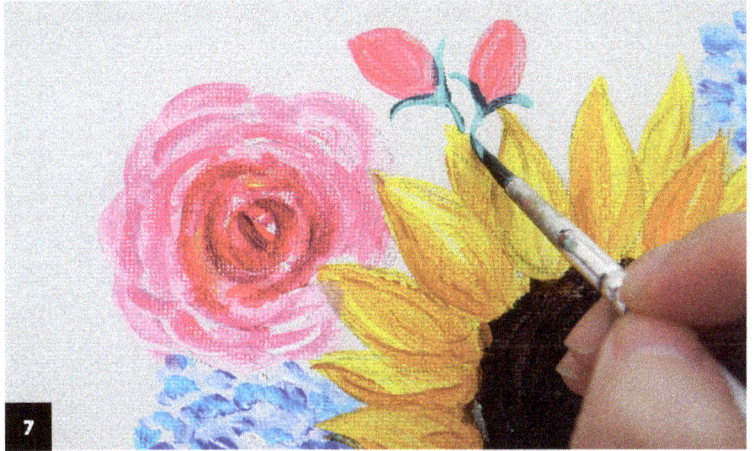

7 Paint a small, oblong shape representing the bud, using the round brush. I usually put two to three buds in an open area that doesn't have any flowers. Paint a thin, curved *V* shape with green paint and the round brush at the bottom of the bud. Then, paint a thin line connecting the bud to the flowers. Paint a couple of tiny buds beside the two roses on the right.

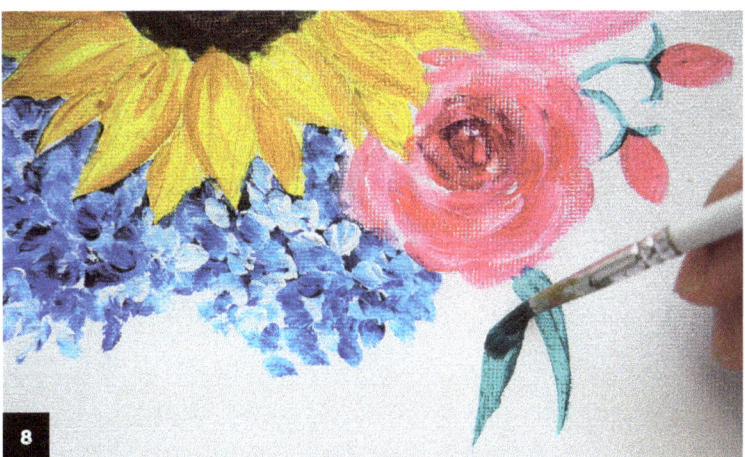

8 A flower cluster would not be complete without some leaves. I like painting two different kinds of leaves in two shades of green; this variety adds interest to the painting. Paint simple leaves first, using the round brush and green paint mixed with a touch of blue. Start painting the tip of the leaf a couple of inches (about 5 cm) away from the flowers with the tip of the brush. Then, gently press the brush down to make the leaf broader until it connects to the flower. Paint these in different lengths and directions around the cluster.

(continued)

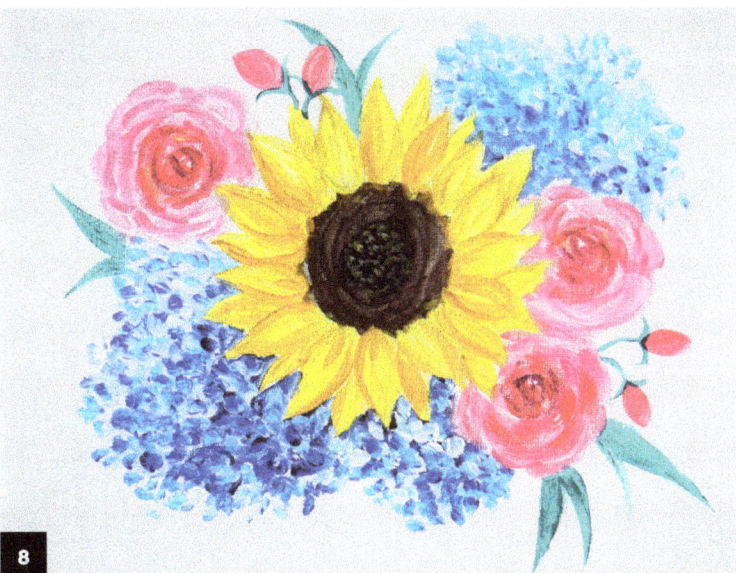

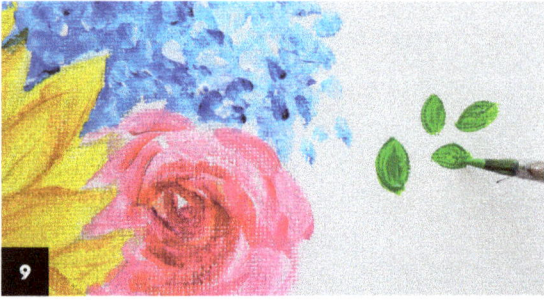

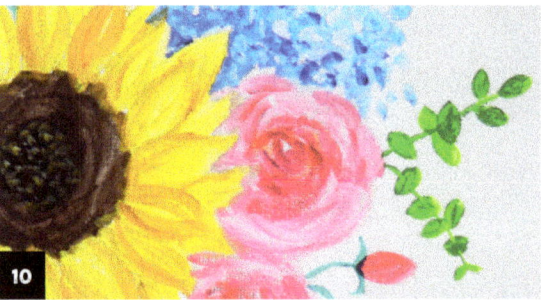

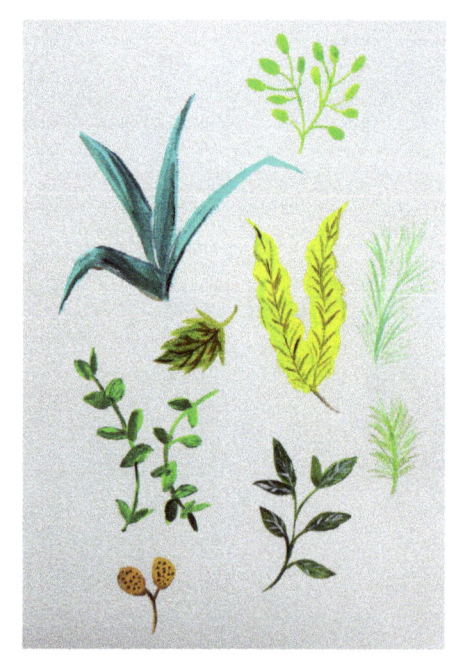

TIP
Leaves can be as interesting and varied as flowers. Try incorporating the simple leaves shown here into your paintings.

9 Paint eucalyptus leaves in yellow-green using the round brush. To create a couple of stems of these leaves, paint a row of several tiny oblong-shaped leaves, slightly opposite each other, and smaller than the buds in step 7.

10 Paint a thin green stem to connect the leaves. You can also paint two additional small leaves and connect the bottom of the leaves with the stem. Try using some of the simple leaves shown in this photo in your paintings.

11 The beauty of acrylics is that you can paint another flower layer even after you've painted the other components. As the final touch, paint an orange dot at the bottom left over the hydrangeas and another one between the two roses on the right. Using white acrylic paint and the round brush, create small, pointed petals surrounding the orange center to make small white flowers. This helps break up the blue of the hydrangea and the red of the roses, allowing the viewers' eyes to explore each element of the flower cluster.

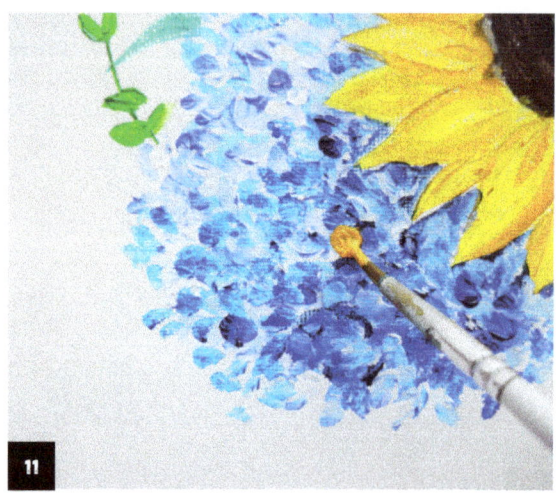

CREATING COMPOSITIONS

Composition may not be the first thing people notice about a piece of art, but it plays a huge role in making or breaking a painting. We all have different aesthetics and tastes, but each painting shares common elements that make it visually appealing. Here are some tips to help you create a successful composition.

- **Create a focal point.** This is the focus of your painting and what the viewer will be immediately drawn to. When I create a floral painting I begin by selecting a flower or two as the focal point. I call these flowers my "superstars," and I build the other elements around them. I rely on different techniques to make these superstars the focal point: Choose a color that will stand out from the rest of the painting, place it near the center or at the center of the paper or canvas, or let the other elements of the painting point toward the focal point.

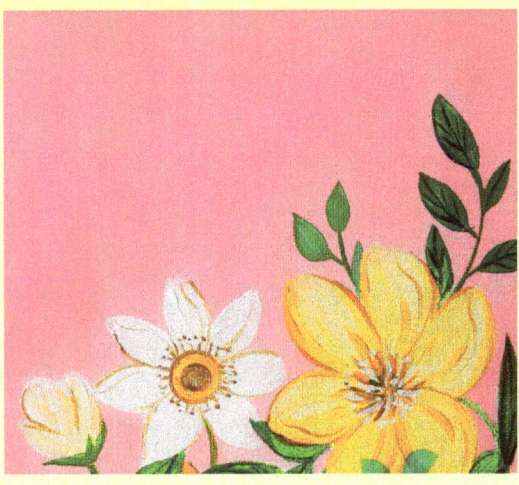

- **Simplify.** Having too many things going on in a painting can leave the viewer confused or overwhelmed. Selecting a limited color palette helps your painting look cohesive and allows the viewer to take in the other elements of the piece.

- **Balance.** Look at your painting at arm's length. Does something seem off? Check to make sure the elements are balanced. Are all the intricate details huddled together on the left side of the painting? Is your subject too close to an edge? Evaluate whether you need to move the subject closer to the center; add or remove elements; or shift the viewer's gaze to another part of the painting—all these factors contribute to a more balanced composition.

Note that these are not strict rules you need to follow. Composition is about understanding how you can best tell your story using the elements in your painting. For a fun exercise, study different kinds of paintings and try to identify how the artists were able to produce a visually balanced composition.

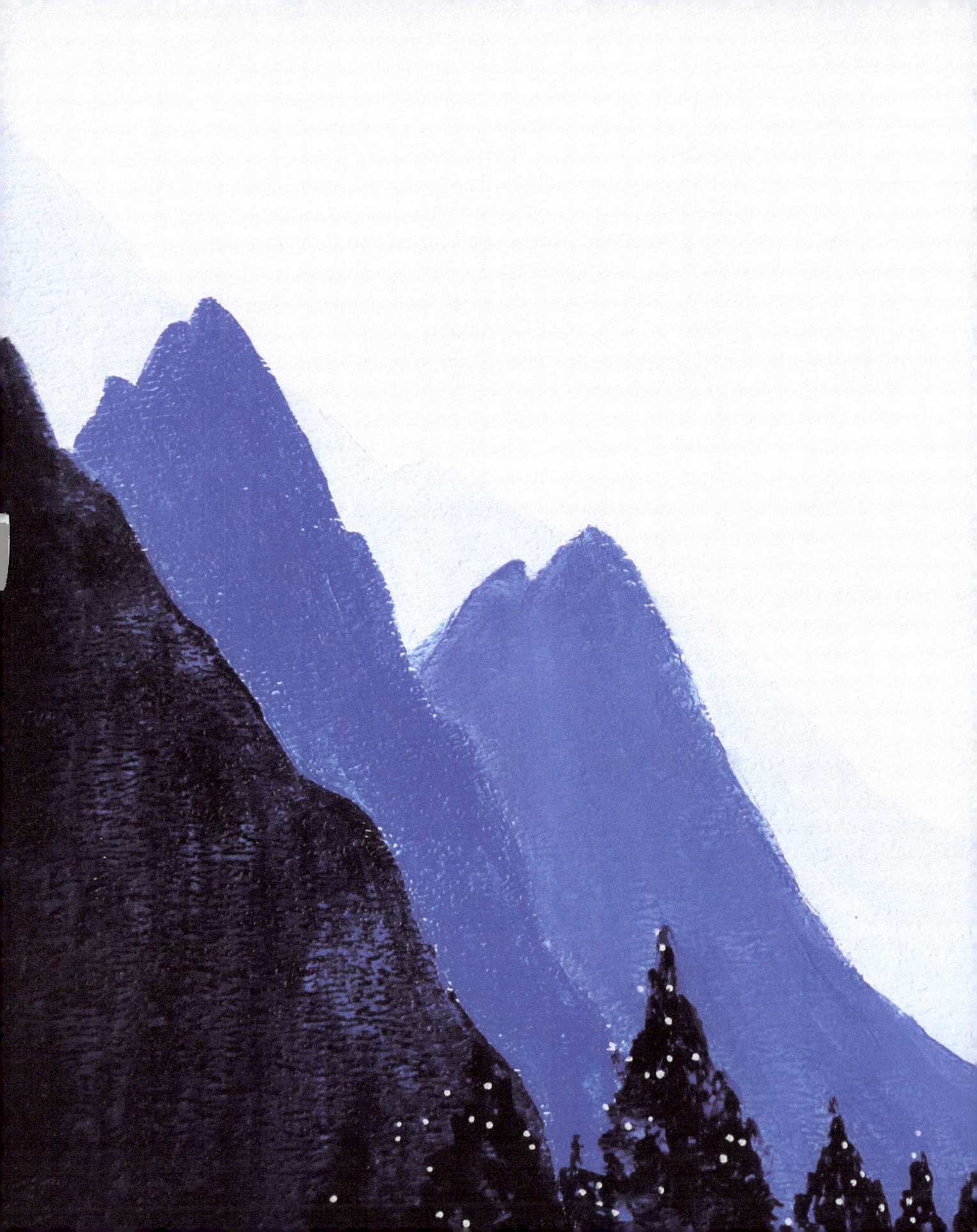

5

LANDSCAPES AND SKIES

Who doesn't like looking up and seeing a beautiful clear blue sky with drifting clouds? Or sitting on a beach, watching a magnificent orange sunset with a nice drink in hand? Just as looking at these beautiful scenes can make you feel peaceful and calm, painting landscapes and skies also lends a sense of serenity. Painting these vistas is like creating a piece of heaven on a canvas that I can look back on when life gets a little too noisy. I'll take you through the process of recreating panoramas such as a cloudy blue sky and an orange sunset using a variety of enjoyable and easy techniques.

SKY AND CLOUDS

MATERIALS

Acrylic paints in blue, white, and black or Payne's gray

Canvas panel (I used an 8" × 10" [20.25 × 25.5 cm] panel.)

Flat brushes, sizes 8 and 10

Filbert brushes, sizes 4 and 8

Round brush, size 2

Mixing palette

For me, painting clouds is therapeutic. In this exercise, we'll keep the sky simple and focus more on the creation of big, white fluffy clouds. The key to achieving this kind of airy effect is how you blend, so let's get right to it!

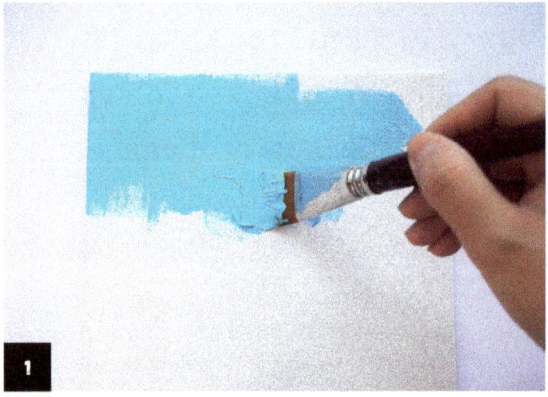

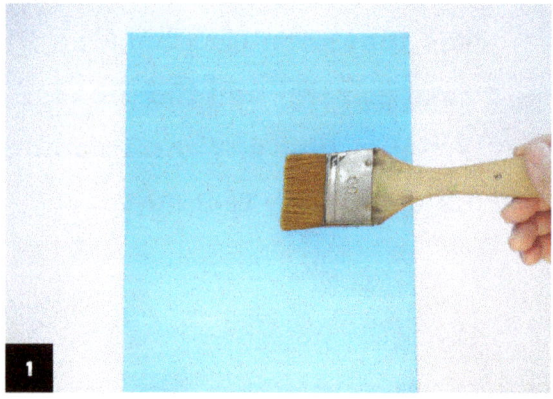

1 Mix blue and white to create a sky-blue color, adjusting the amount of blue or white in the mixture to suit your tastes. The size of your substrate will determine how much of the paint to use; make sure you have enough paint to cover the entire surface, as the color may be uneven if you have to mix more paint.

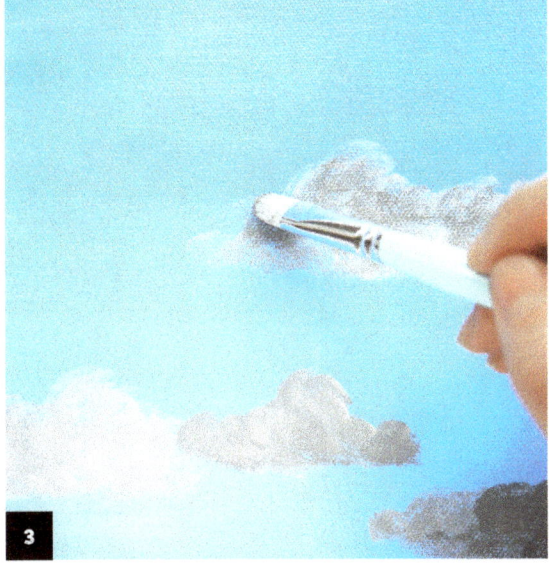

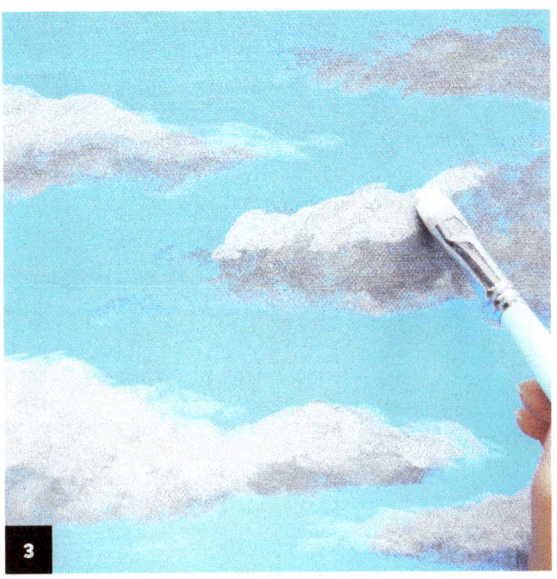

2 Block the entire canvas with the paint, using the size 8 flat brush. Then using the size 10 flat brush with no paint, lightly brush the area with quick sweeping motions, as if you're dusting. The paint should be slightly wet as you do this to achieve the effect of softening and smoothing the background color, blending the hard edges and colors seamlessly. Repeat this dry brushing motion until you get a nice well-blended sky. Allow the paint to dry before moving to the next step.

3 Add some white acrylic paint and a dab of black to the palette. Create light gray by mixing a bit of black with a lot of white, using the size 8 Filbert brush—this will be the cloud color. Lightly paint a cloud using short, quick circular motions with the Filbert brush. Try not to add too much paint to the paper. This allows you to make subtle strokes that make the clouds appear fluffy. While painting the clouds, remember that they come in different shapes and sizes. I added larger clouds on top and wispier clouds at the bottom of the blue sky.

(continued)

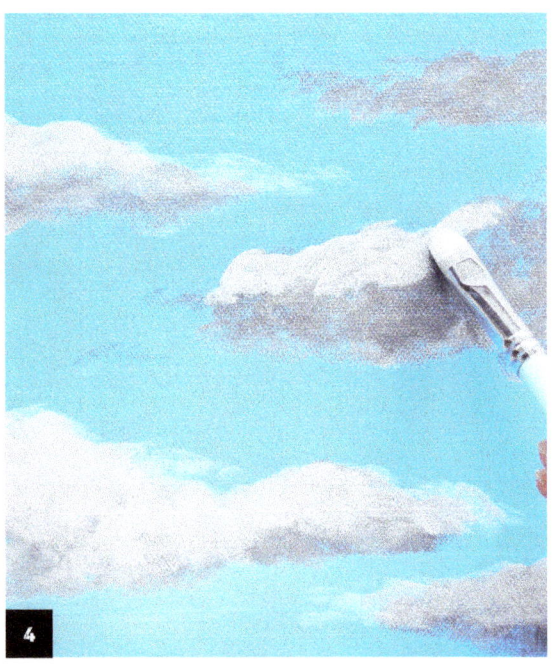

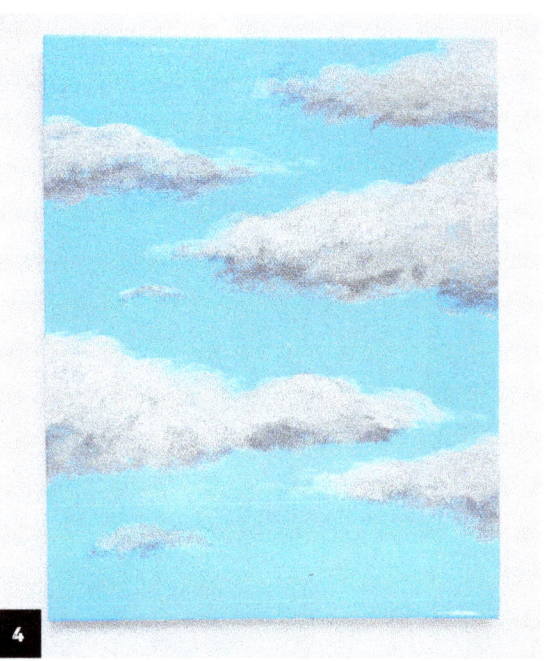

4 Once you're happy with the placement of the light gray clouds, add more white to the gray mixture and paint on top of the gray clouds, using circular motions. This circular blending creates a more airy effect for the clouds as opposed to a horizontal blending. Remember that the paint must be wet in order to make the blending effective, so use quick, short strokes.

5 To paint the edge of the cloud, remove any excess paint on the brush by dipping it in water and wiping it off with a paper towel. Then lightly brush the edge of the cloud as it fades into the blue sky.

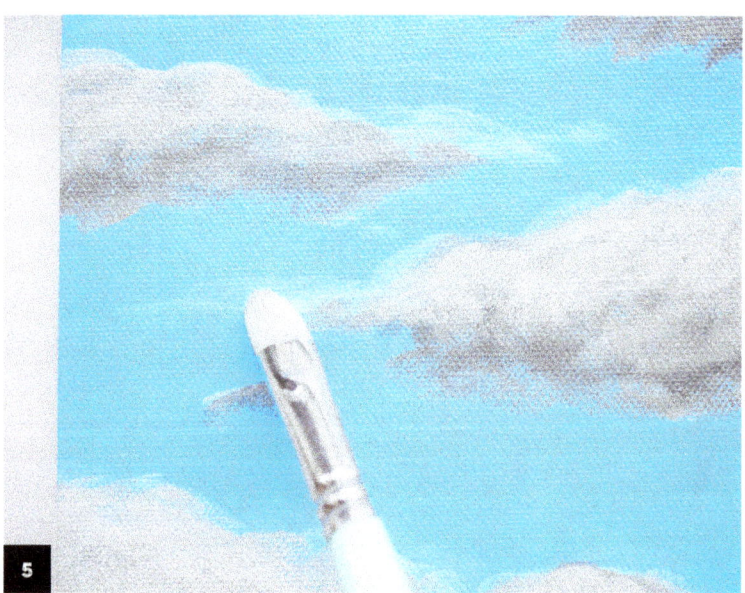

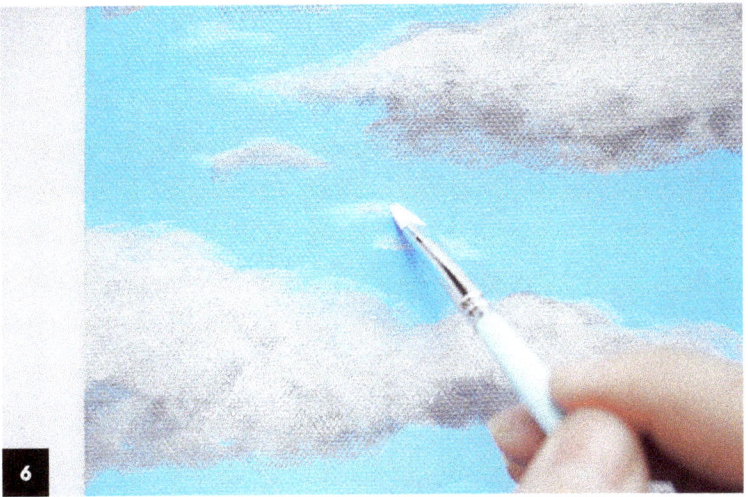

6 Add wispier white clouds in other parts of the sky with the size 4 Filbert brush to create the look of drifting clouds. To do this, use just a touch of white paint mixed with a tiny bit of water and make small circular motions as you move the brush lightly across the background. Wipe off any excess paint on the brush to blend the cloud into the sky as you did in step 5. Pick up some of the light gray paint and use it to add shadows under the larger clouds, giving them a more solid shape.

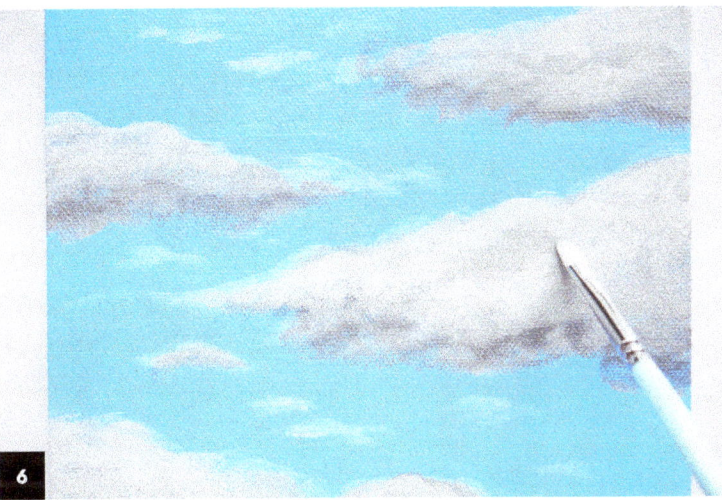

7 Create some tiny birds soaring through the sky and clouds. Add a short dash with a dip in the center near one of the larger clouds, using the round brush and white paint. This forms the silhouette of a bird flying. Add another bird slightly lower so it looks as though the two birds are flying together. To complete the painting, add some tiny scattered white dots in the sky.

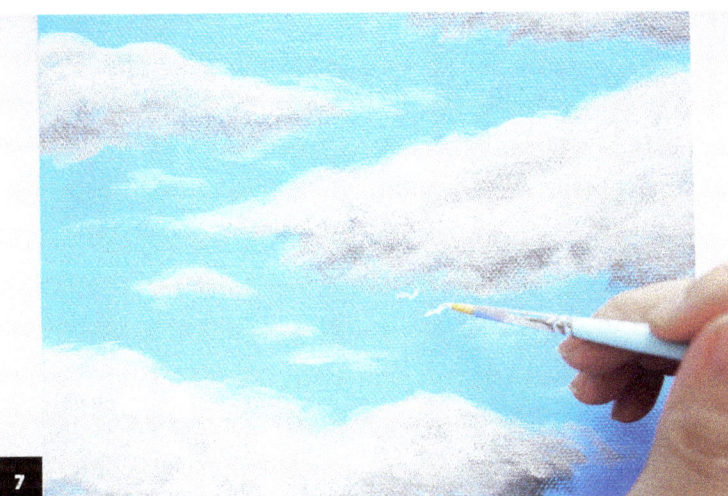

PASTEL EVENING SKY

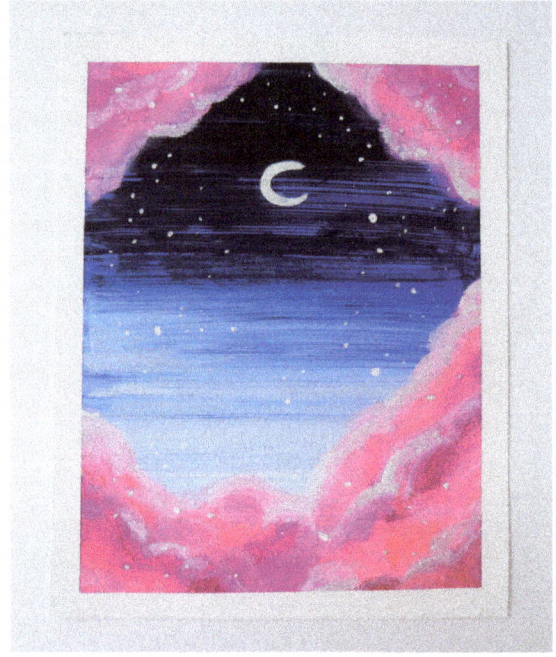

MATERIALS

Acrylic paint in red, blue, violet, white, and black or Payne's gray

300 GSM hot pressed watercolor paper, approximately 5" × 7" (12.5 × 17.75 cm)

Flat brush, size 10

Filbert brushes, sizes 4 and 8

Round brush, size 2

Palette knife

Mixing palette

Paper towel or cloth rag

Now that you've learned how to paint fluffy clouds, let your imagination run wild and create an evening sky filled with pastel-colored clouds. To blend the colors of the evening sky, you'll use a fun tool: the palette knife. Let's start painting!

1 Apply paint directly to the paper. Starting at the middle top and referencing the photo, squeeze out an ample amount of Payne's gray, add ultramarine blue 2 inches (5 cm) below that, sky blue 2 inches (5 cm) below that, and white acrylic paint at the bottom. There should be enough paint to cover the entire canvas, and it's fine if there is excess paint.

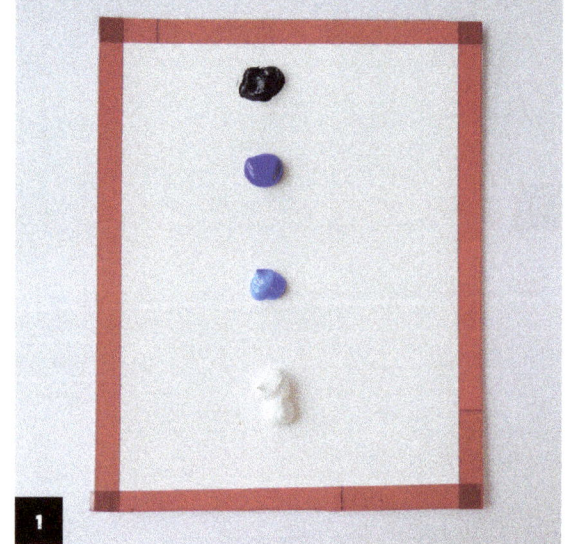

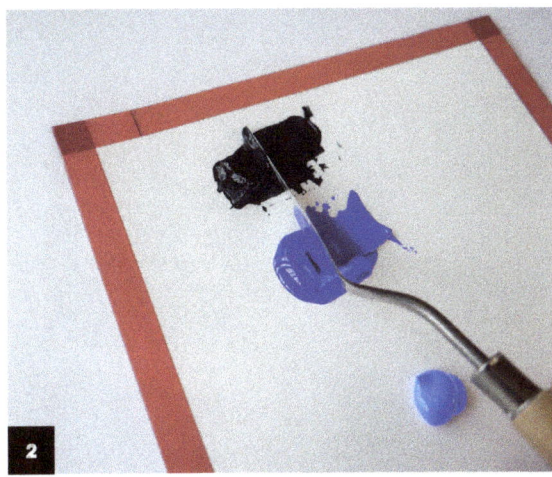

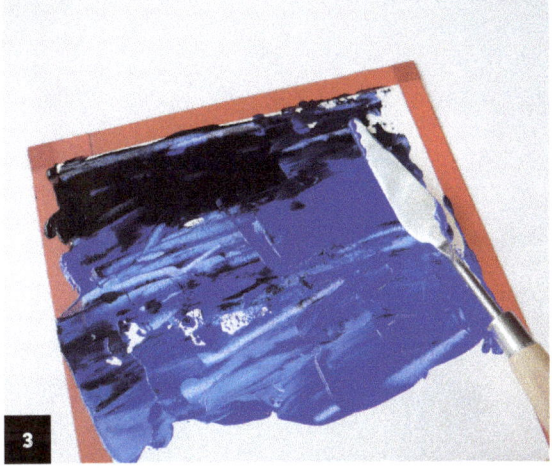

2 Instead of using a brush to spread the paint, use a palette knife. Starting at the top with Payne's gray, spread the color using a back-and-forth motion to move the paint, covering the paper all the way to the sides.

3 Spread the remainder of the paint on the paper. When you reach the ultramarine blue, don't be afraid to mix the residual Payne's gray into it, but be sure to spread the blue so that it also covers the left and right sides of the paper. As you do this, you'll notice the Payne's gray gradually mixing with the ultramarine layer.

(continued)

USING A PALETTE KNIFE TO PAINT

— — —

A palette knife may seem intimidating to use at first, but it's a great tool for blending and applying paint easily. Use the knife to spread and mix paint as you move the tool around the canvas or paper. You can use the top and side of the knife to move the paint on the canvas, but be careful not to scratch the substrate.

With the following tips, you'll be reaching out for this tool more frequently!

- Hold the knife as if you're spreading butter. Be gentle as you hold it so you can move the knife freely, without dragging or scratching the canvas.

- Tilting the knife allows you to pull the paint sideways and spread it evenly.

- Use the bottom part of the knife to transfer and spread paint, not the top. It's easier to pick up the paint by tilting the blade and scraping the paint at the bottom of the knife.

- Clean the knife by wiping off the blade, especially the sides. If the knife has a wooden handle, simply wipe it off—don't let it soak in water, as that may loosen the blade's attachment to the handle.

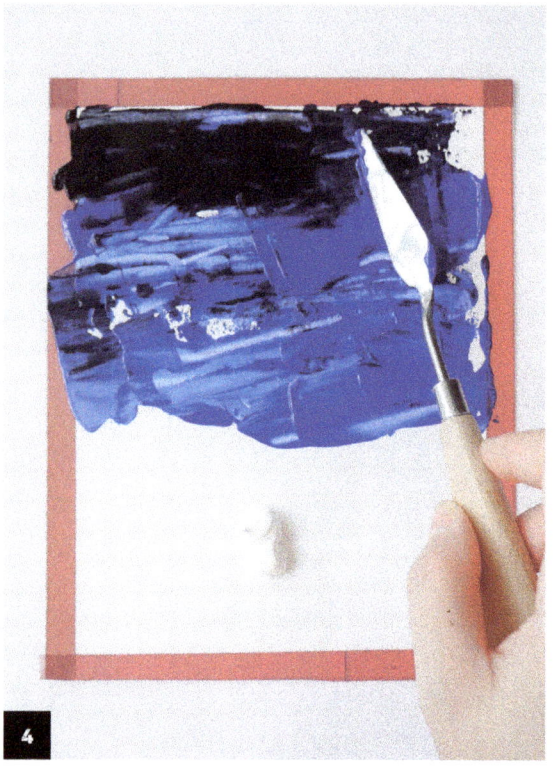

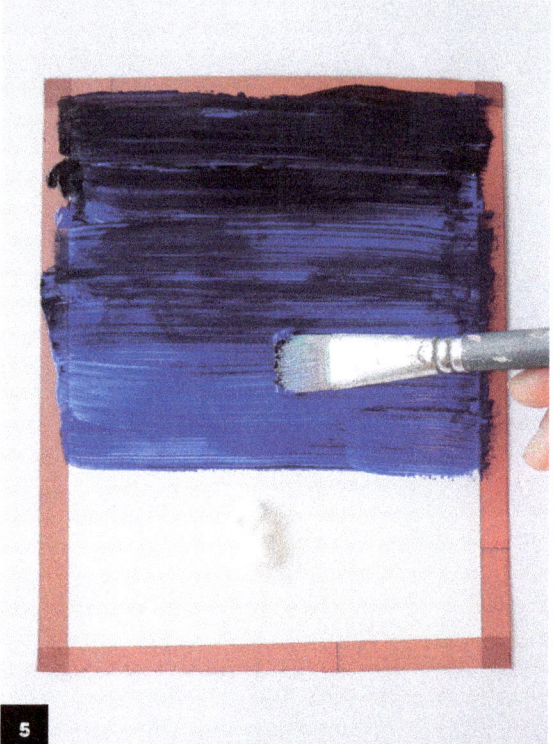

4 Continue to use the palette knife to spread each layer of paint except for the white—that area should be fairly pristine, so a flat brush will be used later.

5 Once the gray and blues have been spread out, and while the paint is still wet, switch out the knife for the size 10 flat brush. Without adding more paint, sweep the paint back and forth with the brush. This helps remove any excess paint and evenly mixes the sky background. You should have a nice gradient blend of Payne's gray and darker and lighter blues.

6 Continue to work while the paint is still wet. Clean the flat brush and use it to spread the white paint at the bottom of the paper, making sure to blend it with the blue above it to create a transition for the sky. As the sky blue is still a bit wet, the white paint will incorporate a light touch of it as you blend it all the way to the bottom of the paper. Allow the paint to dry.

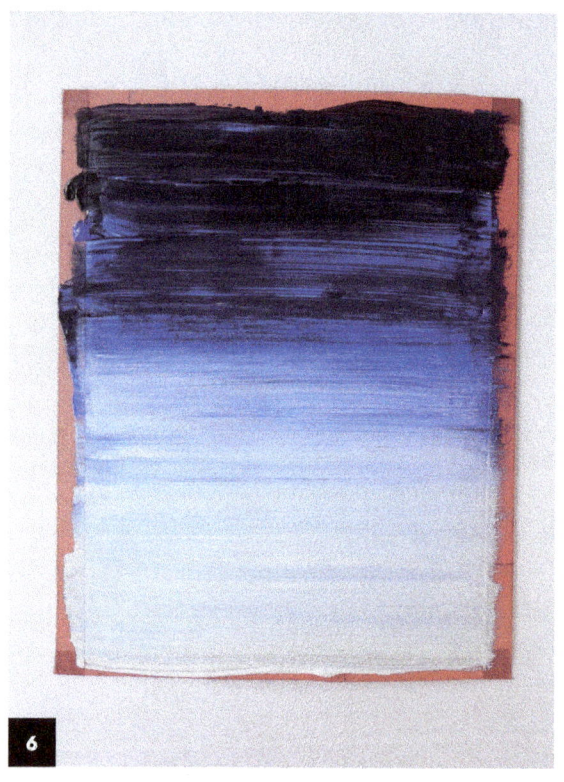

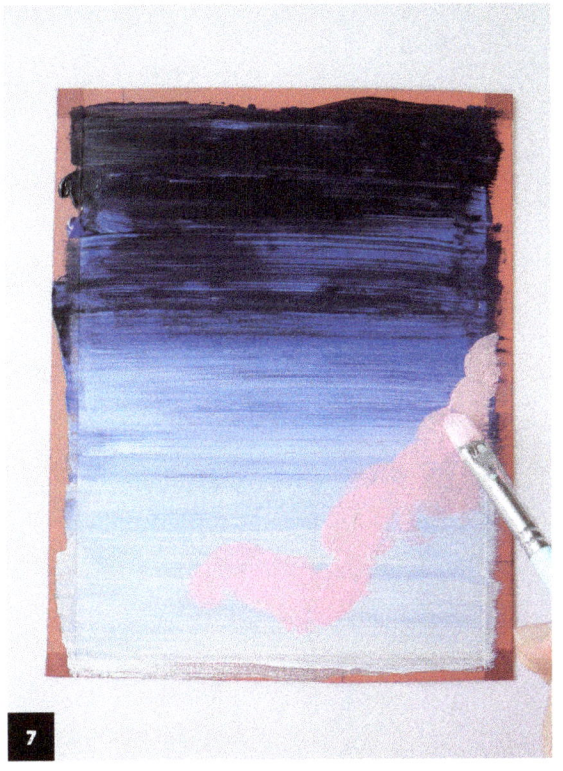

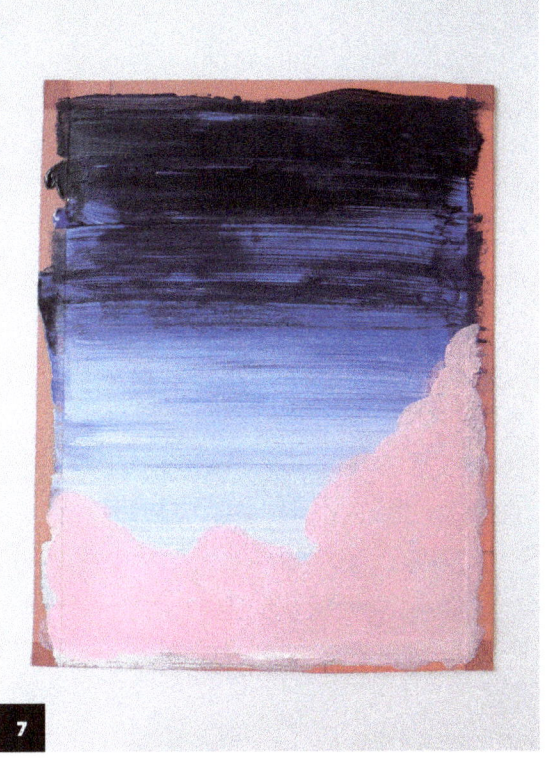

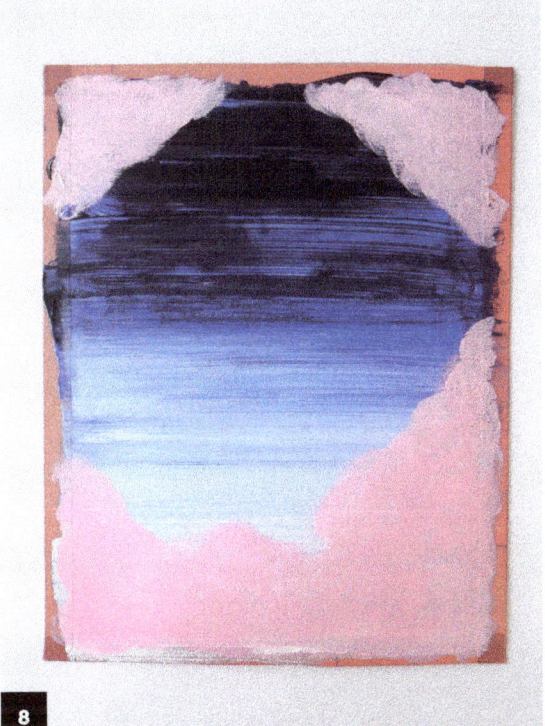

7 To paint the clouds, mix a little red paint with a lot of white to create a medium pink shade. Paint the outline of the clouds with the size 4 Filbert brush, using short strokes. Begin applying the pink at one side of the paper in the middle and angle the brush downward toward the opposite corner. The bottom clouds should be larger than the ones at the top corners. Apply the paint using small circular motions to make the clouds appear fluffy. Painting the clouds with an uneven edge makes them look more natural.

8 Paint more clouds peeking in at the top corners. This layer doesn't need to be opaque as you'll continue to layer other colors. Allow the paint to dry.

(continued)

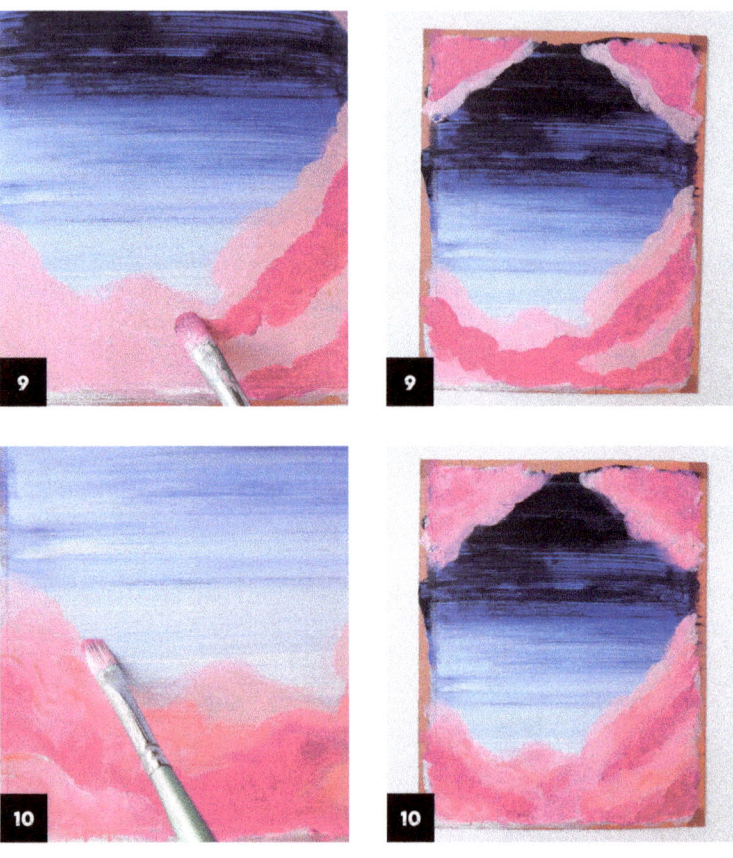

TIP
This color swatch shows the three shades of pink that make up the clouds.

9 Mix red, violet, and white on the palette to create a medium magenta shade for the darker portions of the pastel pink clouds. Begin painting about an inch (2.5 cm) below where you started painting the first pink cloud, using the size 8 Filbert brush. Apply the paint with small circular motions; this provides depth to the clouds and the purple shade works well with the pink. Create an uneven edge, as you did in step 7, keeping in mind that the pink clouds should be more dominant than the purple.

10 Create the medium transition color for the clouds by adding a bit of red to the pink shade. Use this color to blend the lighter pink and dark purple together. Apply this medium pink between the two other shades using the size 4 Filbert brush. Using light, short strokes, gently blend this transition color with the light pink on top, the medium shade in the middle, and the dark purple at the bottom. If the brush has too much paint, wipe off the excess on a paper towel or cloth and continue blending until the clouds look airy and fluffy. Repeat steps 9 and 10 for the clouds in the top corners.

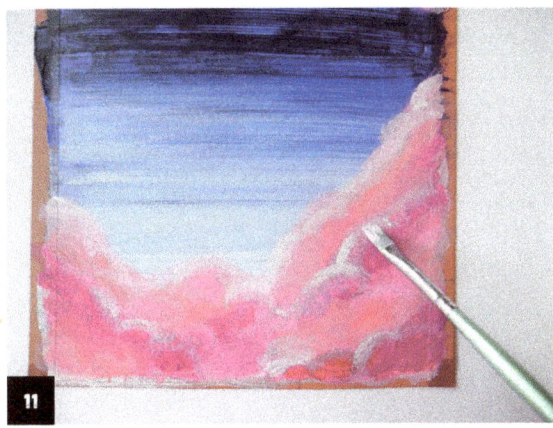

11 Add highlights to the top part of the clouds using white paint and a clean size 4 Filbert brush. Blend the edges of the clouds so the outline looks less defined and sharp. Continue blending until the clouds are to your liking. Allow the paint to dry.

12 Paint tiny white dots around the canvas to represent stars, using the size 2 round brush. Create a crescent shape in the center of the sky for the beautiful moon that graces your evening pastel sky (see finished image, page 84).

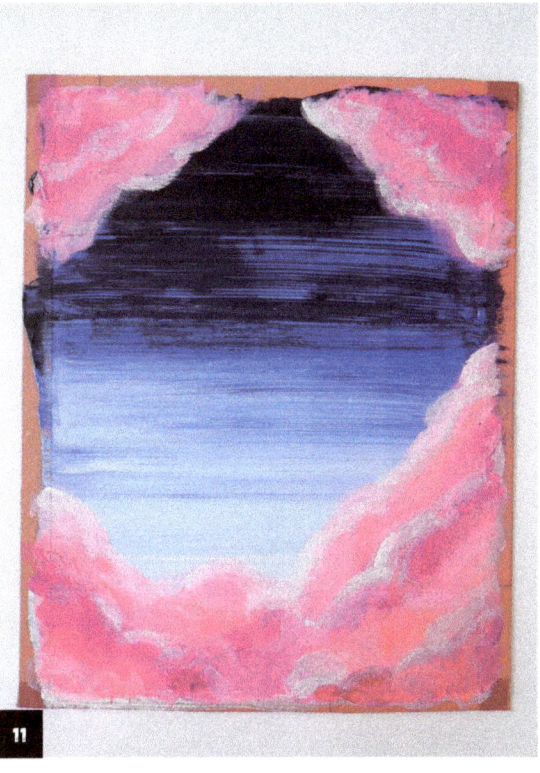

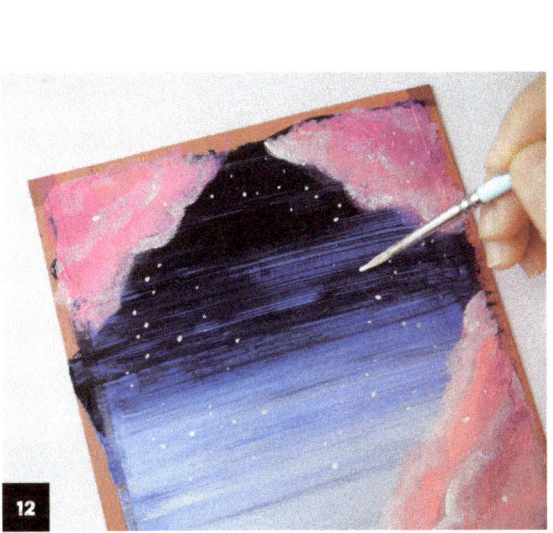

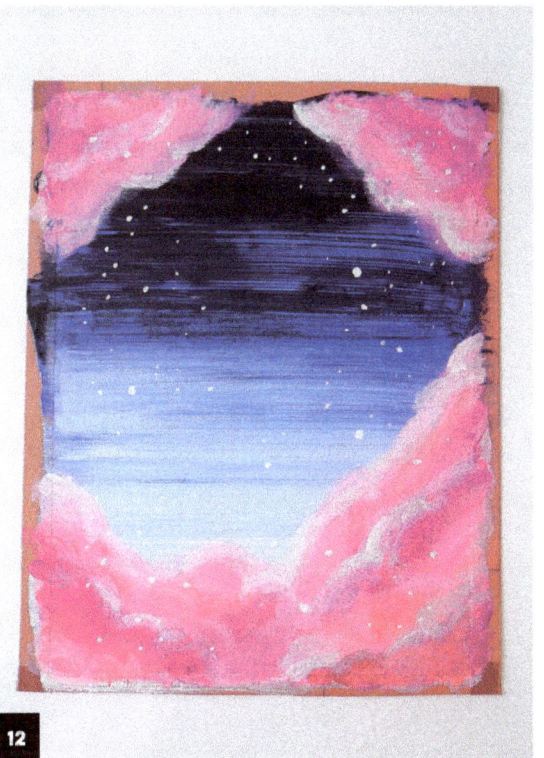

SUNSET CITYSCAPE

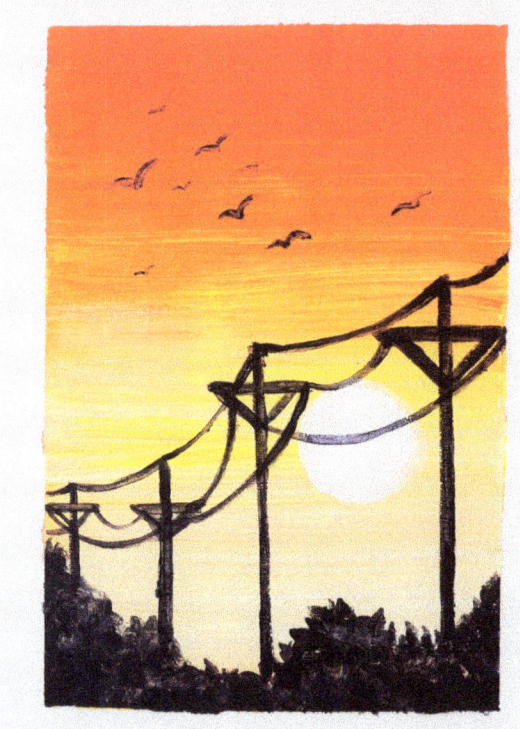

Sunsets are one of nature's most beautiful phenomena. We love watching the skies go from red to orange to yellow until the mighty sun sinks beneath the horizon and the evening begins. In this lesson, you'll paint a gradient with the colors of the setting sun and depict a cityscape with some guidance on perspective.

1 Apply a pea-size amount of several paint colors in descending order on your canvas, making sure they're equally spaced: red, orange, yellow (with a bit of white), and white at the bottom.

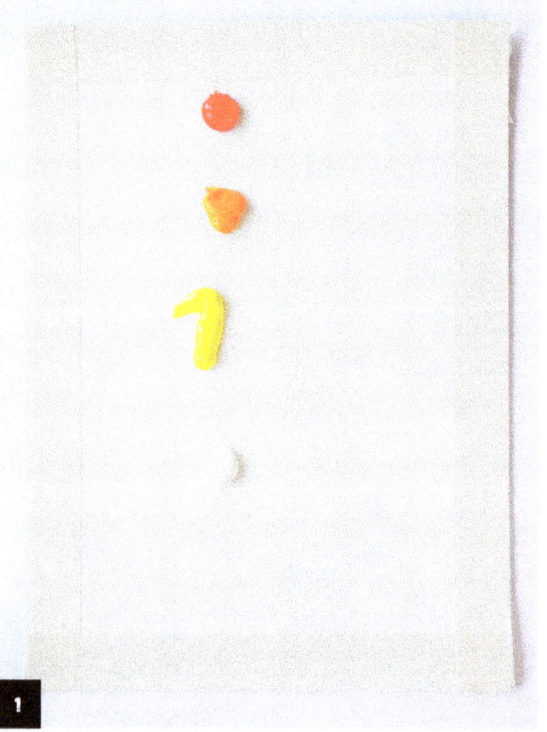

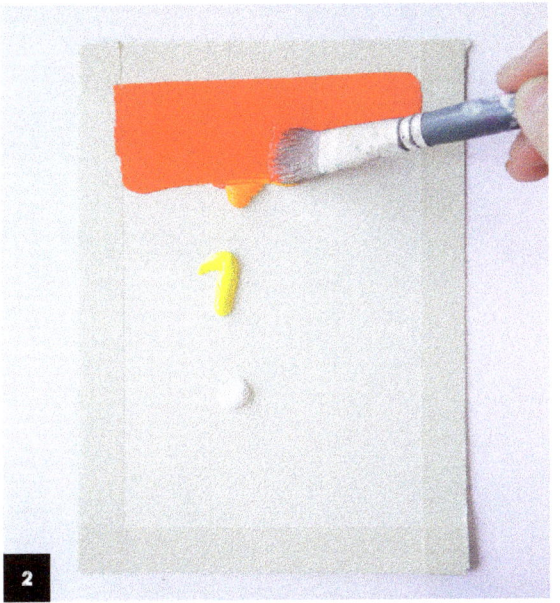

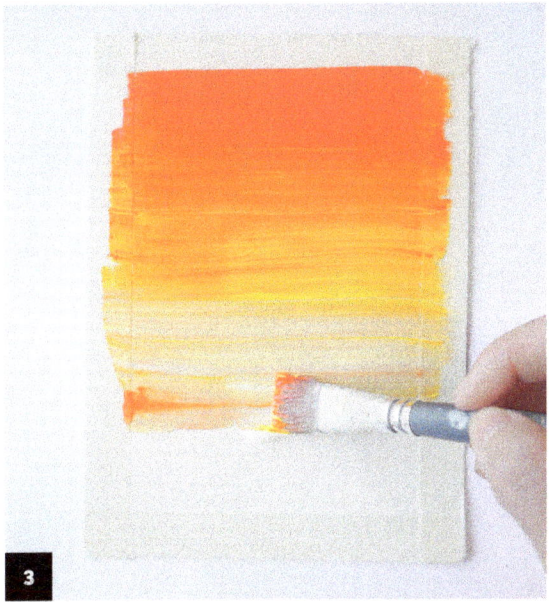

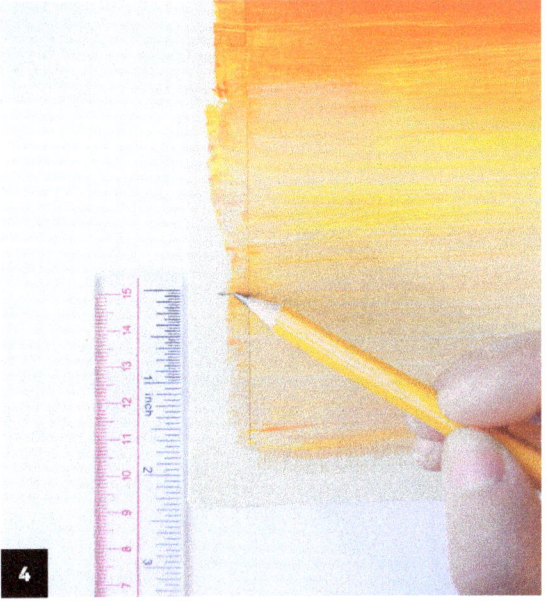

2 Starting at the top with red, sweep the paint from side to side, using the size 10 flat brush.

3 Continue this technique, working your way down the canvas, blending the colors as you move and not cleaning the brush between colors. By the time you reach the bottom of the canvas, you will have created a gradient of the colors. Allow the paint to dry.

4 Lightly draw a light horizontal line an inch (2.5 cm) from the bottom of the paper for the horizon line, where the sky meets the land. This will be your guide for painting the setting sun.

(continued)

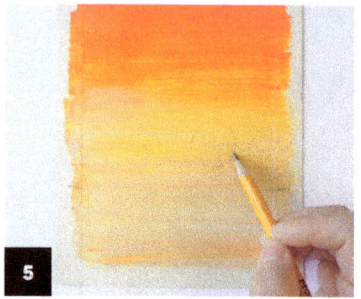
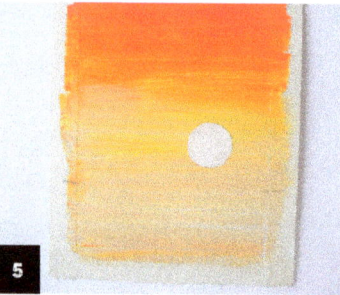
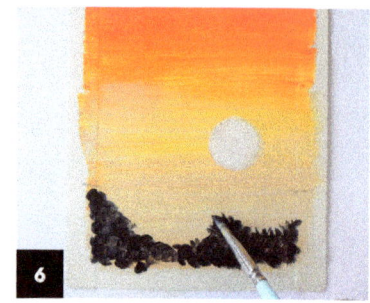

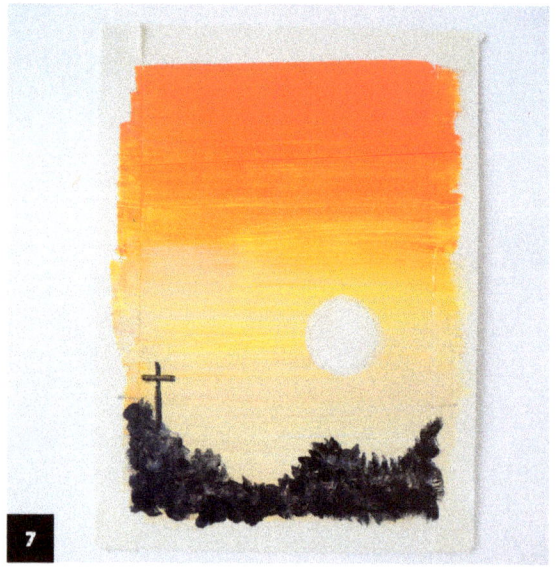
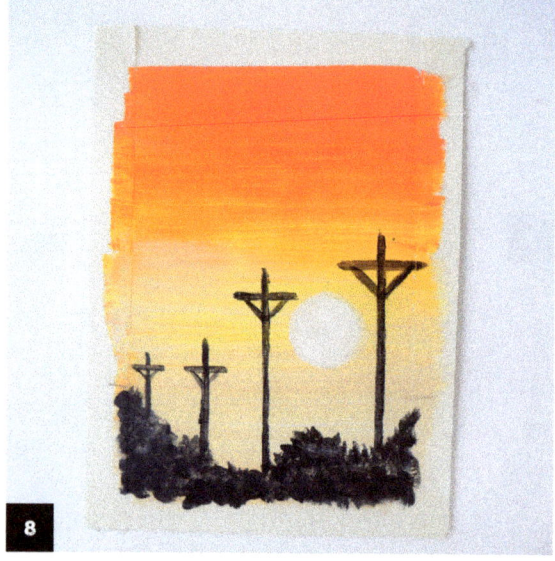

5 Draw a circle about the size of a dime right above the horizon line with a pencil to represent the sun. Make it slightly off-center, toward the right, and paint it an extremely pale yellow—almost white.

6 Create some treetops a little below the horizon. Paint a silhouette of rolling hills with Payne's gray; this will be a row of trees. Use the edge of the size 8 flat brush to make short, thin strokes at the top of the trees to create leaves. Allow the paint to dry.

7 As noted in "Getting Some Perspective," opposite, the vanishing point is where the outermost object in my perspective disappears, so that power pole will be very small. To create the pole, paint a vertical line at the left of the canvas, almost at the border, and then paint a short horizontal line near the top.

8 As you move back from the vanishing point, paint another pole slightly larger than the first one. Notice that this second pole is spaced a bit farther apart than the first, using the invisible parallel lines of the vanishing point as a guide. Paint two more electric poles, making sure they are bigger and farther apart than the previous two. The last pole is the largest one, as it is closest to the viewer. Paint a *V* under the horizontal line of each pole.

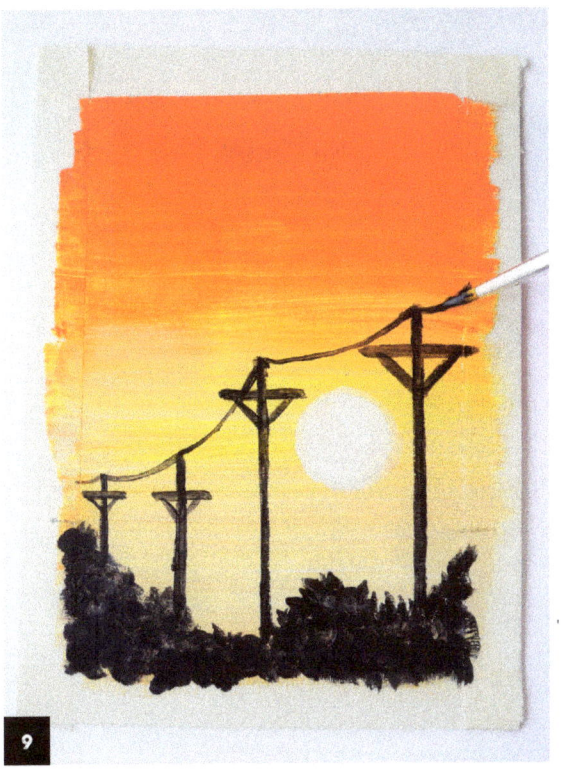

GETTING SOME PERSPECTIVE

In simple terms, perspective is the point of view that you want the viewer to see in your landscape. Perspective allows the artist to convey three-dimensional distance and space with a two-dimensional medium.

For this painting, the perspective is represented by the power poles, which are trailing off in the distance. My point of view, called the vantage point, is from the lower right corner looking up. The area to the left where the power lines disappear is called the vanishing point.

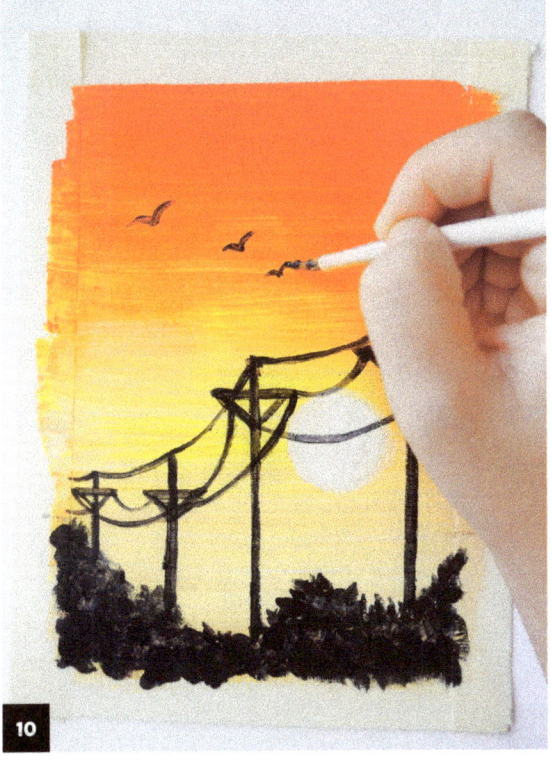

9 Using the round brush and Payne's gray, add a thin swag connecting each power pole all the way to the vanishing point. Make sure that the line becomes thinner as you move toward the vanishing point.

10 Paint some small birds in the sky, creating a curved *V* with the round brush and Payne's gray.

SNOWY MOUNTAINS

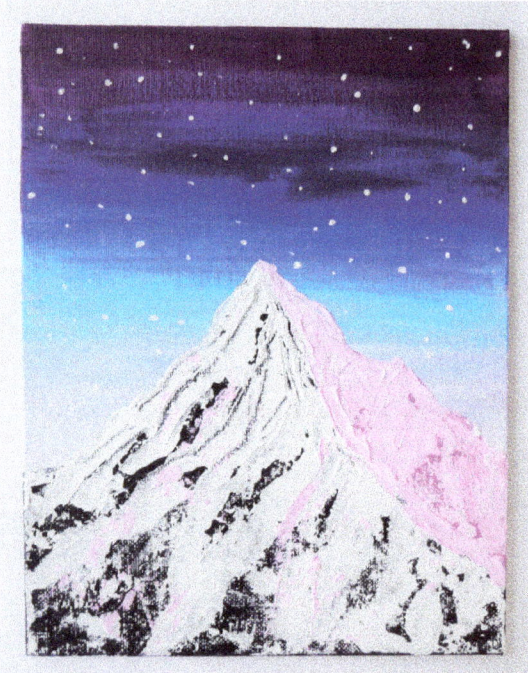

MATERIALS

— • • —

Acrylic paint in blue, violet, white, and black or Payne's gray

Canvas panel, 8" × 10" (20.25 × 25.5 cm)

Flat brush, size 8

Round brush, size 6

Filbert brush, size 4

Mixing palette

Palette knife

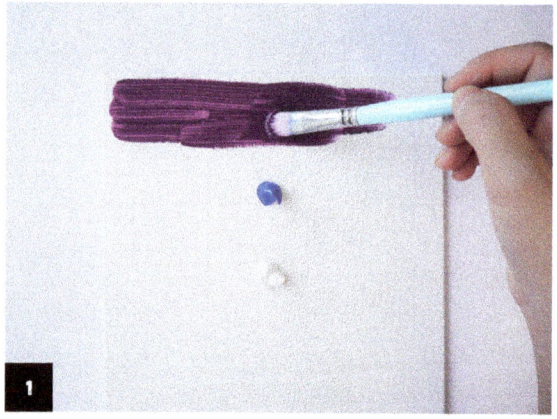

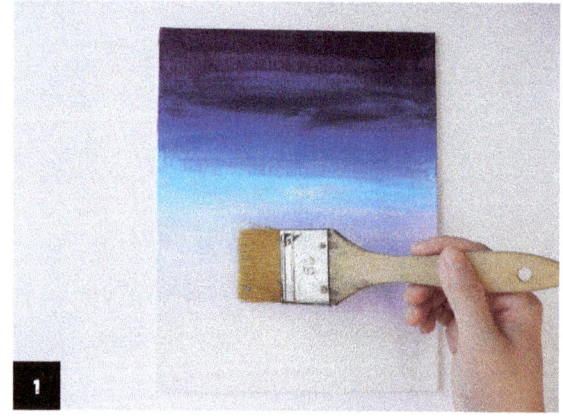

For this lesson, you'll combine the techniques you've learned from painting skies to create this beautiful snowy mountain range. You'll add to your palette knife skills by using the tool to create a snowy mountain cap.

1 Prepare the paint for creating a gradient of the sky by adding these paint colors to the canvas, in order from the top: violet, blue, light blue (mix blue and white), and white. Using the flat brush, spread the paint across the canvas, starting with violet and gradually mixing each succeeding color until you've reached light blue. Clean the brush and spread the white paint until the bottom part of the canvas is covered. Brush back and forth with the flat brush to soften the gradient on the painting. Allow the paint to dry.

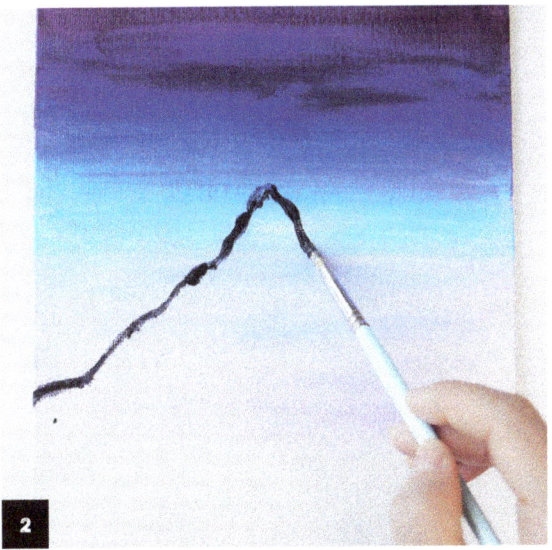

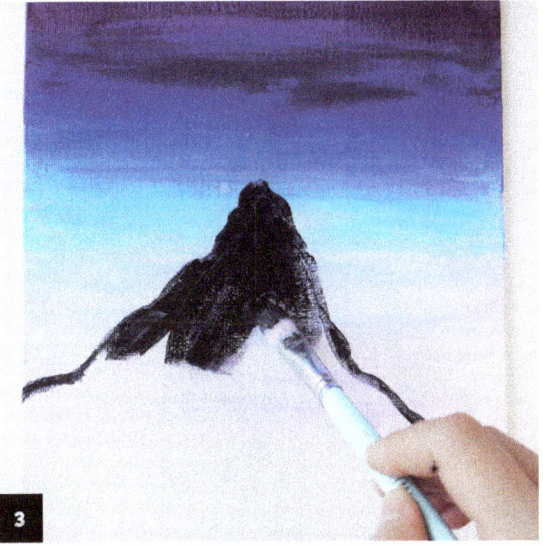

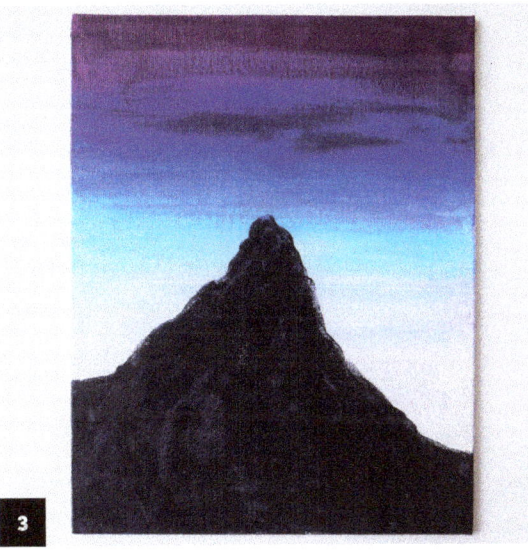

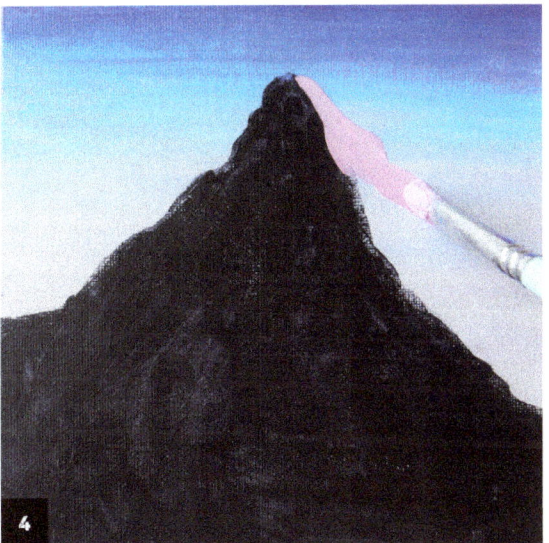

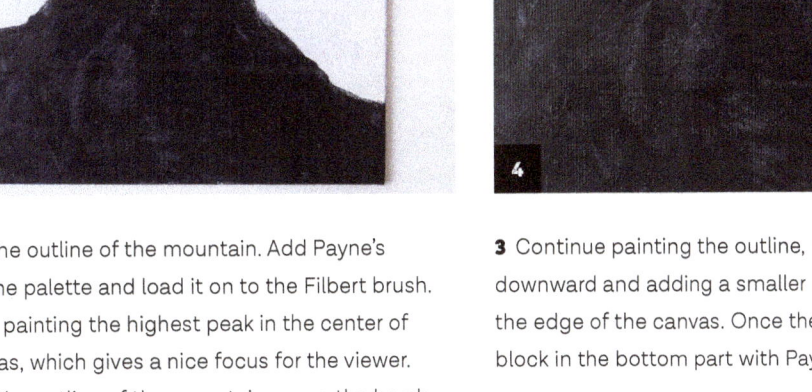

2 Paint the outline of the mountain. Add Payne's gray to the palette and load it on to the Filbert brush. Begin by painting the highest peak in the center of the canvas, which gives a nice focus for the viewer. To paint the outline of the mountain, move the brush in a jagged motion, at an angle, giving the outline a rough-edge feel.

3 Continue painting the outline, moving the brush downward and adding a smaller peak before reaching the edge of the canvas. Once the outline is complete, block in the bottom part with Payne's gray.

4 Use a brighter color to add contrast on the mountain's right side. Mix violet and a little white to create a soft purple color. Begin painting the tip of the mountain, using the round brush.

(continued)

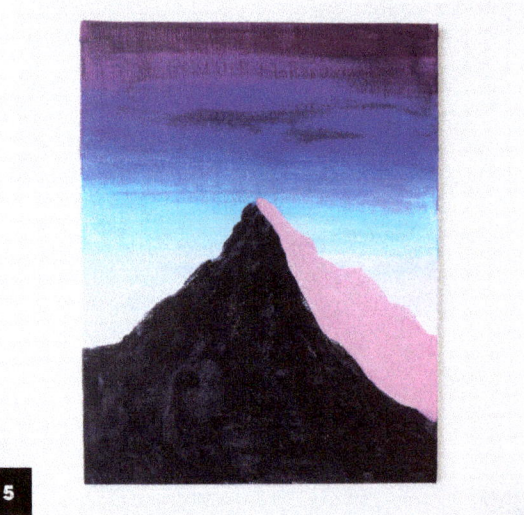

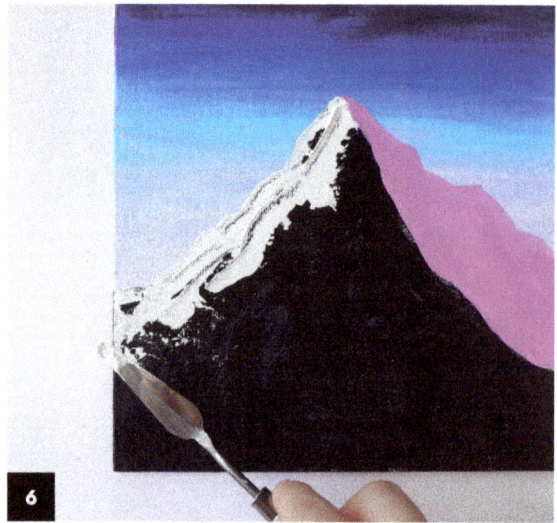

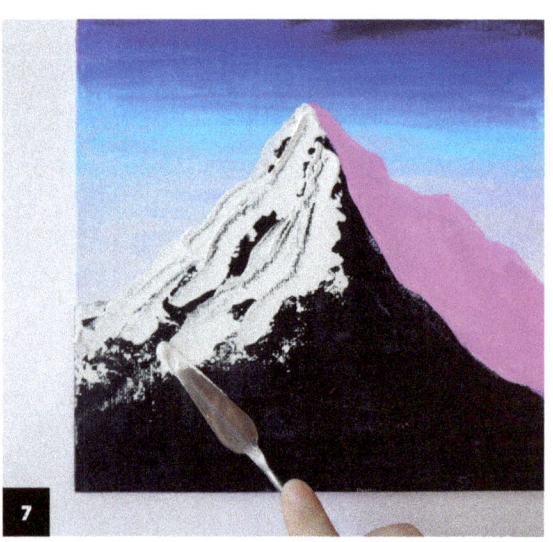

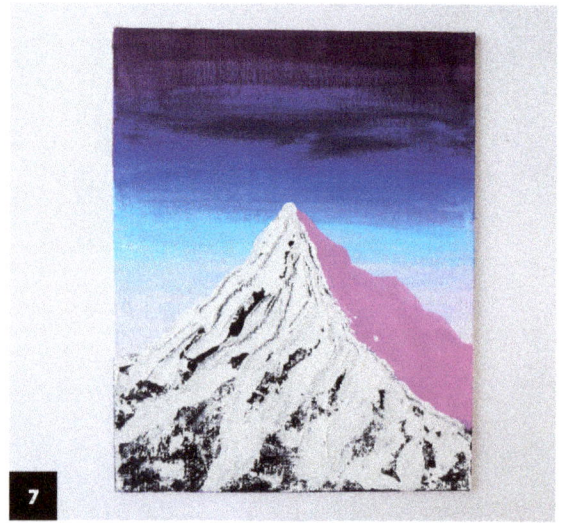

5 Sweep the brush down the slope to about an inch (2.5 cm) above the dark area you painted in step 3. Allow the paint to dry.

6 Add white paint to the palette and, using the palette knife, pick up a substantial amount of paint with the back of the knife. Starting at the mountain peak, gently move the edge of the knife in a zigzag motion to the left, bringing the paint down to the left edge of the painting.

7 Apply another layer; pick up more paint from the palette and start at the top of the outline, gradually pulling down the paint. In the image, you can see that I've moved the white paint to the left using the palette knife, while leaving the right side of the mountain bare. Using the palette knife lends a ragged snowy effect to the mountain.

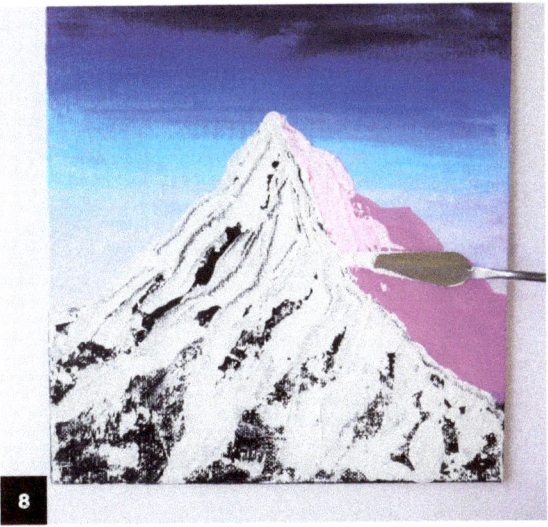

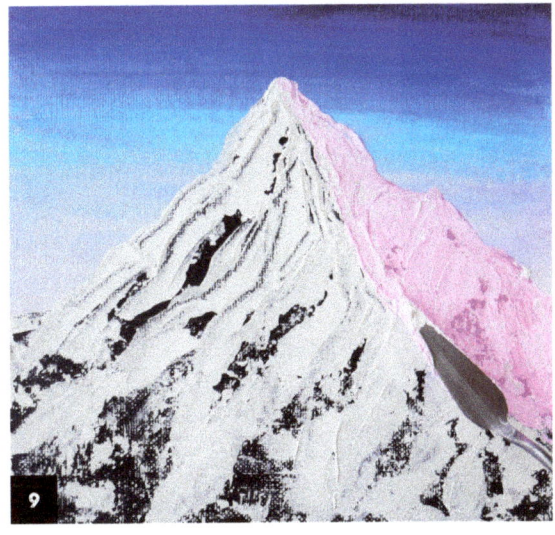

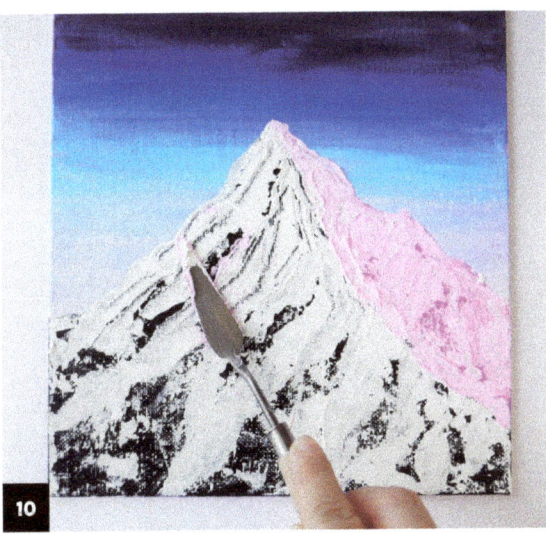

8 Add more white paint to the light purple mix to create a snowy effect on the right side of the mountain. Using the same method as in step 6, pick up some of the light purple paint using the back of the palette knife and, starting at the top of the mountain, move the knife in a zigzag motion to the right until you reach the edge. It should feel as though you're spreading butter on toast.

9 Add more paint to the edge of the palette knife and lightly drag the edge of the knife from the tip of the mountain to the bottom, following the line where the black and purple shades meet. Allow the paint to dry.

10 Create more contrast on the snow on the left side of the mountain. Pick up some of the purple mixed in step 8 with the palette knife. Employing the same technique you used to create the snowy texture in step 6, gently run the knife through the paint diagonally. Dip the round brush in white paint and add tiny dots in the sky to represent snow falling over the mountaintop (see the finished image, page 94).

TIP
Applying paint with a palette knife adds texture and dimension to a painting. Here the technique gives the mountain a layered effect and the feeling of height.

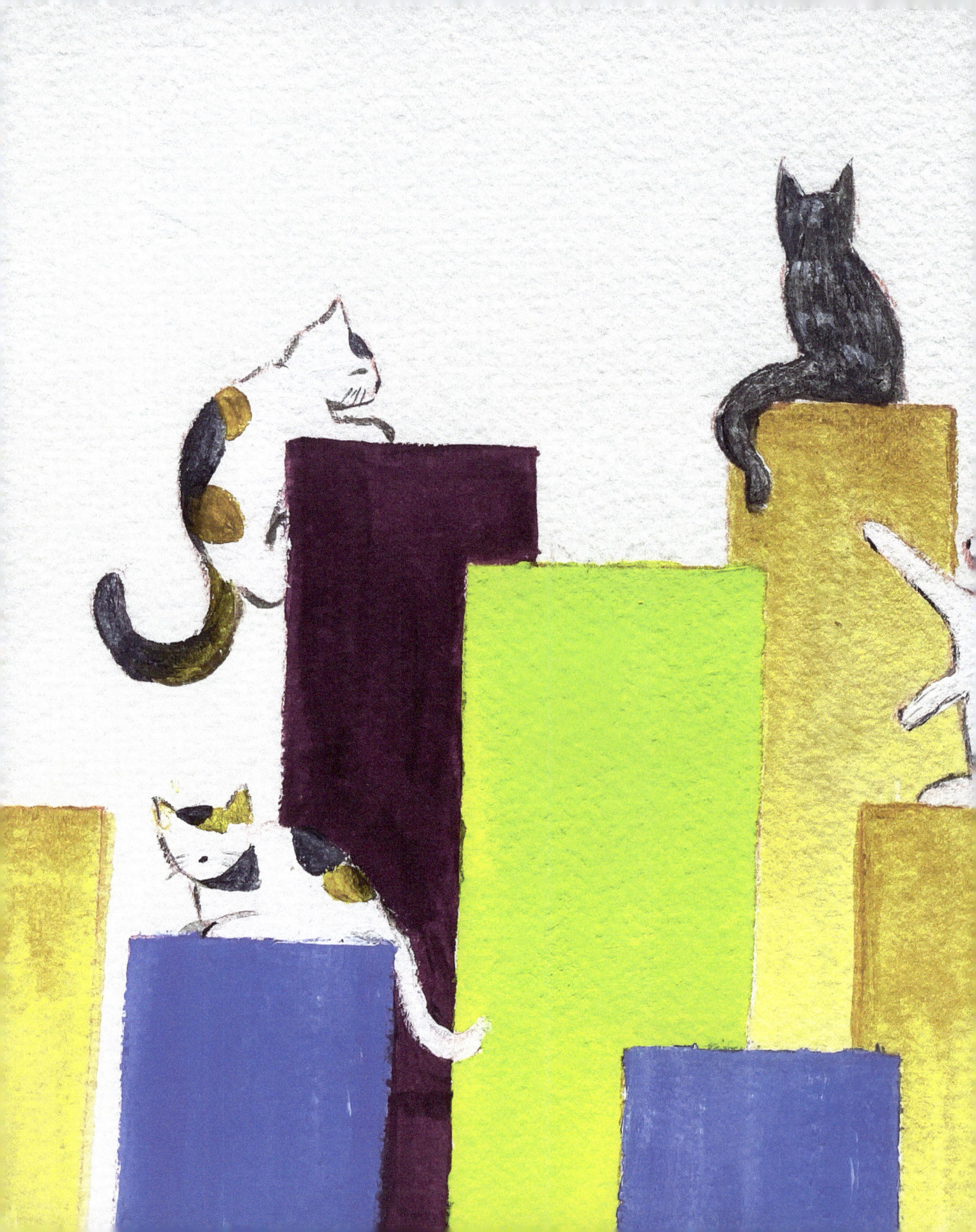

6

ADORABLE ANIMALS

— — — — — —

Capturing the likeness of small creatures in a painting is super fun and exciting. I often get requests from people for paintings of their adorable pets that they can treasure as keepsakes for years to come. I've done several acrylic paintings of my own lovable companions that I display in my home. Painting animals can be challenging because they're living creatures with unique features, even within the same species. Our goal as artists is to capture the most identifiable traits in our paintings. In this chapter, we'll learn how to render fur, feathers, scales, and other unique animal characteristics using the acrylic techniques we've learned so far, as well as new ones.

KOI FISH

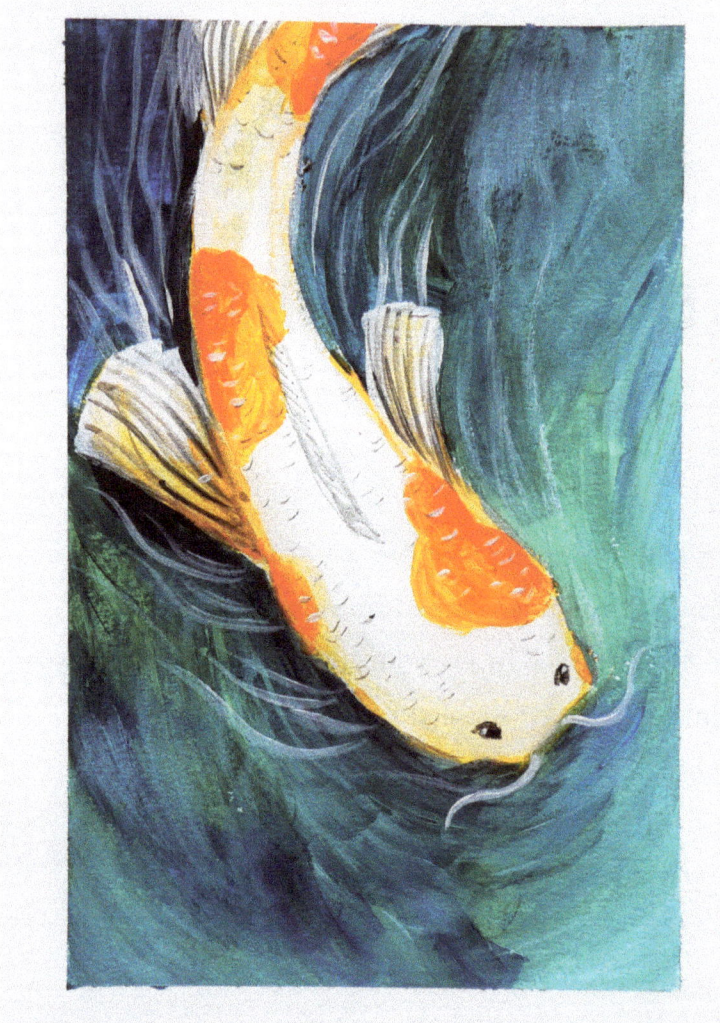

MATERIALS

- - -

Acrylic paint in red,
orange, blue, green,
white, brown,
and black

Canvas paper, 5" × 7"
(12.5 × 17.75 cm)

Round brush, size 2 with
soft synthetic bristles

Flat brush, size 4

Koi fish symbolize abundance and good luck, and I love incorporating them in my paintings. These prized fish are not only celebrated for their symbolism but also for their beautiful and distinctive colorations. You'll learn how to paint a simple koi fish, rendering its colorful scales and depicting how the fish moves in water.

1 Apply a small amount of orange paint to the palette and dilute it with water, using the flat brush. Paint the outline of the koi fish on the paper, including the fins and tail. The body of the fish should be a modified S shape to convey the flow and movement of the fish in water.

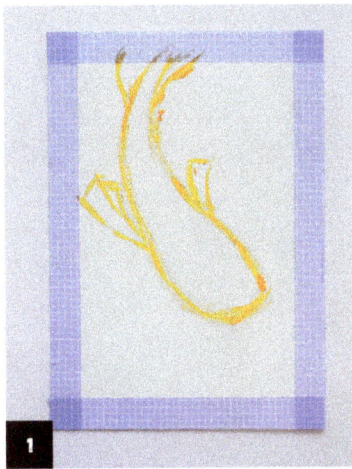

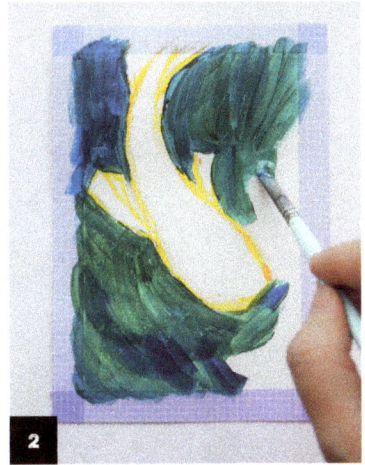

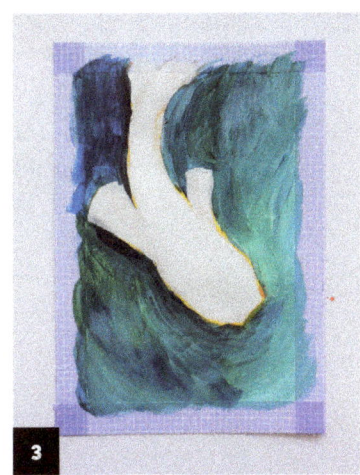

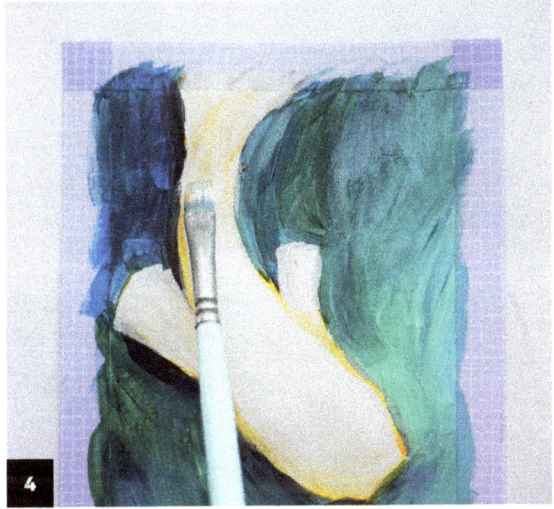

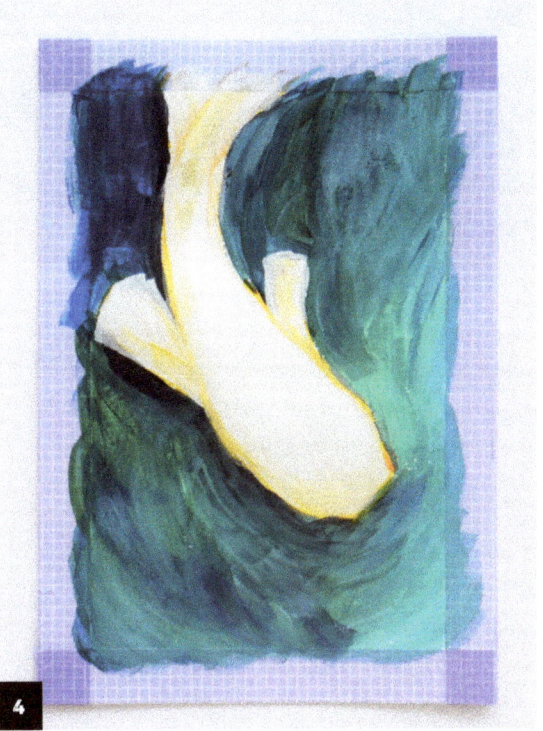

2 To paint the pond background the fish is swimming in, add equal amounts of blue, green, and white paint to the palette and lightly mix them together. Don't worry about blending the colors too much, as this makes the water look more realistic. Clean the brush and begin blocking in the background with these shades, being careful not to paint over the koi fish outline.

3 Darken the background color by adding a small amount of black and a little water. Add this color under the fish's belly to represent its shadow, using the flat brush. Add a bit of this color under the fins and tail as well. Allow the paint to dry. Clean the brush for the next step.

4 Add white paint to the palette and block in the koi fish, using the flat brush. Before the paint dries completely, dilute a small amount of brown paint with water on the palette and brush it on one side of the fish, adding a bit of warmth to the painting. Allow the paint to dry.

(continued)

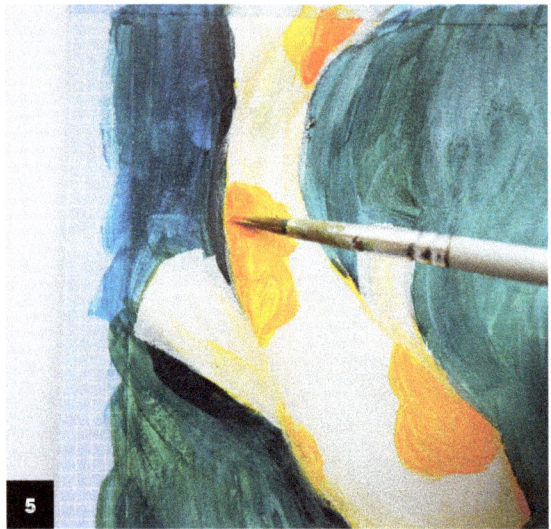

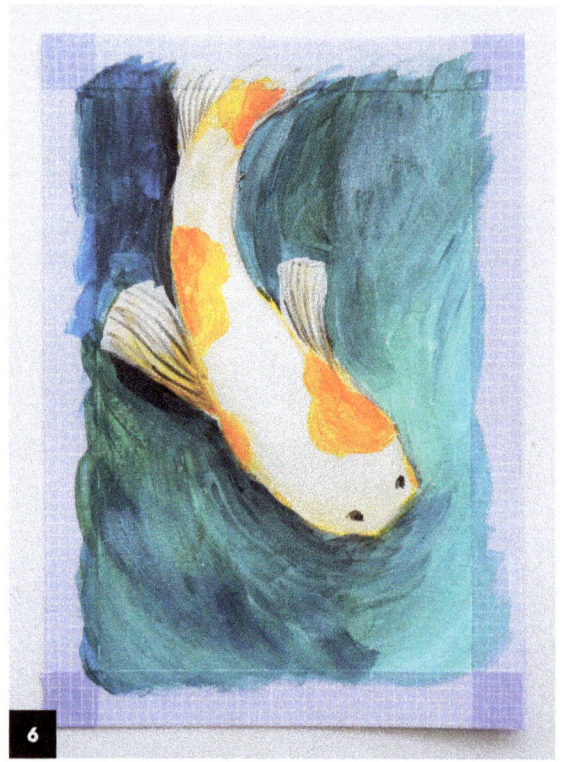

5 Add orange paint to the palette and add markings to the fish's head, body, and tail with the round brush. Mix a bit of red with the orange and add this color to the markings near the edge to give them more depth. Allow the paint to dry.

6 Add black paint to the palette and use the round brush to carefully paint small dots for the fish's eyes. Add a small amount of water to the black paint and add details to the fins and tail. Create flowing lines that begin at the center of the body and go toward the edge, ending at the fin and tail tips.

7 Make scattered small comma strokes on the side of the fish to create the scales, using the same diluted black paint and the round brush. Clean the brush.

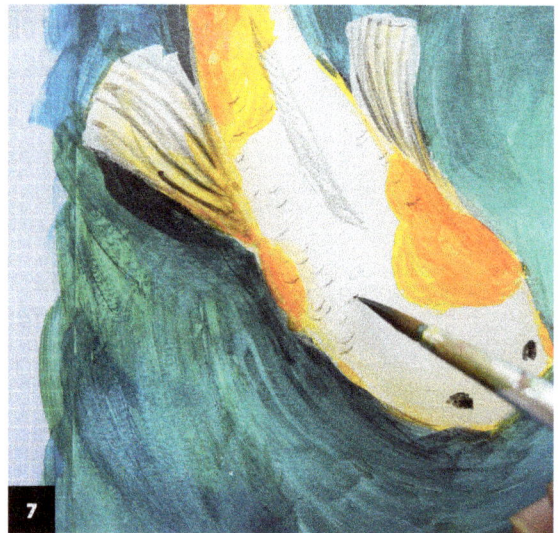

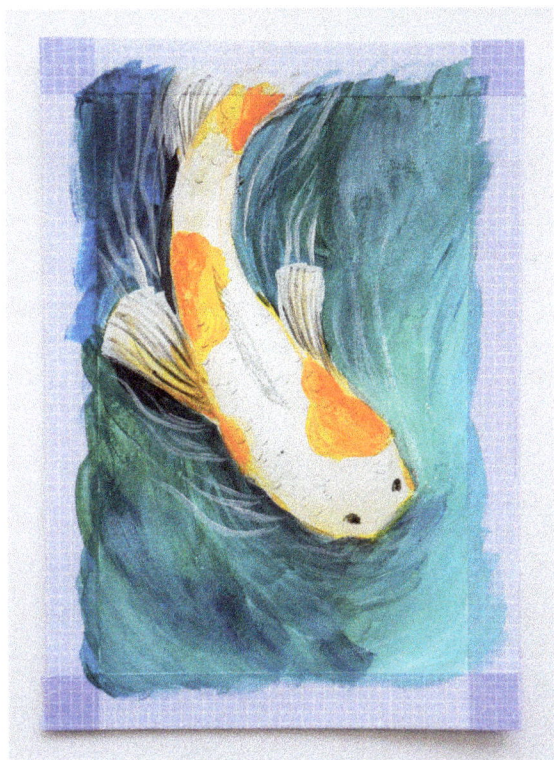

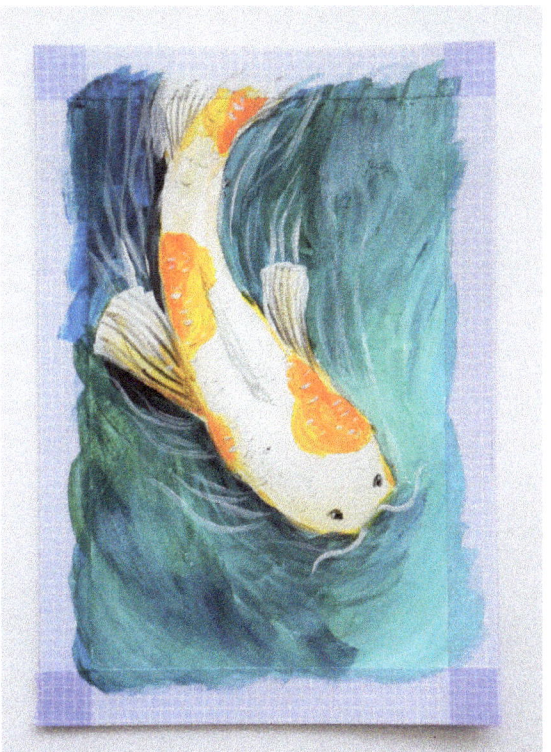

8 Add highlights to the painting. Using white acrylic paint and the round brush, add thin flowing lines at the side of the fish that move toward the tail. This accentuates the fish's movement.

9 With white paint and the round brush, add the koi fish's wispy moustache around its mouth. Create highlights on the scales you painted in step 7, adding smaller comma strokes in white on top of the scales. Add a tiny white dot to the black area of the fish's eye; this highlight makes the fish look more realistic.

FLUFFY PUPPY

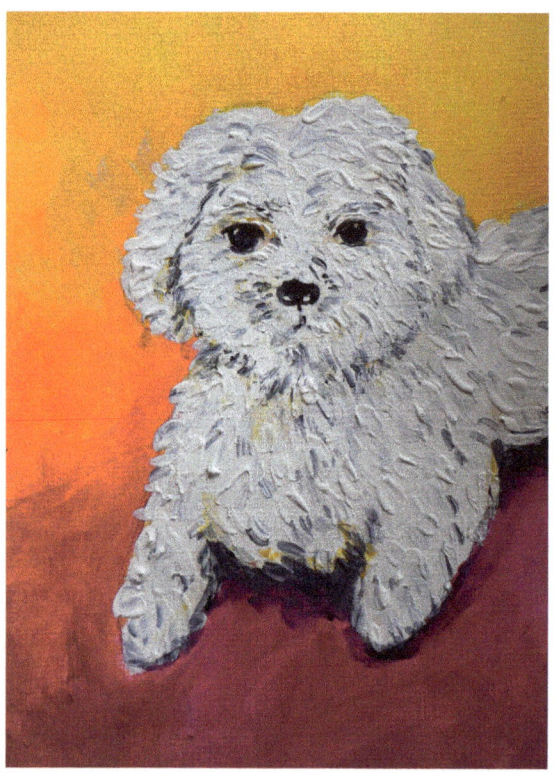

MATERIALS

- - -

Puppy template (see page 139)

Acrylic paints in yellow ocher, red, orange,
Payne's gray, and white (Heavy-body
paint is recommended for painting the
dog's fur, but if not available, modeling
paste or a similar medium can be added
to the paint to give it thickness and body.)

Glazing medium

Canvas paper, 6" × 5" (15.25 × 12.5 cm)

Pencil

Flat brush, size 4 or 6

Round brush, size 2

Mixing palette

Creating texture with acrylic paint is easy and
lends an eye-catching effect. Texture can add
a new dimension to your artwork and can be
added to a variety of subjects. This lesson is
perfect for beginners.

1 Sketch a puppy in pencil, using a photo for inspiration
or the template, and draw a diagonal line to delineate
the foreground and background.

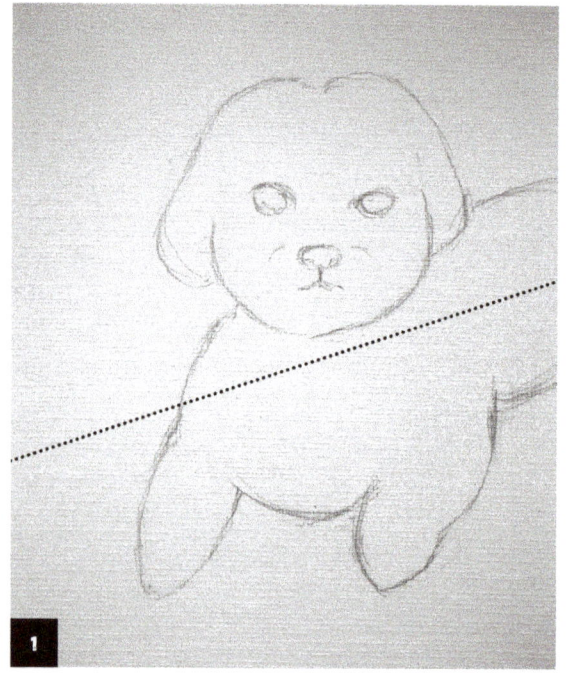

1

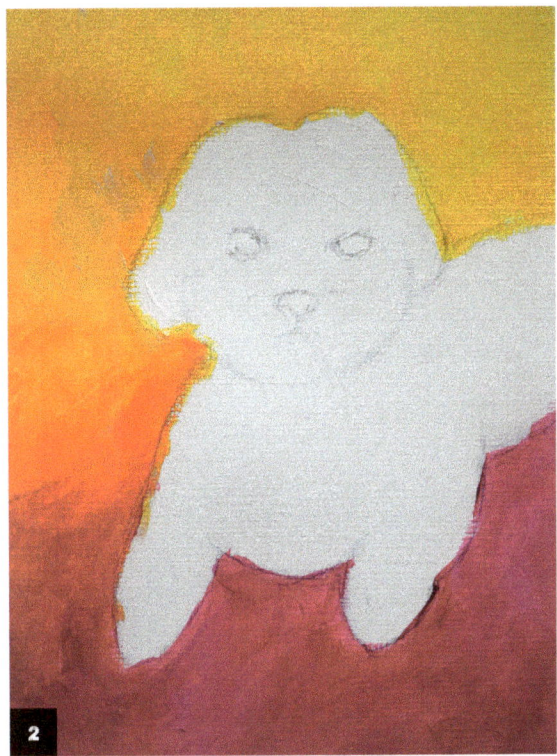

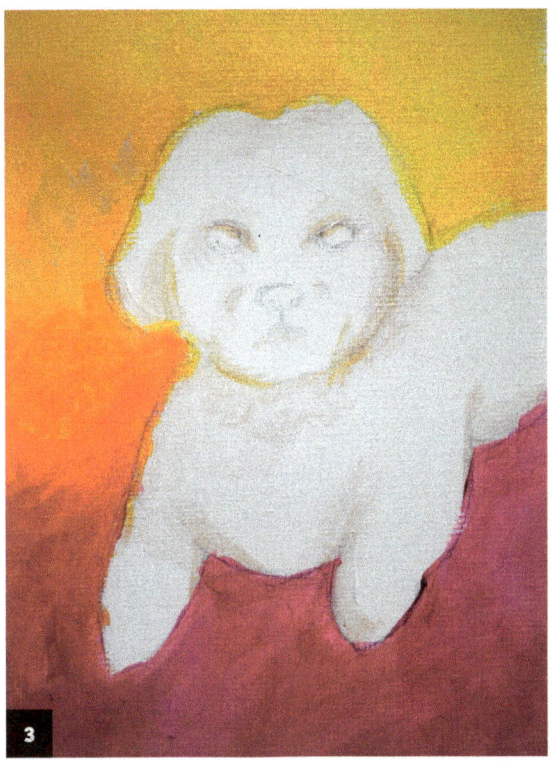

2 Block in the outline of the puppy, using white paint and the flat brush. Paint the background and foreground, using orange for the background and bright pink for the foreground. (I mixed red and white to create pink.) Use quick brushstrokes while the paint is still wet to blend the areas. Allow the paint to dry.

3 Add a yellow ocher glaze (see the glazing technique on page 34) to outline the face, features, and body to create depth. Adding this layer prevents the puppy from looking too stark against the background.

(continued)

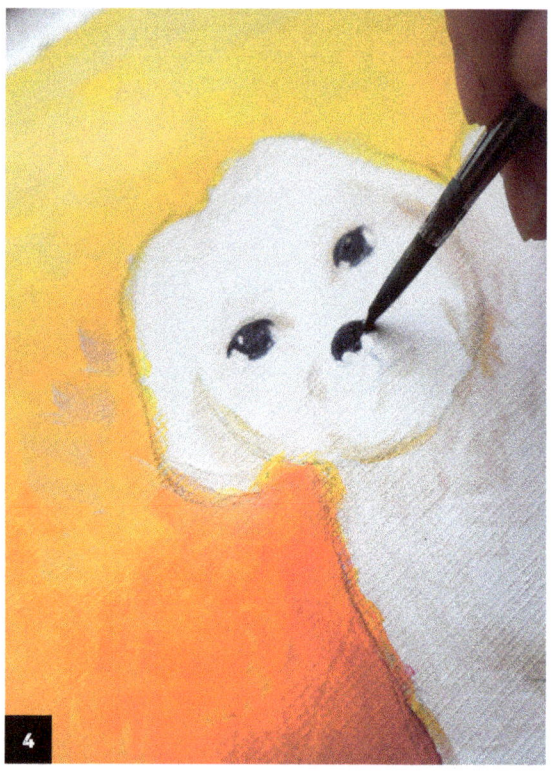

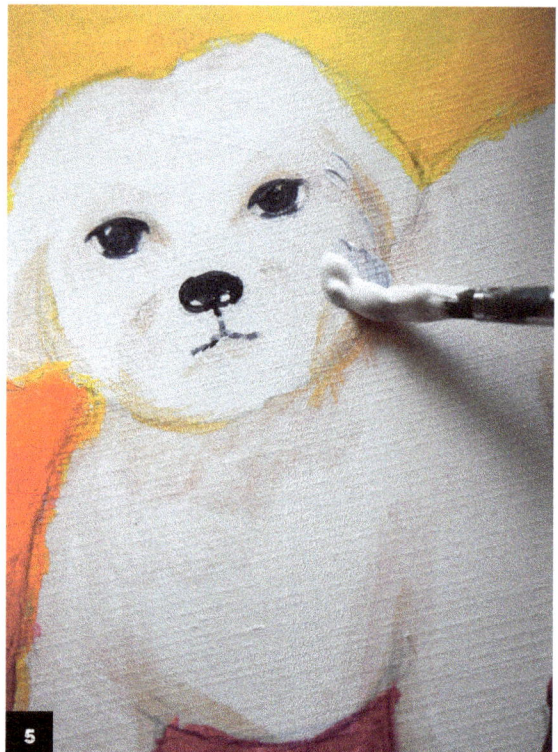

4 Paint the eyes and nose using Payne's gray and the round brush. Add a pinpoint of white to the upper corners of the eyes. Eyes reflect light, and this will give life to the subject. Add two dots of white to the nose for nostrils.

5 Begin to build up the fur texture, using the round brush and starting with a mixture of white with a little Payne's gray. Don't fully mix the colors; when the paint is applied, there should be streaks of white and gray, which mimic the look of fur. Start with lighter colors when creating texture on the puppy because its dominant color is white. You can easily adjust the color later by adding more Payne's gray if necessary.

To create the fur texture, move the brush in short strokes in the direction of the fur. For example, the fur on the body angles downward, while the fur around the eyes is in a circular pattern.

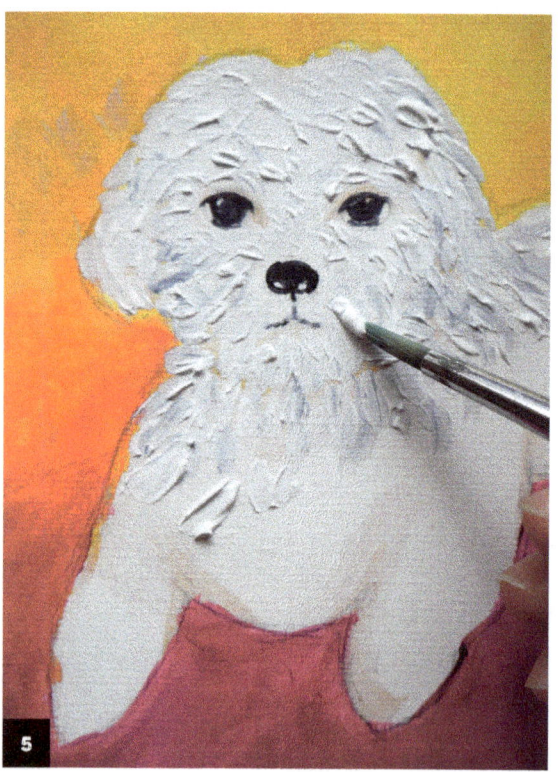

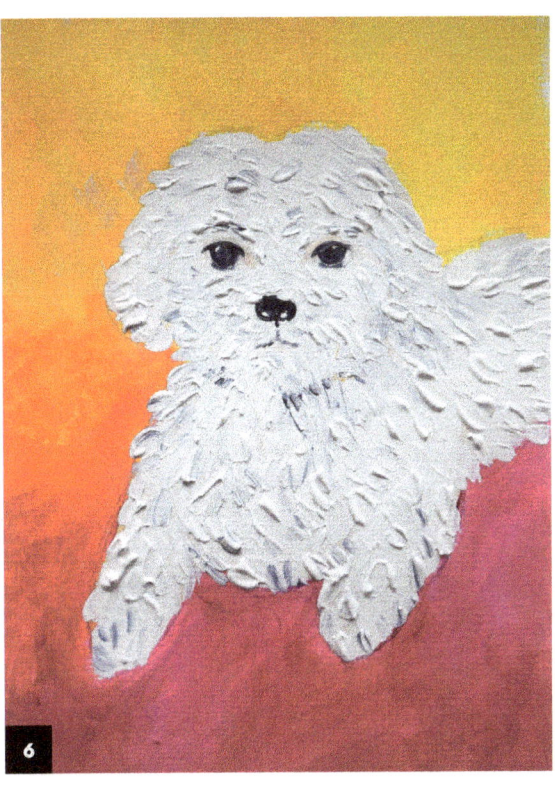

6 Imagine a light source and think about where the shadows would be, such as underneath the chest, belly, and face; where the ears meet the head; and under the chin.

7 Create a glaze with Payne's gray by adding a small amount of glazing medium to the acrylic paint. Use the mixture to paint the areas where the subject and the foreground meet to emphasize the shadow underneath the puppy. Wash your brush to remove some of the paint and soften the edges of the Payne's gray glaze.

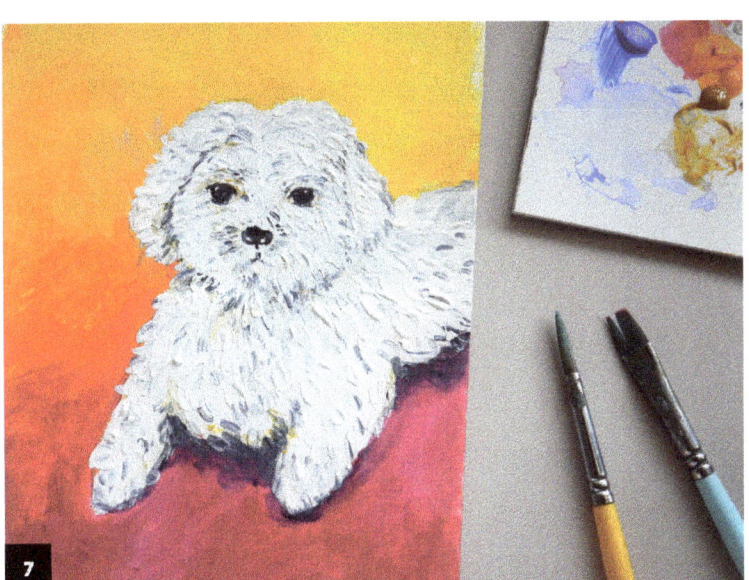

TIP
Creating textures calls for a lot of paint, so make sure you have enough on your palette. I use heavy-body paint straight out of the tube for this technique.

COLORFUL PARROT

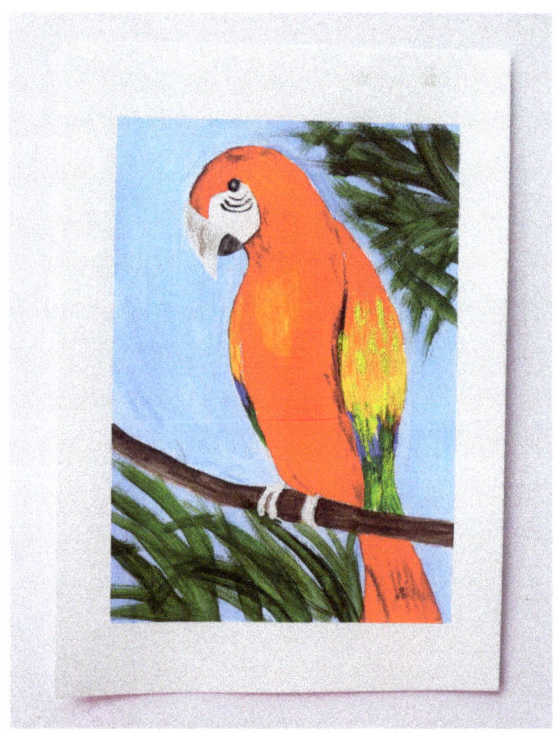

MATERIALS

Parrot template (see page 140)

Acrylic paint in red, orange, yellow, green, blue, white, brown, black, and Payne's gray

Canvas paper, 5" × 7" (12.5 × 17.75 cm)

Scrap paper

Round brushes, sizes 2 and 6 with soft synthetic bristles

Round brush, size 4 with stiff bristles

Flat brushes, sizes 4, 6, and 8

Pencil

Eraser

Mixing palette

A bird's colorful feathers are always mesmerizing, and these bright plumes can be easily depicted by layering acrylics. This lesson features a parrot hanging out in a palm tree. You'll learn how to layer shades of acrylic paint using a dry-brush technique that adds texture and suggests numerous brightly colored feathers. This technique offers so many possibilities. Experiment with different types of brushes and test various effects before applying them to your paintings.

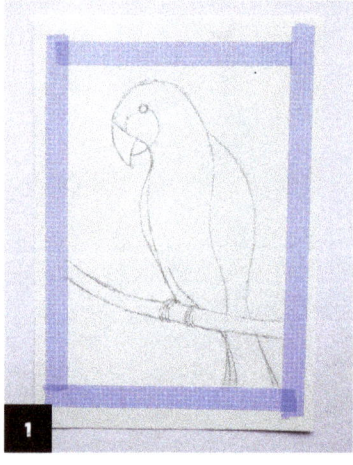

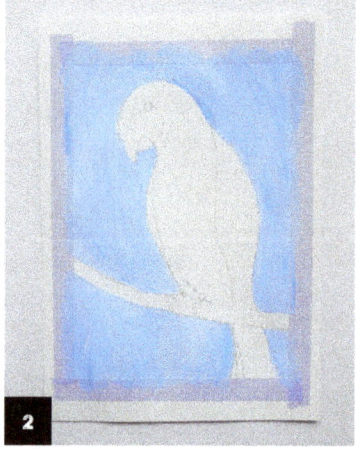

1 Sketch a parrot sitting on a branch in the center of the paper and include details such as the eye, beak, etc. Use the template on page 140, a photo, or your imagination as inspiration.

2 Mix blue paint with a larger amount of white to create a sky-blue shade, and paint the background, using the size 8 flat brush. Be careful not to paint over the parrot and the branch. Allow the paint to dry.

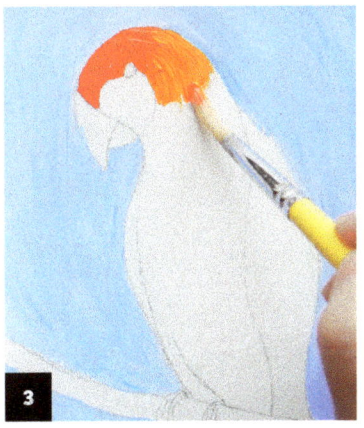

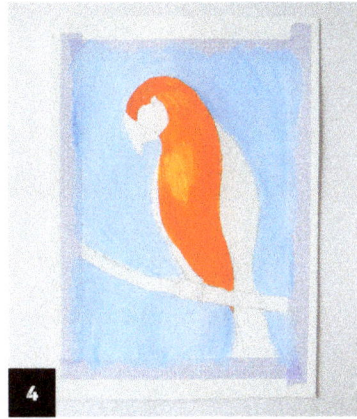

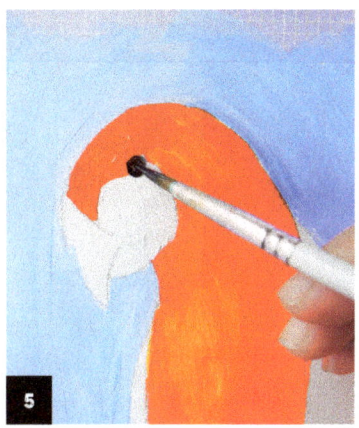

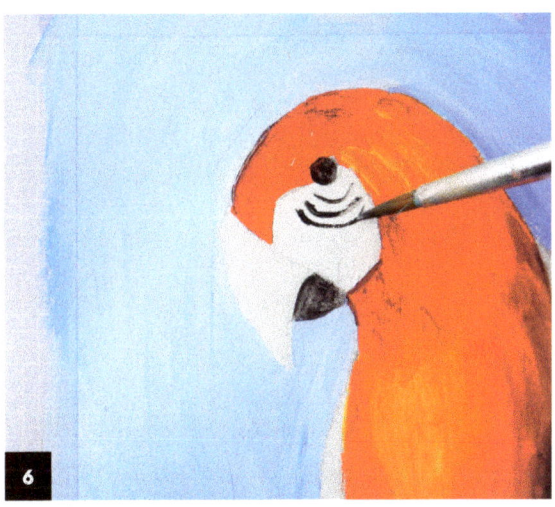

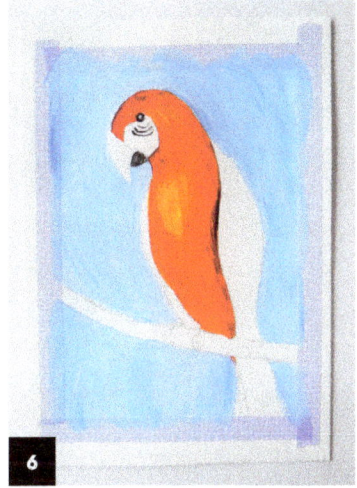

3 Blend equal parts red and orange paint on the palette to create a red-orange shade and paint the head of the parrot with the size 6 round brush, being careful not to paint the area around the eye. Without rinsing the brush and while the paint is still wet, pick up some orange paint and create a gradient in the area beside the parrot's eye.

4 Clean the brush, pick up some red paint, and paint the parrot's body. When you get to the chest, add orange paint to the brush and paint the area with that color. Paint the area around the eye white and allow the paint to dry.

5 Add details and shadows. Add black paint to the palette, mix it with a little water, and paint the bottom part of the bird's beak and round eye with the size 4 round brush.

6 Add some red paint to the black to create a dark red color and brush on a light wash of this color at the top of the parrot's head and underneath the white area of the eye, using the same brush. Paint the top part of the beak white and the bottom part black. Paint three thin black half-circles under the eye. Add a dot of white paint to highlight the center of the parrot's eye. Using the size 2 round brush that's mostly dry and Payne's gray, add vertical streaks on the parrot's back.

(continued)

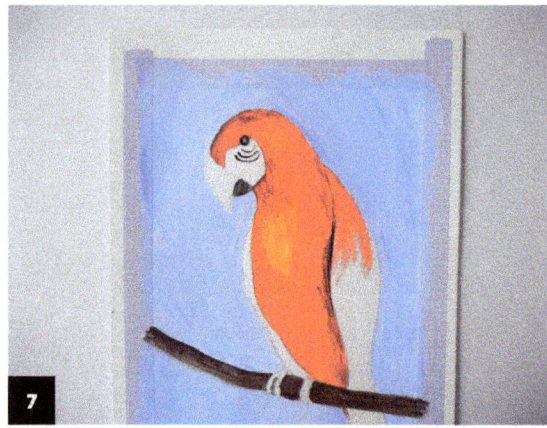

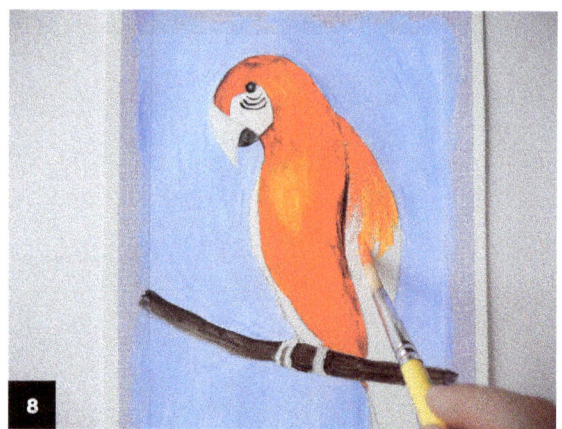

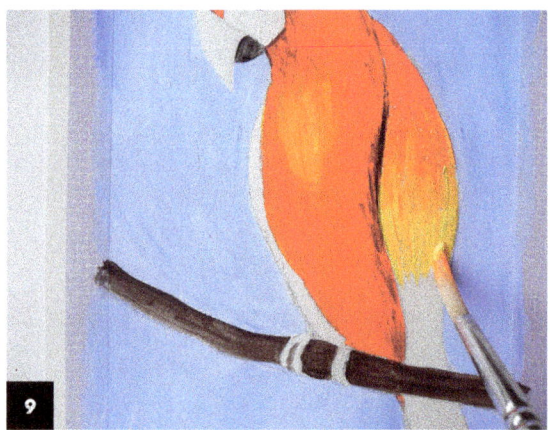

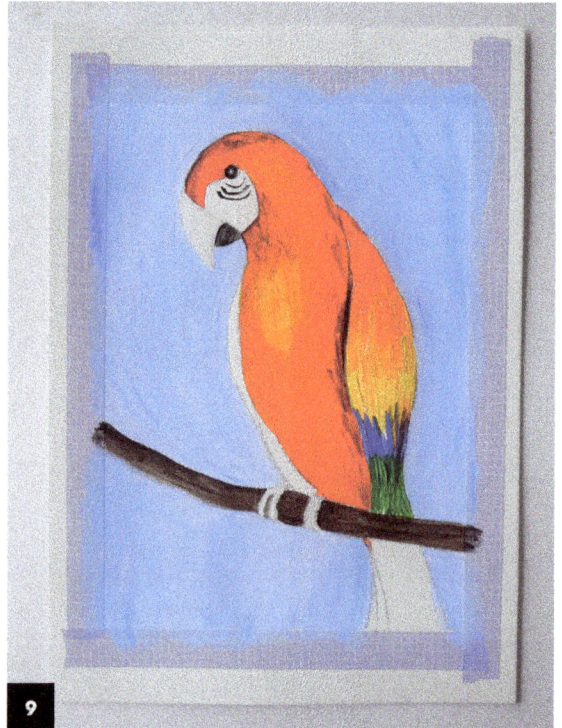

7 Add a small amount of brown paint to the palette and paint the branch using the size 6 round brush. Paint the tiny claws of the bird white.

Add the following colors to the palette in preparation for painting the feathers: red, orange, yellow, blue, and green. Beginning at the top part of the wing, pick up some red paint with the round brush and make long downward strokes, going about a quarter of the way down the wing.

8 While the red paint is still semi-wet, clean the brush, pick up some orange paint, and paint with the same downward strokes on the wing. This time, however, start from the middle of the red area.

9 Continue painting the wing, adding yellow, blue, and green in the same way. Paint the bottom part of the wing below the branch red. Paint these colorful layers the same way on the bird's other wing. Allow the paint to dry.

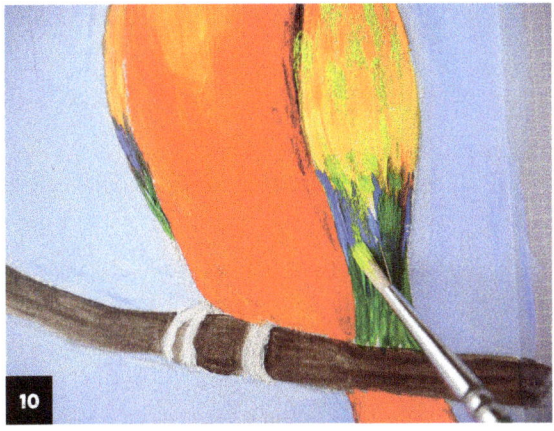

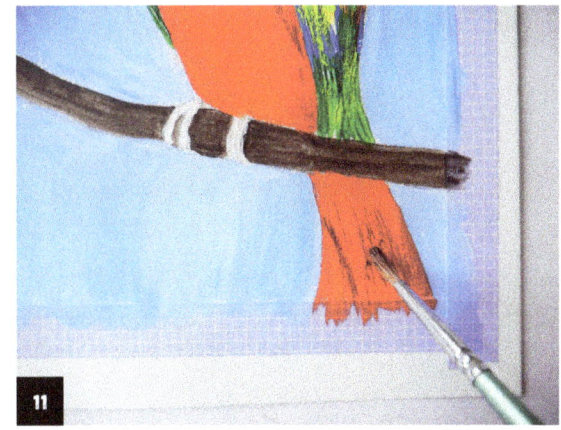

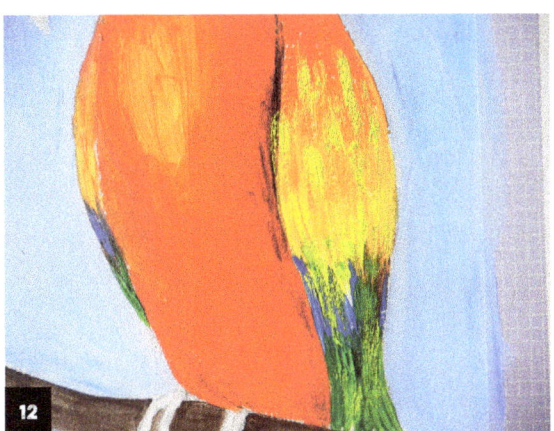

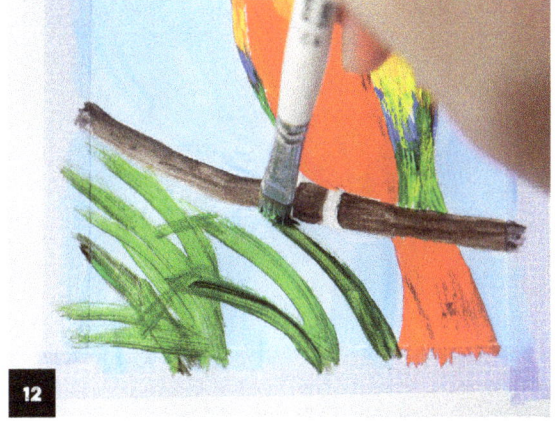

10 Mix a small amount of yellow paint with green on the palette to create a bright green and pick up some of the paint with the tip of the stiff round brush. Test the dry-brush technique (see page 35) on a piece of scrap paper before trying it on the painting.

Paint short, quick strokes on top of the yellow, blue, and green layers. This gives the impression of the feathers subtly alternating colors.

11 Clean and dry the brush and blend red and black paint on the palette to make a dark red. Brush this color toward the end of the bird's tail, adding shadow and depth in that area.

Make several vertical strokes toward the end of the parrot's tail, right below the log where the bird is perching. The dry brush will make dark red shadow lines that will look like individual tails of the bird.

12 The dry-brush technique can be used with different types and sizes of brushes. Add green paint to the palette and pick up some of the paint with a dry, size 4 flat brush. Starting at the bottom of the painting, press down on the edge of the brush and drag it up to make a short upward stroke. Continue making these strokes in a fan shape to create palm leaves. Do the same at the top right corner of the paper (see finished image, page 108).

TIGER

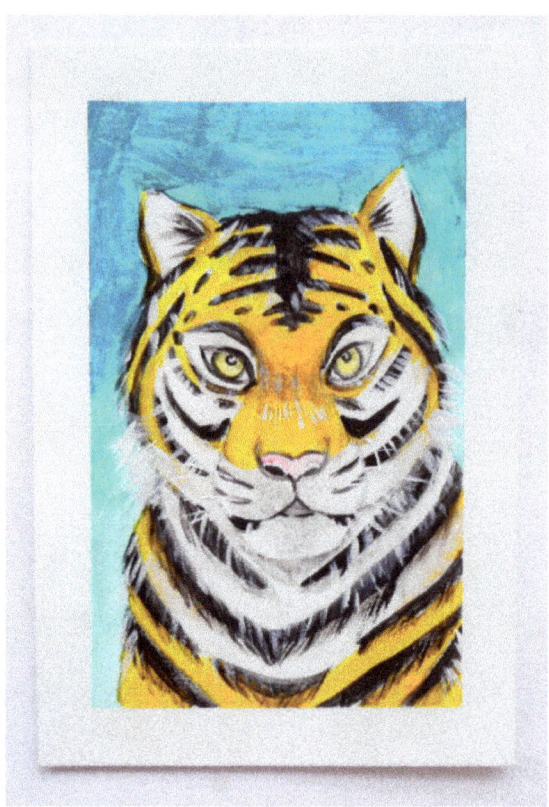

MATERIALS

– – –

Tiger template (see page 140)

Acrylic paint in blue, green, yellow, orange, brown, black, and white

Canvas panel, 5" × 7" (12.5 × 17.75 cm)

Pencil

Eraser

Round brush, size 4

Flat brush, size 4

Scrap paper

This not-so-small creature is part of one of my favorite animal families, the cat. Tigers may seem intimidating to paint, but with a step-by-step guide you'll be able to create your own big cat using techniques for layering and dry brushing.

1 Sketch the tiger using the template, a photo, or your imagination as inspiration. Make sure to include details such as the eyes, nose, and mouth, and the placement of the stripes.

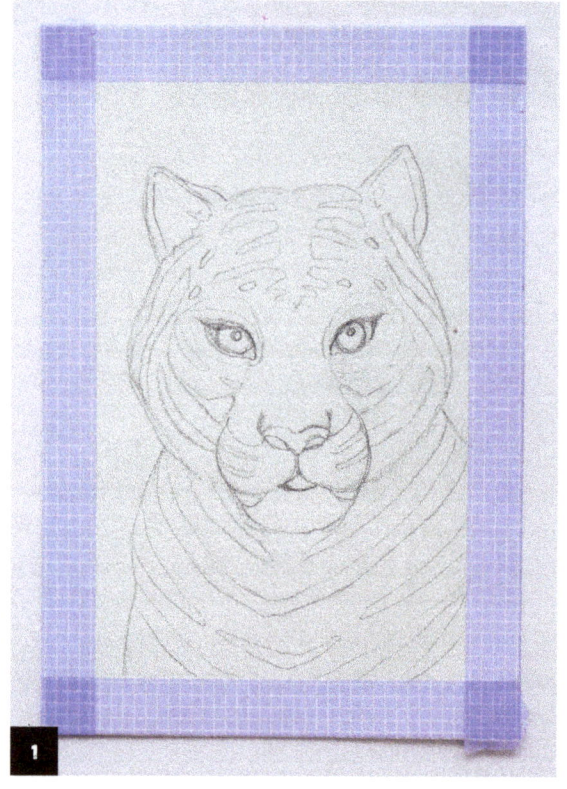

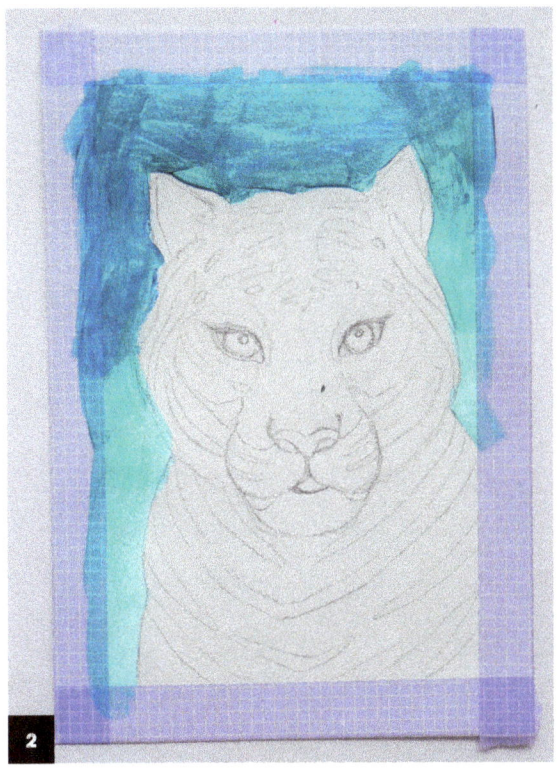

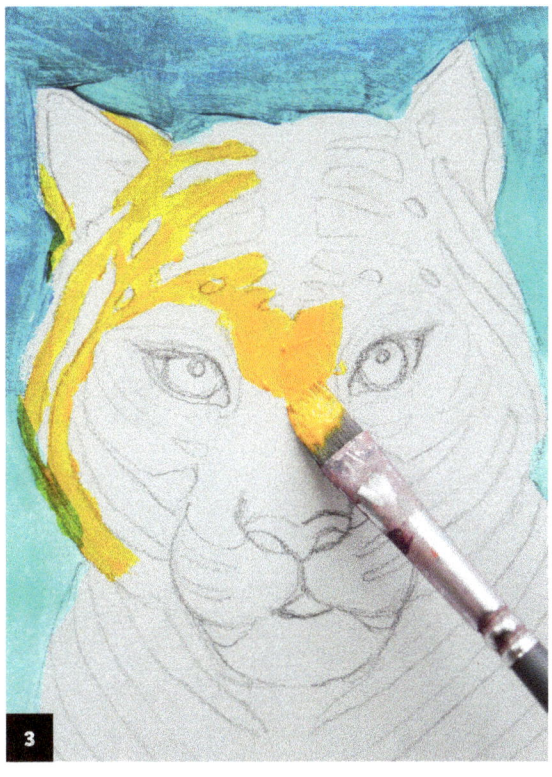

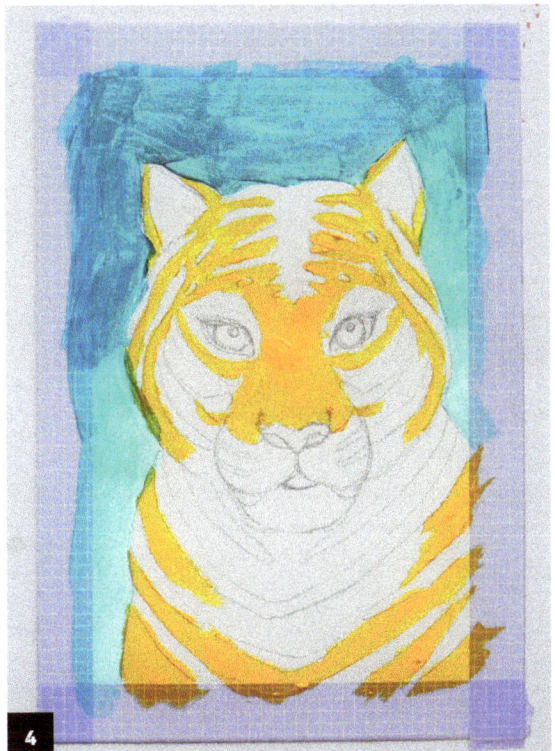

2 Blend green and blue paint on the palette to make a cyan color and paint the background, using the flat brush. Create a gradient on the paper, starting with a darker shade at the top and gradually lightening it toward the bottom. Make the blue-green shade lighter by adding more water to it. Allow the paint to dry.

3 Mix yellow and orange paint on the palette to create the bright yellow-orange base color of the tiger. Paint the tiger's face and body using the edge of the flat brush, being careful not to paint any of the stripes. The tiger's chest area, cheeks, mouth, inner ear, and outer eye areas should also be left unpainted.

(continued)

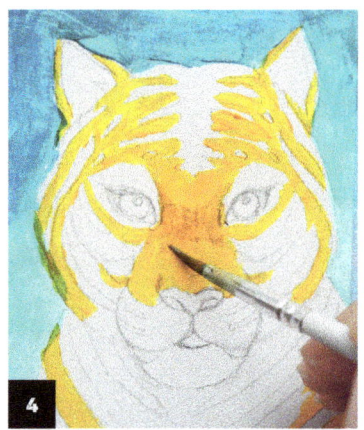

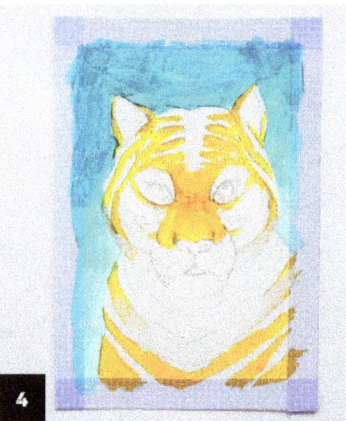

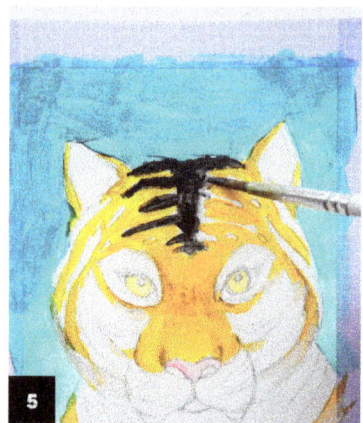

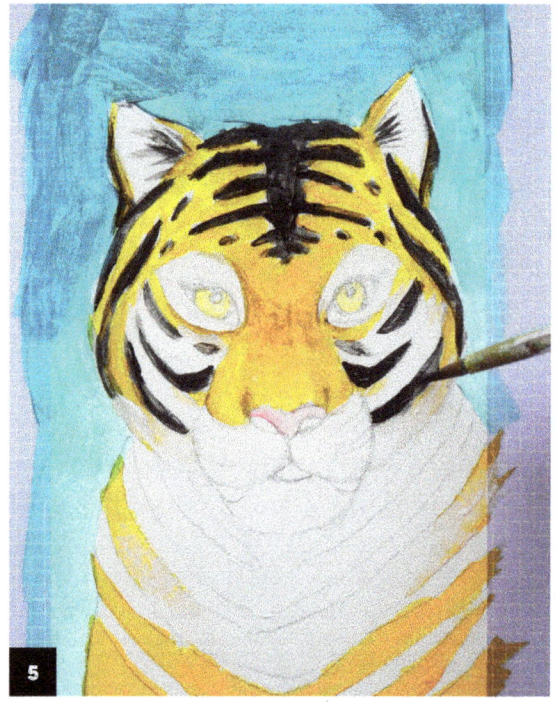

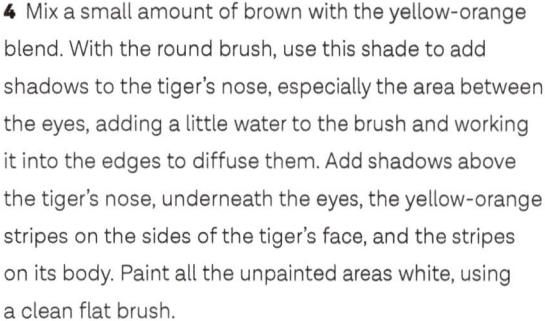

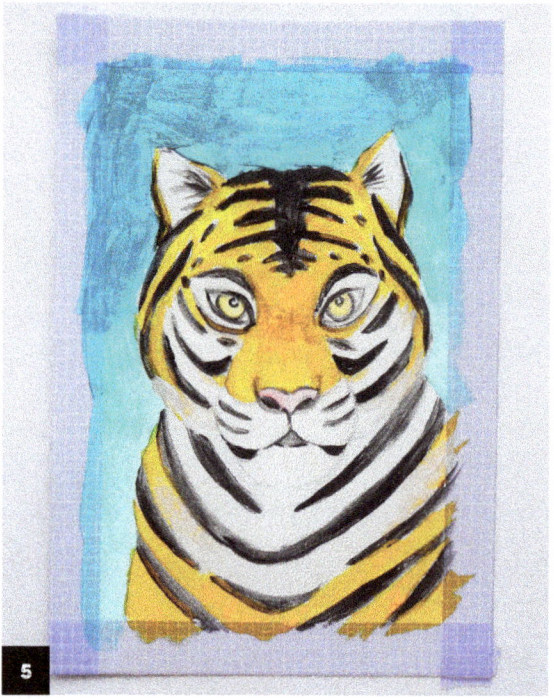

4 Mix a small amount of brown with the yellow-orange blend. With the round brush, use this shade to add shadows to the tiger's nose, especially the area between the eyes, adding a little water to the brush and working it into the edges to diffuse them. Add shadows above the tiger's nose, underneath the eyes, the yellow-orange stripes on the sides of the tiger's face, and the stripes on its body. Paint all the unpainted areas white, using a clean flat brush.

5 Pick up some black paint from the palette with the round brush and paint the black stripes on the face and body. Use black to outline the eyelids, nose, ears, and mouth. Allow the paint to dry.

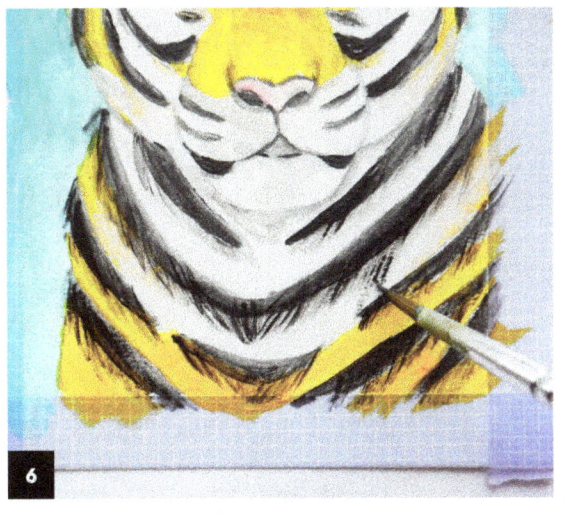

6 Create the fur texture using a dry-brush technique (see page 35). Wipe off any excess water from the round brush and pick up some black paint. Test the brush on some scrap paper to make sure you have the right amount of paint on the brush. Beginning with the tiger's cheeks, brush outward on the stripes. Use downward brushstrokes for the stripes on the body. Don't worry if the brushstrokes aren't the same length—this better imitates the fine hairs of the fur. Allow the paint to dry.

7 Paint the tiger's eyes and nose; for the eyes I used light yellow, and for the nose, light pink. Allow the paint to dry.

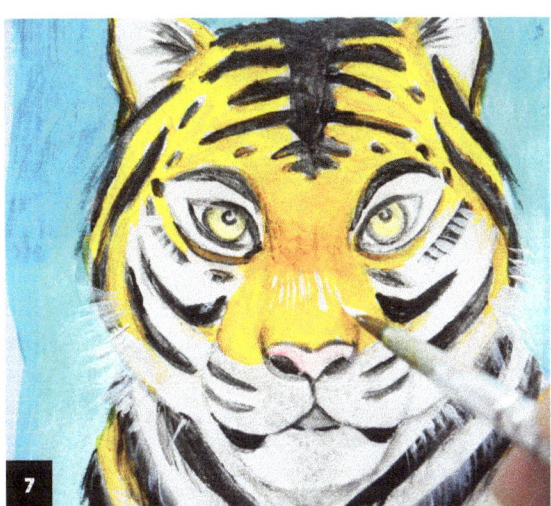

TIP

To add even more texture to the fur, use the dry-brush technique with white paint. Pick up white paint with the brush and lightly scratch the paper in short downward strokes on different parts of the painting. Vary the amount of paint on the brush to add thicker amounts in some areas, making the fur stand out. This also creates texture. I added white fur near the tiger's cheeks—extending outward to give a sense of fuller fur around the face—chest, face, nose, and mouth.

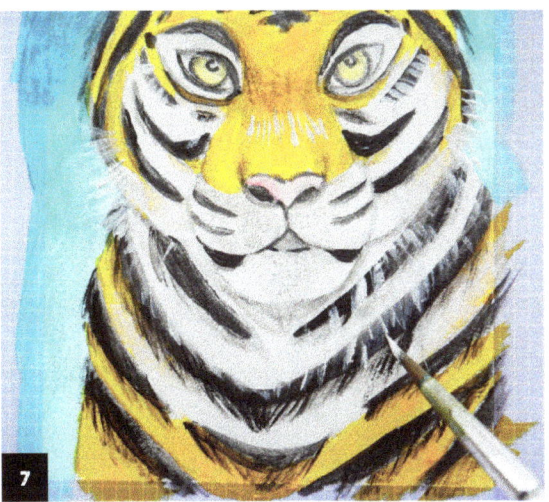

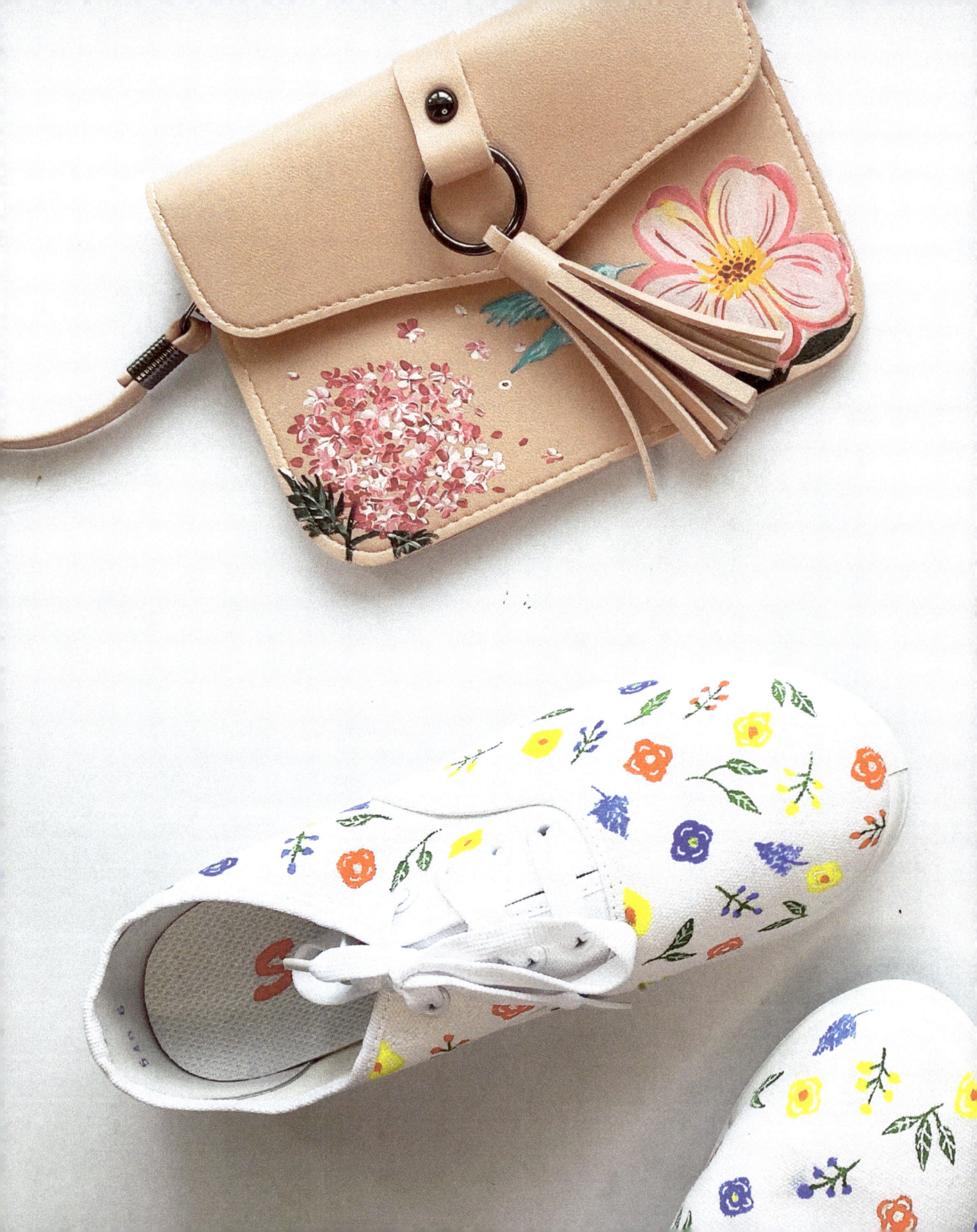

7

PROJECTS

- - - - - - -

You've come to the most exciting part of the book where you'll challenge yourself to use what you've learned so far to paint a variety of subjects on different substrates. One of the reasons I'm drawn to acrylics is because I can use them to paint practical, everyday items. I've use them for home decorating, craft projects, and even handmade gifts for friends. In this chapter, you'll learn how to spruce up objects such as wooden bowls, canvas sneakers, a leather tote bag, and more. This is where the versatility of acrylics truly shines.

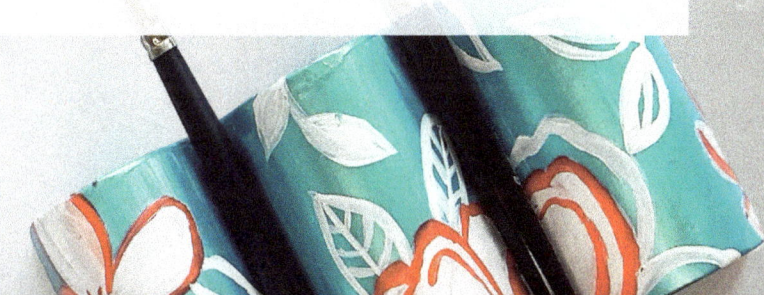

CUPCAKE APRON

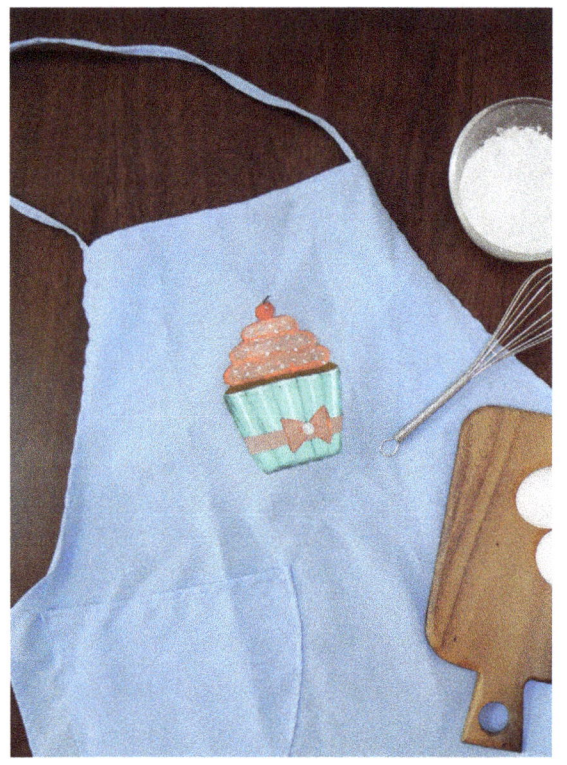

MATERIALS

— — —

Plain cotton apron

Acrylic textile paint in red, green, white, brown, Payne's gray, and black

Textile medium (This can be found in art stores and online and added to regular acrylic paint to make it suitable for painting fabric.) (optional)

Piece of cardboard, about 8" × 10" (20.25 × 25.5 cm)

Large binder clips

Iron and ironing board

Round brushes, sizes 4 and 6

Mixing palette

Customize different types of fabric with acrylic textile paint—add unique designs to a plain T-shirt or pair of jeans. The medium added to the paint makes the fabric washable and helps prevent cracking once the paint is set. In this project, you'll decorate an apron with a cute cupcake motif. You'll incorporate the techniques you learned in the still life lessons to make this treat look real and good enough to eat!

1 Wash, dry, and iron the apron before painting, making sure any stains or dirt are removed. Washing helps expand the cloth fibers so they're better able to absorb paint. Place a piece of cardboard behind the apron to make it more stable for painting and to prevent the paint from seeping through and staining your work surface. Secure the cardboard to the apron with binder clips so it doesn't move as you paint.

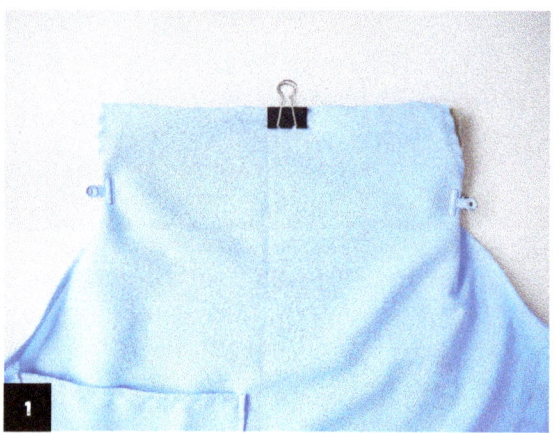

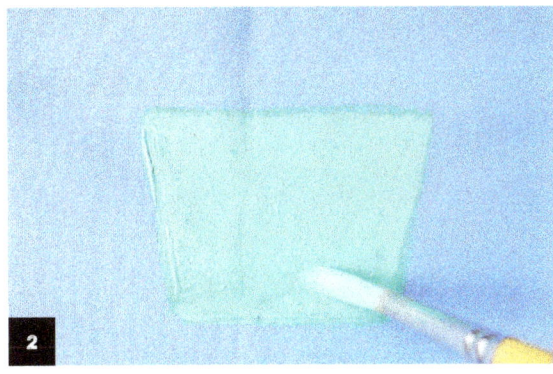

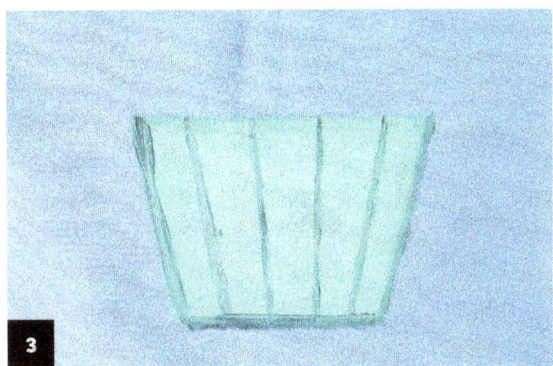

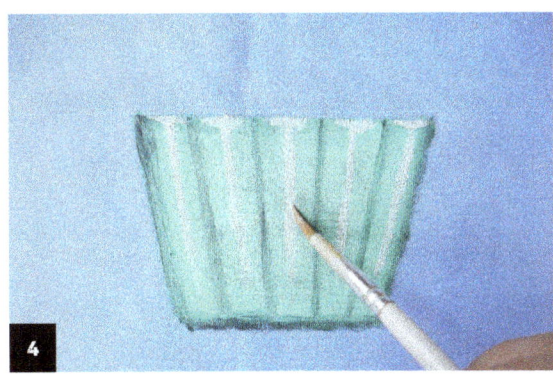

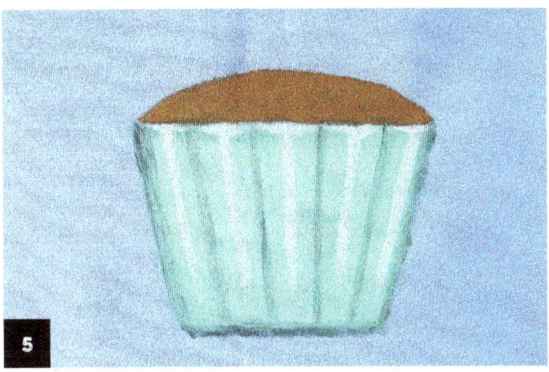

2 Paint the cupcake using a photo, drawing, or your imagination for inspiration. Paint the cupcake liner first. Mix green and white paint on the palette to create a light green and load the size 6 round brush with the color. Paint a symmetrical trapezoid shape 2 to 3 inches (5 to 7.5 cm) wide, making it wider on the top and narrower on the bottom. Because fabric absorbs textile acrylic paint, your initial applications may not appear as opaque as you'd like. Simply apply more coats to cover the area. When painting on fabric, don't mix a lot of water with the paint, as it may bleed or make the paint run. Allow the paint to dry.

3 Add dimension by painting alternating shadow and highlight lines to represent the cupcake liner folds. Mix the light green you blended in step 2 with a tiny amount of Payne's gray to make a shadow color. Using the size 4 round brush, paint a thin downstroke at the left end of the wrapper that's parallel to the side. Move about ⅓ inch (0.85 cm) to the right, and paint another downward stroke, also parallel to the side. Continue this pattern until you reach the opposite side. There should be three to four lines in the center of the liner that are parallel to the side they're closest to. Use the shadow color to paint a line at the bottom of the wrapper.

Before the shadows dry completely, clean the brush, wipe off any excess water, and use the brush to soften the edges of the shadows.

4 Load the size 4 round brush with white paint. To create the highlights, paint parallel lines between the existing ones, starting at the top and ending just short of the bottom of the liner. Add a small white horizontal line above each of the vertical lines at the top of the liner.

5 Paint the rounded cupcake using brown acrylic paint and the size 6 round brush; it doesn't have to extend too much above the liner, as you'll paint frosting on top. Allow the paint to dry.

(continued)

6 Mix red paint with white on the palette to create pink. Paint frosting on top of the cupcake, using the size 6 round brush. Create an oblong shape that extends almost to the edge of the liner, and layer it over the brown cupcake just a bit. Paint two more similar frosting layers, making each one slightly shorter than the one below it.

7 Add shading to the frosting with red paint and the size 4 round brush. Paint an *S* shape to outline the frosting layers, starting at the top.

8 Clean the brush, wipe off any excess water, and use it to soften the edges of the red line. Softening the red color makes the frosting look more lifelike.

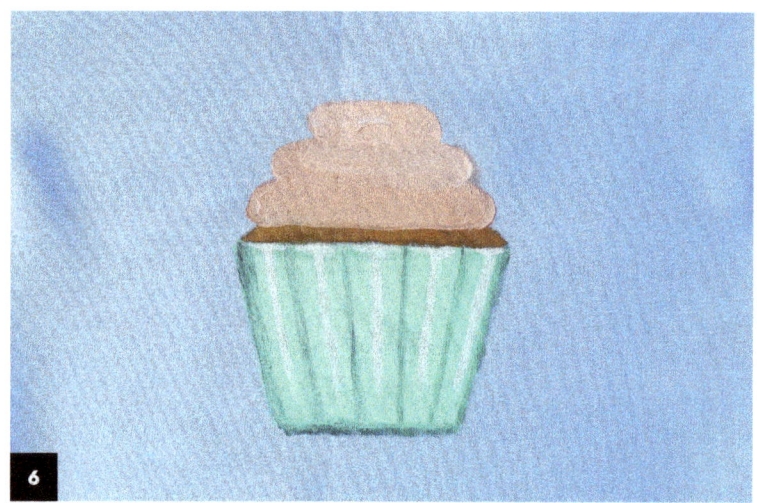

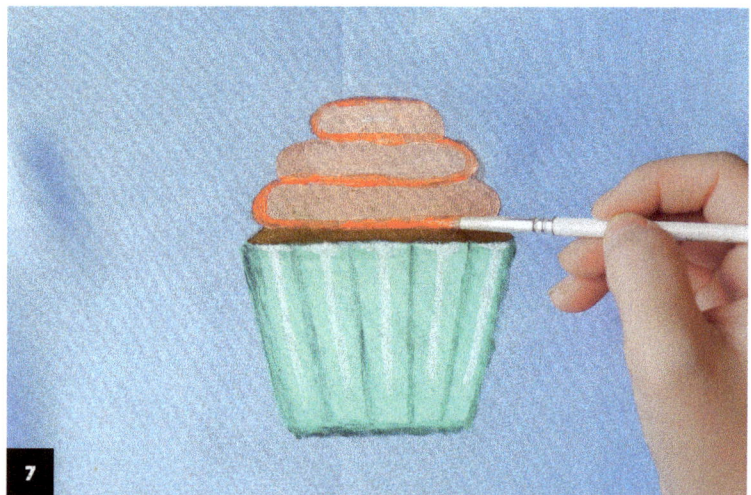

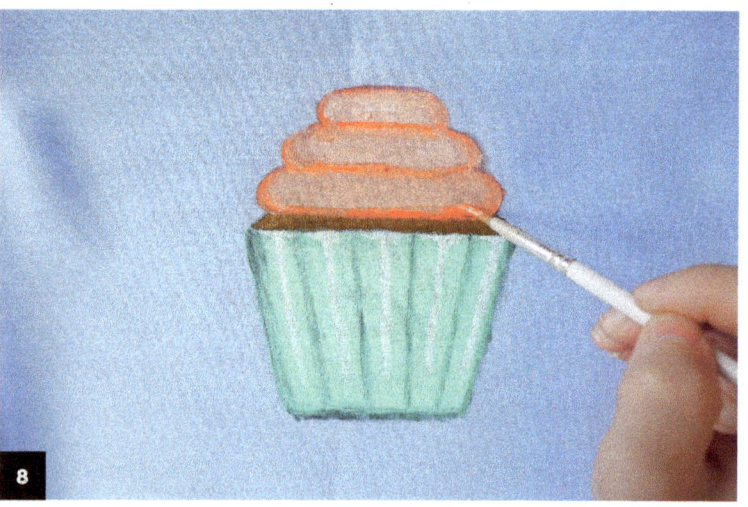

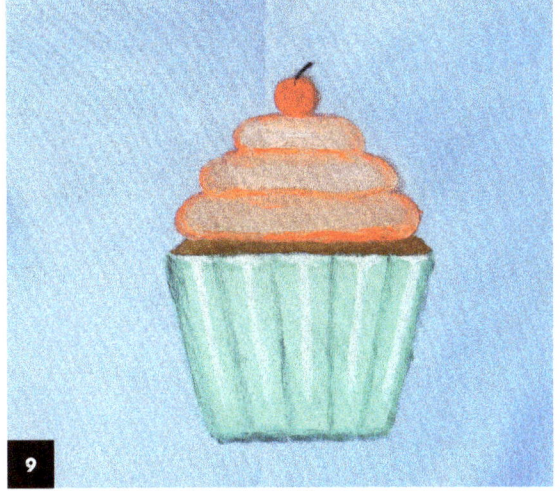

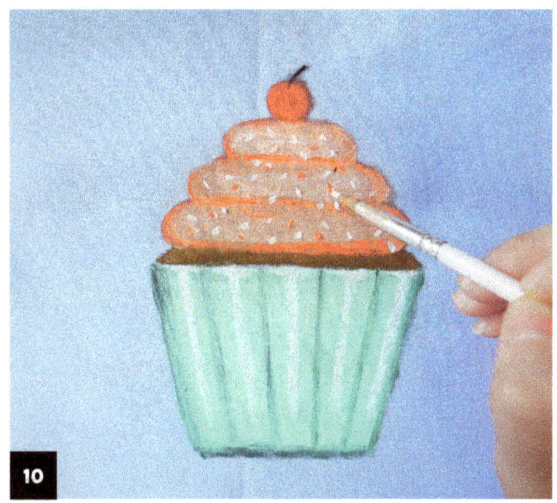

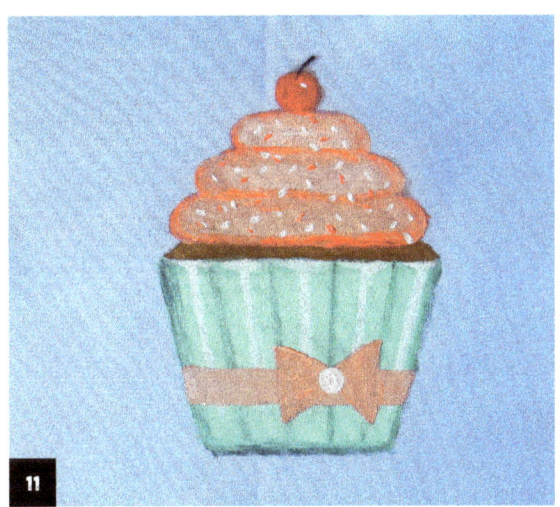

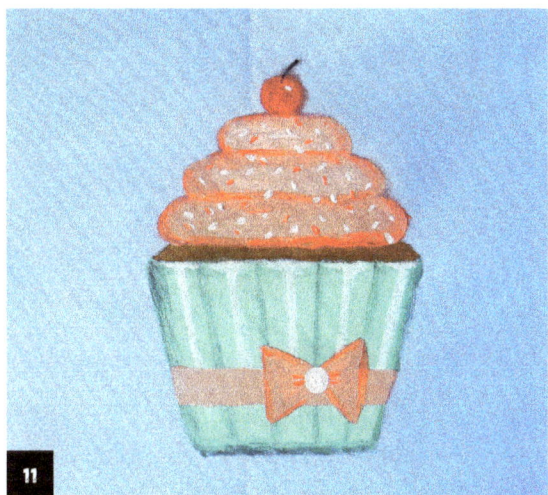

9 Paint a cherry at the top of the cupcake by adding a red circle and a thin black line for the stem with the size 6 round brush. Add a small white dot highlight at the top right, below the stem of the cherry, as a highlight.

10 Add sprinkles to the frosting by painting tiny red and white lines and dots at different angles with the round brush.

11 Paint a thick horizontal line just below the center of the wrapper and add a bow in the middle. Outline the bow with red paint, add a small white circle in the center, and paint two thin short lines in red beside the white circle on either side of the bow. Wait 24 hours for the paint to dry and follow the manufacturer's instructions for setting the paint.

KOI POND WOODEN BOWL

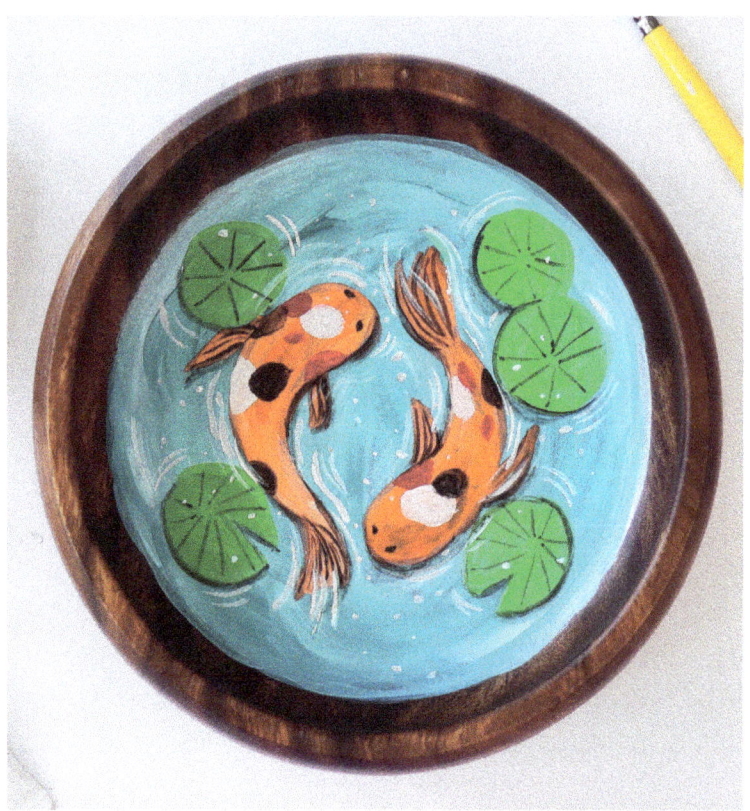

MATERIALS

- - -

Koi fish template
    (see page 140)

Wooden bowl with a
    flat bottom

Acrylic paints in red,
    orange, green, blue,
    white, and black or
    Payne's gray

Indoor varnish

Flat brush, size 6

Round brushes, sizes 2
    and 6

Pencil

Mixing palette

This decorative bowl features beautiful koi fish swimming in a pond. You'll paint on wood and learn how to create depth and movement with a few brushstrokes, just as you did in the painted koi lesson (see page 100).

Note: This item is for decorative purposes only and should not be used for food.

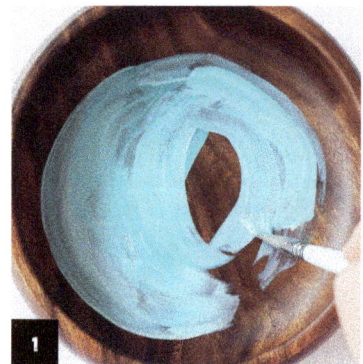

1 Mix green, blue, and white paint to create the color of an aqua blue pond. Don't mix the paint too thoroughly; there should be streaks of dark and light values visible. Paint the inside bottom of the bowl with the flat brush, moving the brush to create parentheses shapes. This gives the illusion of moving water. Allow the paint to dry.

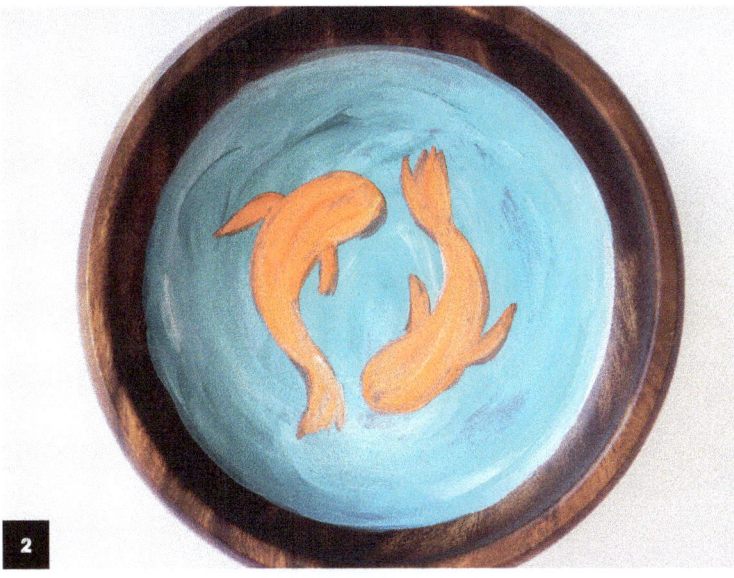

2 Sketch the koi fish on the blue paint with the pencil. Block out the shape of the fish with orange paint and the size 2 round brush.

3 Add markings on each fish using the size 2 round brush. I used red, black, and white to create spots.

(continued)

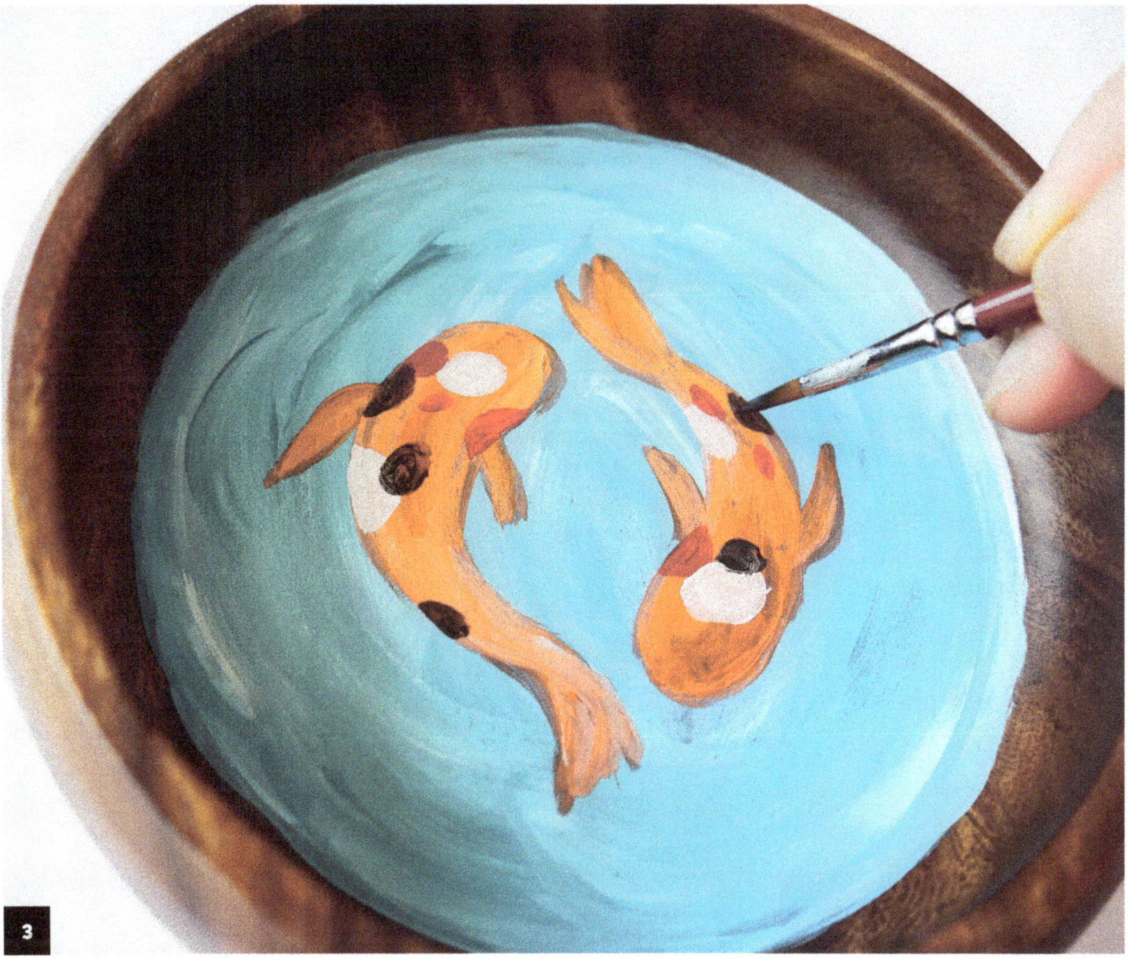

4 Paint eyes on the fish and lines on the tails and fins using black paint and the same brush used in step 3.

5 Paint green lily pads on the sides of the fish using the size 6 round brush. Some lily pads can be complete circles, while others can be incomplete, as if a pie slice has been taken out. Allow the paint to dry.

6 Add veins to the lily pads with black paint and the size 2 round brush. Create water ripples using white paint and the size 2 round brush. Paint the lines following the contours of the fish and lily pads to give the feeling of motion.

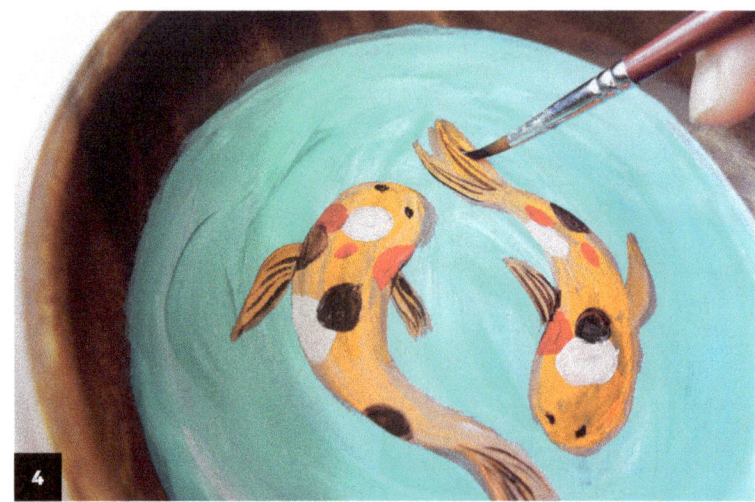

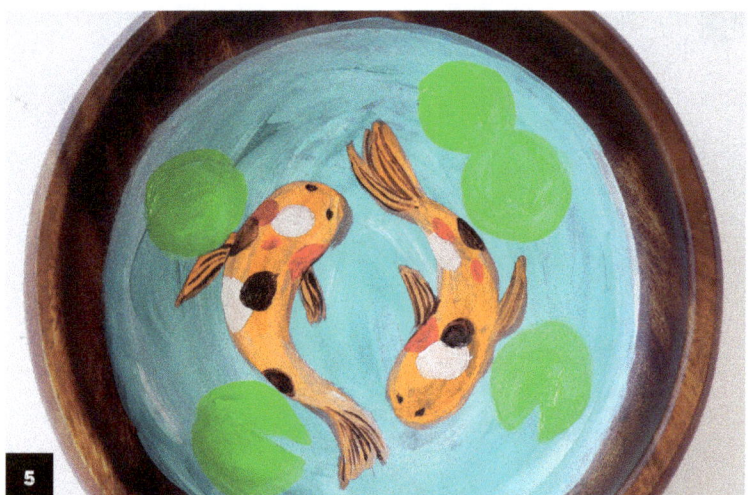

TIP
Koi fish come in a range of shades and patterns, including orange, red, white, black, gray, and yellow. Express your creativity and paint the fish in your favorite colors.

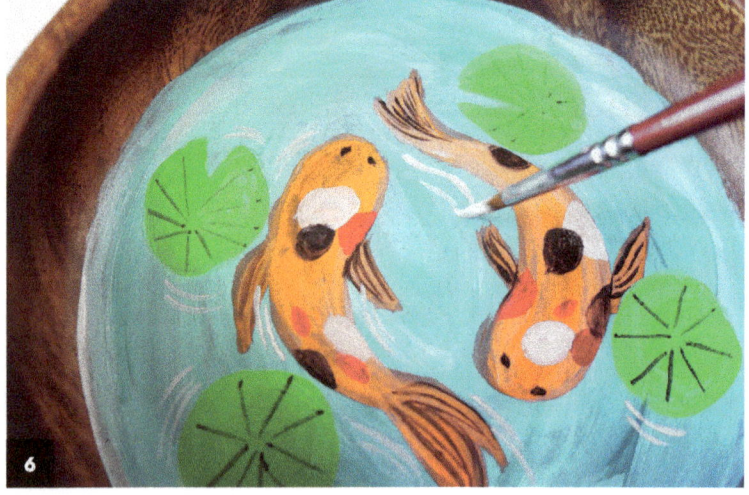

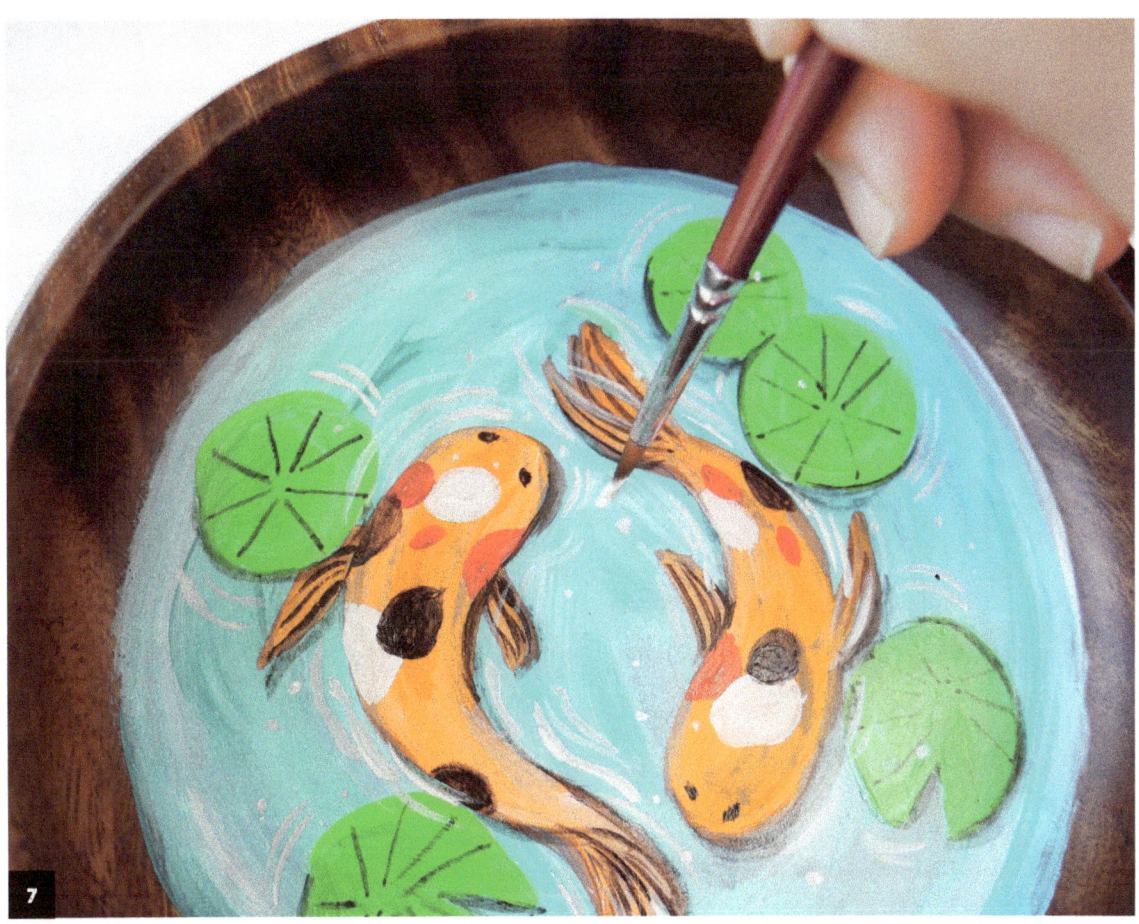

7 Create shadows to bring depth to the painting, using black or Payne's gray thinned with a little water and the size 2 round brush. Orient the bowl so the fish are vertical and add the paint to the bottoms of the lily pads; this makes them appear as though they're floating on the water. Add more shadows to one side of each fish's head, body, and tail. Allow the paint to dry and then use the tip of the brush to add tiny specks of white paint, creating air bubbles in the water.

8 When the paint is completely dry, brush on a coat of indoor varnish, following the manufacturer's instructions.

FLORAL SNEAKERS

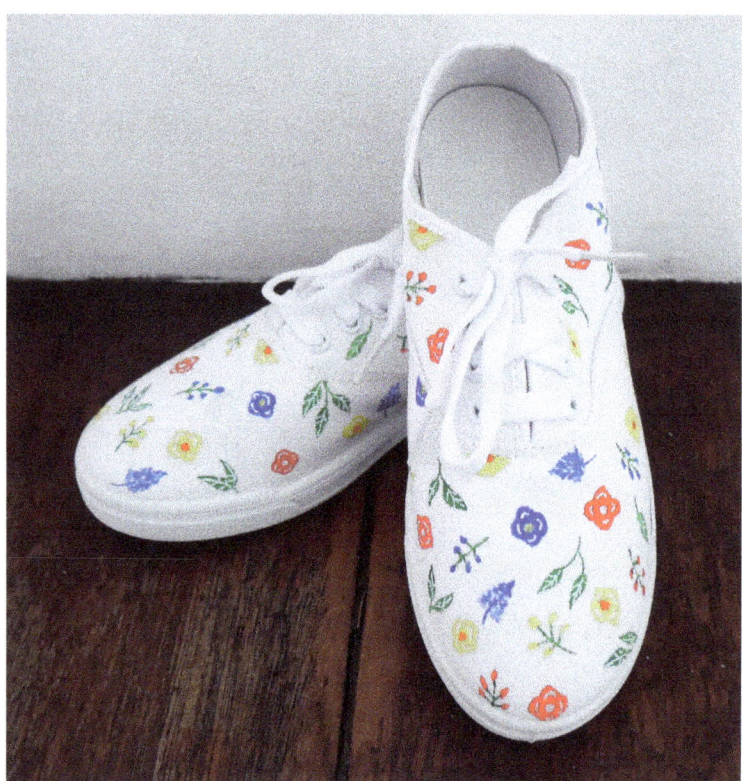

Clean white canvas
    sneakers

Tissue paper

Paper or plastic for
    covering worktable

Acrylic textile paint in
    red, yellow, green,
    cobalt blue, and
    white (optional)

Textile medium. (Found
    in art stores and
    online, textile medium
    can be added to
    regular acrylic paint
    to make it suitable
    for painting fabric.)
    (optional)

Acrylic clear spray sealer

Acrylic ink pen in white
    (optional)

Masking tape

Round brushes, sizes 2
    and 4

Mixing palette

White canvas sneakers are the perfect blank canvas for painting. Let's dress some up to make them ready for summer—or any season!

1 Cover your worktable with paper or plastic and remove the laces from the sneakers. Make sure the sneakers are clean and free of dirt and stains. This will help the paint adhere. Cover the soles of the shoes with masking tape to prevent paint smudges and stains. If there are other areas of the sneakers that you'd like to remain paint-free, such as the logo or a design, cover those with tape as well. Stuff the shoes with tissue paper to give them some stability as you paint.

2 When working with textile paint, don't add too much water or the paint will bleed and run when applied to the fabric. The paint should be thick enough to easily adhere to the fabric.

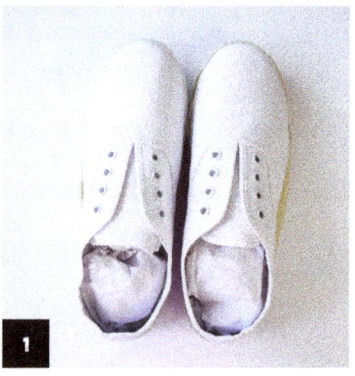

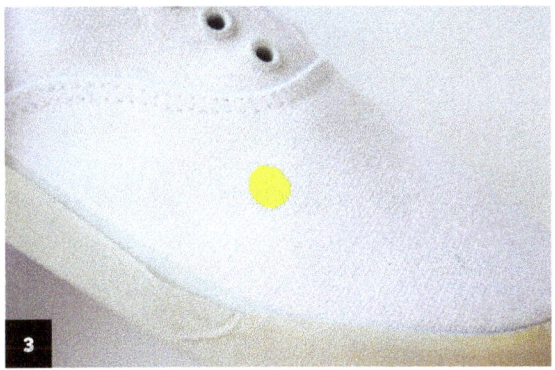

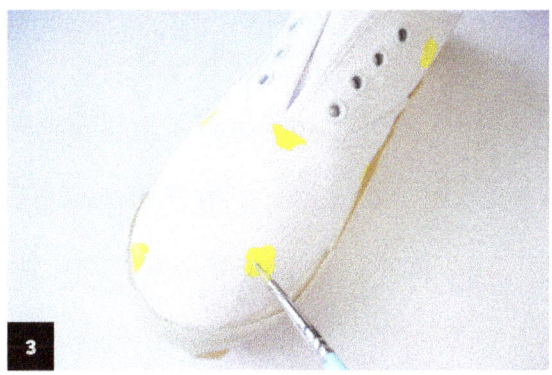

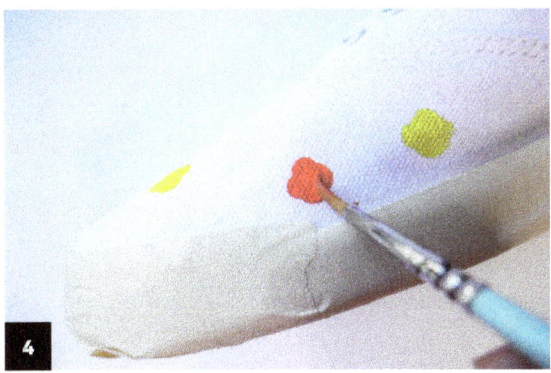

3 Add each color of paint to the palette. For this all-over floral design, I started with yellow paint and the size 4 round brush. Start by painting the largest area of the sneakers with the most prominent designs. For one of the flowers, paint a small circle and then slightly expand the shape to form a four-petal flower.

4 Wash and dry the brush and paint that same four-petal flower in another area in cobalt blue. Make another similar flower in red. Paint a small circle in the middle of each flower, using another color. I painted yellow centers for the red and blue flowers and red centers for the yellow flowers. Depending on the size of your sneakers, you can fit two to three of these four-petal flowers each in yellow, blue, and red. Don't place the florals too close together because you'll add more designs later.

(continued)

TIP

It's difficult to remove acrylic paint from fabric, so I recommend planning your design before committing to painting the sneakers. For this project, I chose an all-over floral design. If you do have to re-move paint from the shoes, dip a cotton ball in acetone and gently rub it on the paint to remove it. Afterward, wash the area with warm water and allow it to dry.

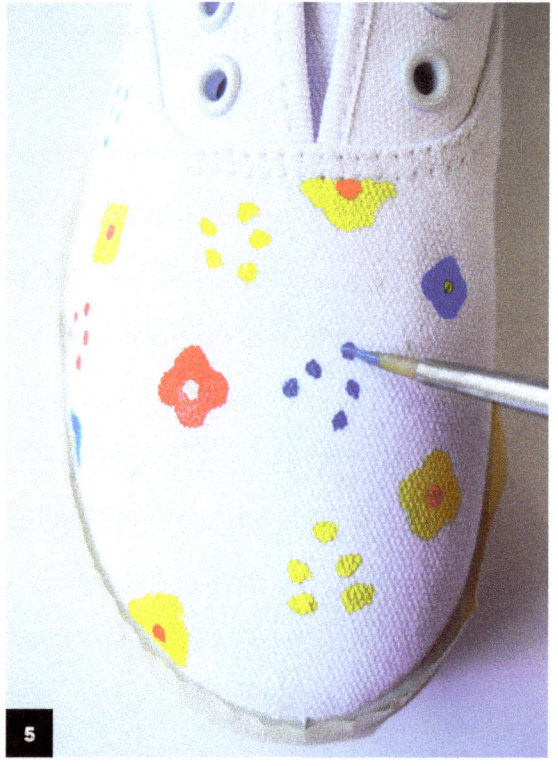

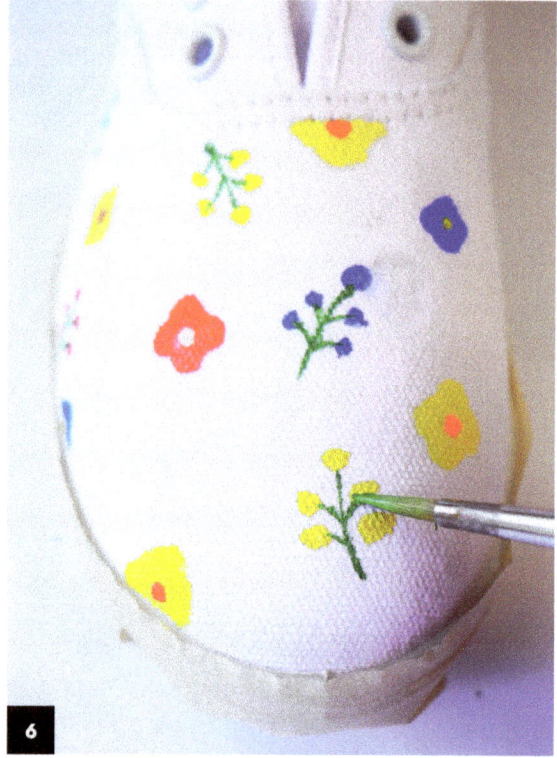

5 For the second design, paint flower buds in the same three colors. Make five tiny circles (representing the buds) in a triangle or pyramid shape. Make another cluster of buds in another area of the shoe.

6 Wash the brush and paint a stem in green, creating a thin line down the center from the top bud and then paint additional stems to connect the other buds with the main stem. Do the same for the other bud clusters. The bud branches don't have to face the same direction; you can rotate them or paint them off the edge of the shoe.

TIP
When painting a matching pair of something, I like to paint the entire design on the first piece and then paint the same design on the second one. The designs don't have to be perfectly symmetrical, but they'll look coordinated when worn together.

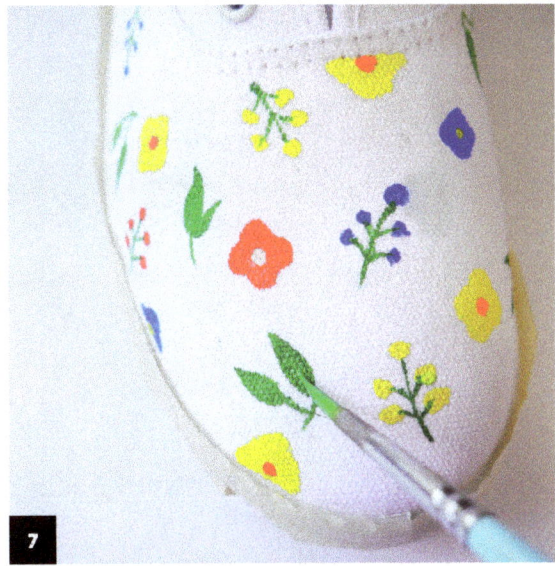

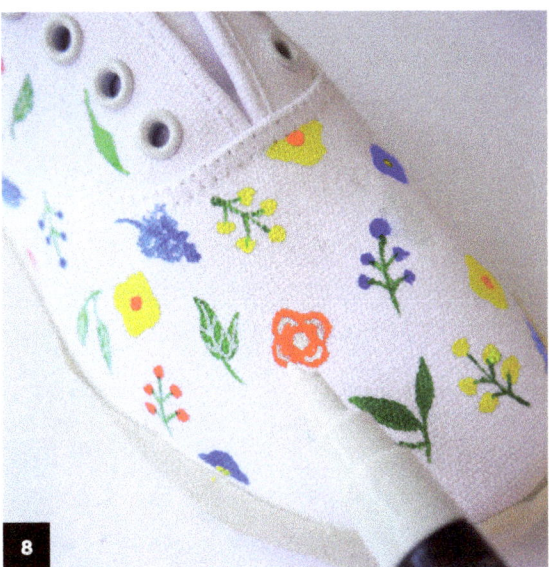

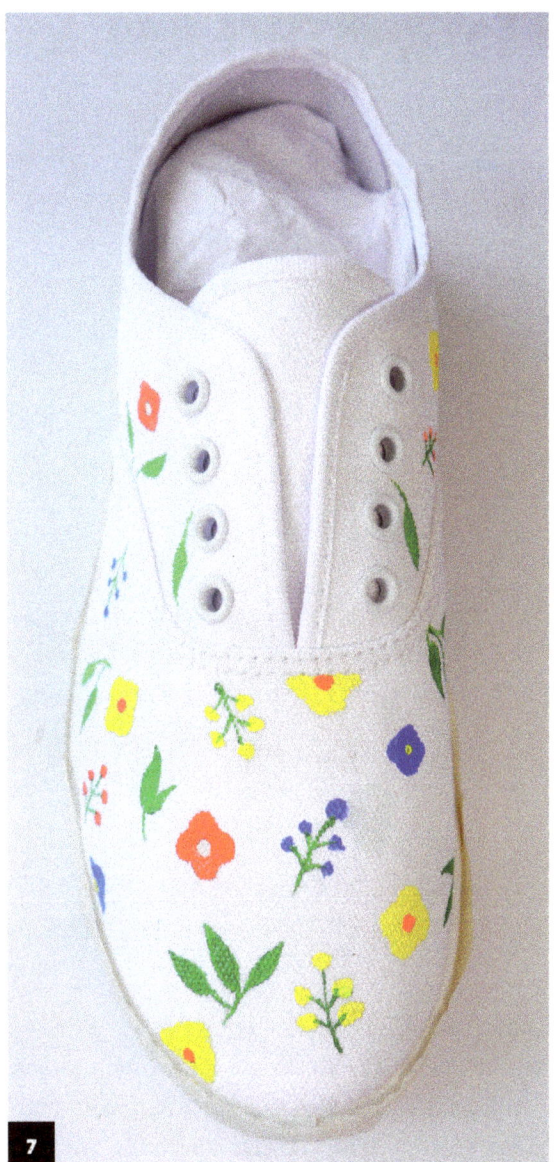

7 Create tiny leaves in the areas surrounding the floral designs in green, using the size 2 round brush (see techniques for painting leaves on page 36). Paint two or three leaves on one stem if there's room.

8 Add tiny curved lines to the flower petals with an acrylic ink pen to enhance their shape. Alternatively, you can use a thin brush and white acrylic to create the curved lines. Add the lines to each four-petal flower and to the leaves to create veins. Allow the paint to dry.

9 Spray the sneakers with acrylic sealer in a well-ventilated place or outside, following the manufacturer's instructions. Wait until fully dry, and your newly painted sneakers are ready to rock!

LEATHER TOTE BAG

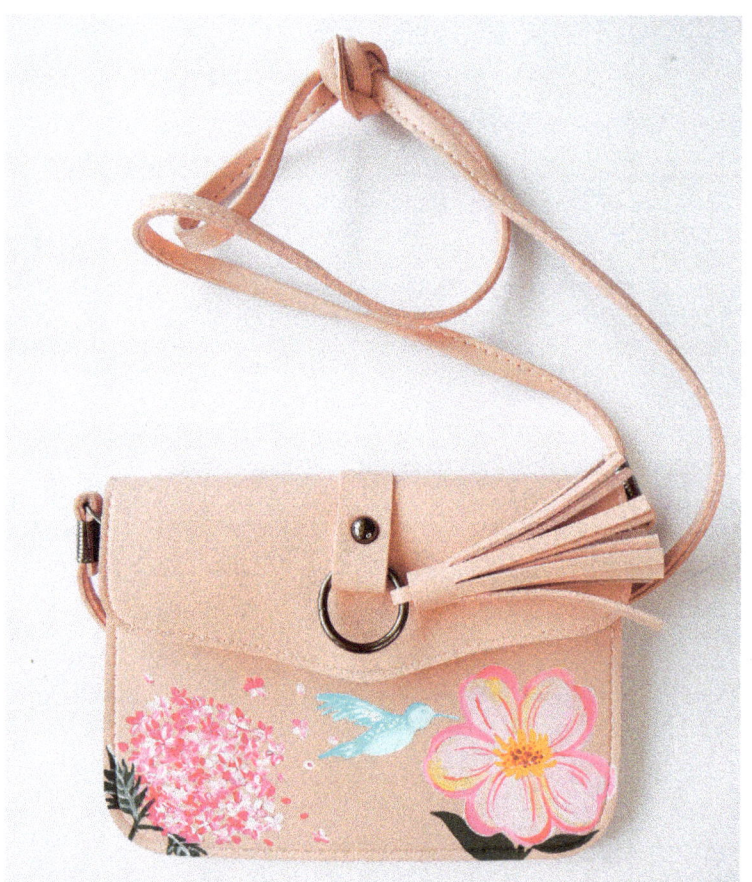

MATERIALS
- - -

Leather tote bag

Acrylic paints in red, yellow, green, blue, magenta, and white

Acrylic leather sealer

Clean cloth

Round brushes, sizes 2, 4, and 6

Mixing palette

One of the unique substrates that acrylic can adhere to is leather. A simple leather item can be easily transformed into a personalized piece with paint. Discover how to create a beautiful floral and bird design on a plain leather bag using acrylic paints made specifically for leather.

1 Prepare the leather bag for painting by wiping it down with a clean cloth to remove any dirt or stains. I used a leather bag in a pretty pink color, and I tied the straps together to make it easier to handle.

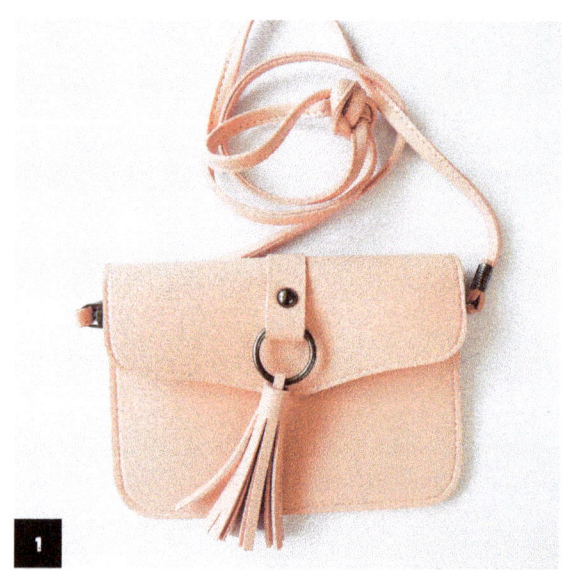

1

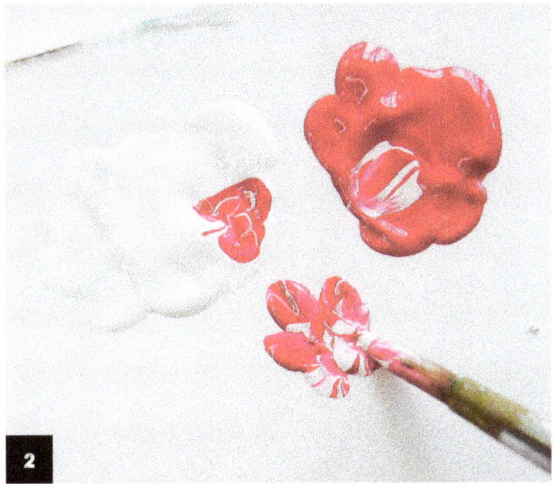

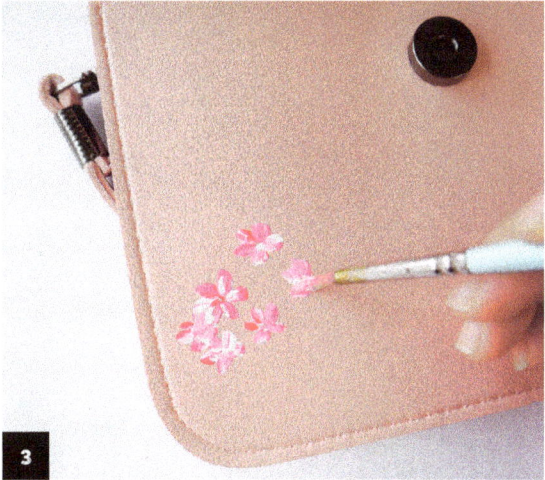

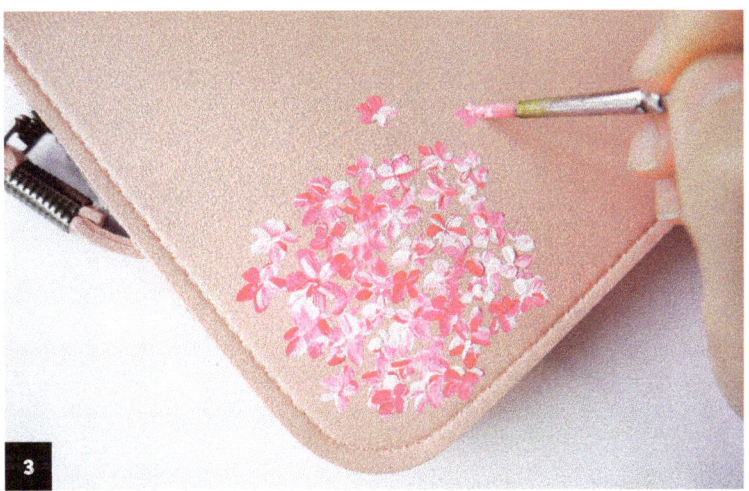

2 The design for this bag includes two kinds of flowers—a hydrangea (see pages 60–63) and a peony—and also a hummingbird. To paint the hydrangea, add red and white paint to the palette, but don't blend them. Dip the size 4 round brush into the red and then into the white paint, creating a red-white mixture on the brush that is not fully mixed.

3 Holding the brush at an angle, dab it onto the leather to create a small four-petal flower. Continue making tiny, four- and five-petal flowers to form a round hydrangea flower.

(continued)

WORKING WITH ACRYLIC LEATHER PAINT

— • • • —

The paint for this project is made especially for leather, but you can use regular acrylic paint—just note that acrylic leather paint will offer better results. Most leather paint is more fluid than heavy-body acrylic paint, and most brands are permanent and waterproof when dry. When working with lighter colored paint, it may take a few layers before it appears truly opaque. Apply a thin layer and wait for it to dry before applying the next one.

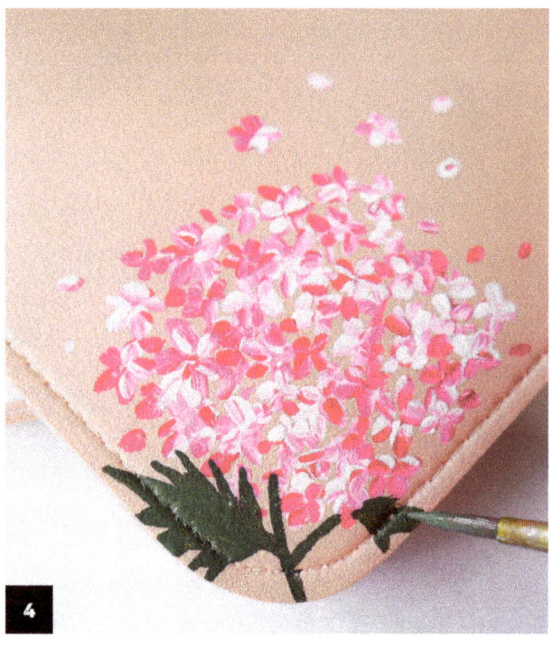

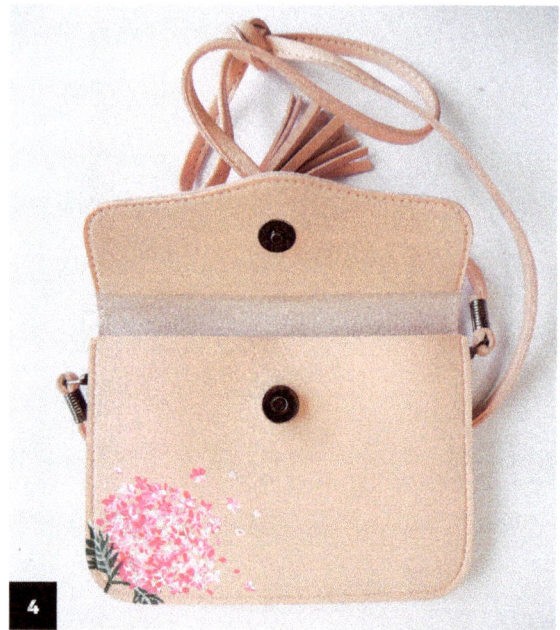

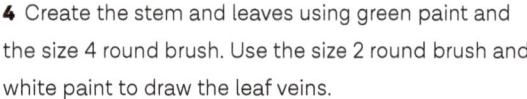

4 Create the stem and leaves using green paint and the size 4 round brush. Use the size 2 round brush and white paint to draw the leaf veins.

5 Blend a little magenta with white paint to create a light pink for the five-petal peony on the other side of the bag. Paint the outline of the peony with the size 2 round brush and then fill in the flower with the same light pink paint. Allow the paint to dry.

6 Paint a thicker outline around each of the petals with the magenta.

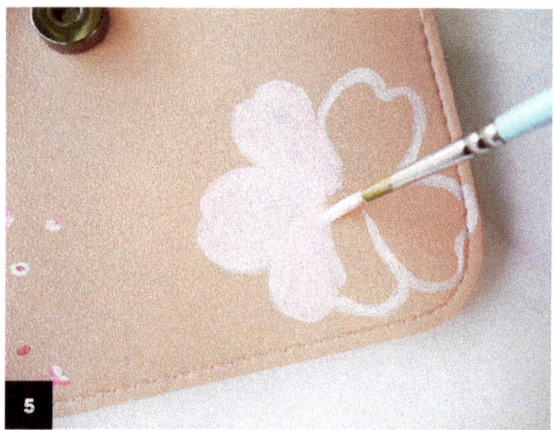

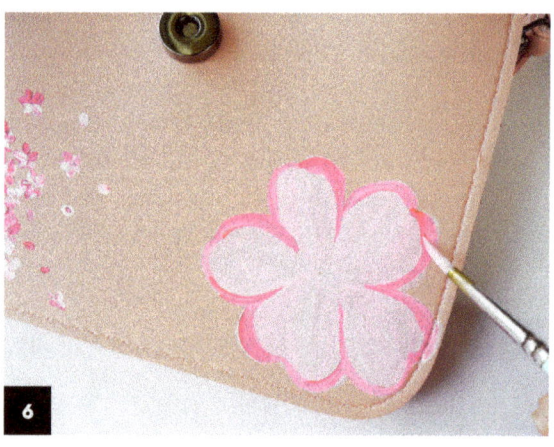

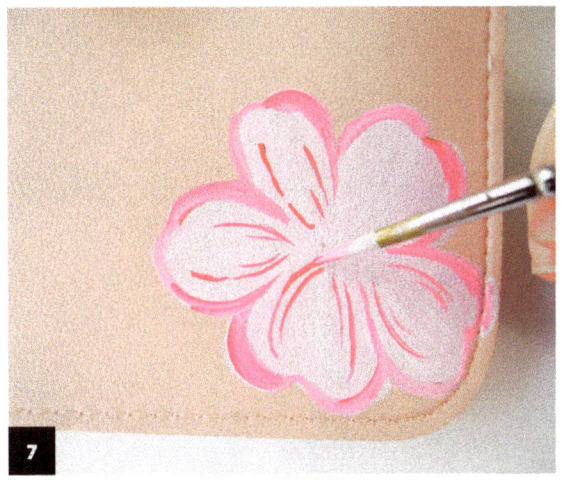

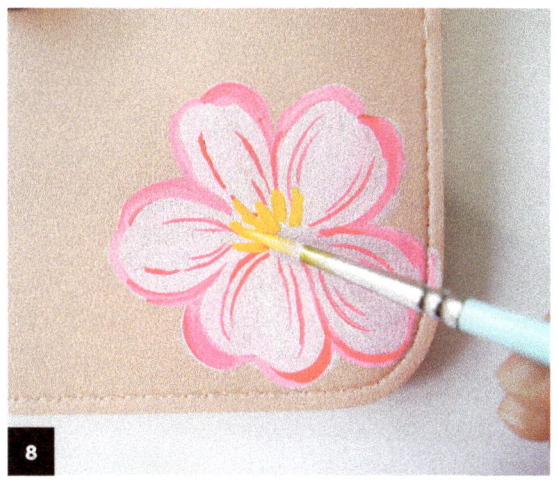

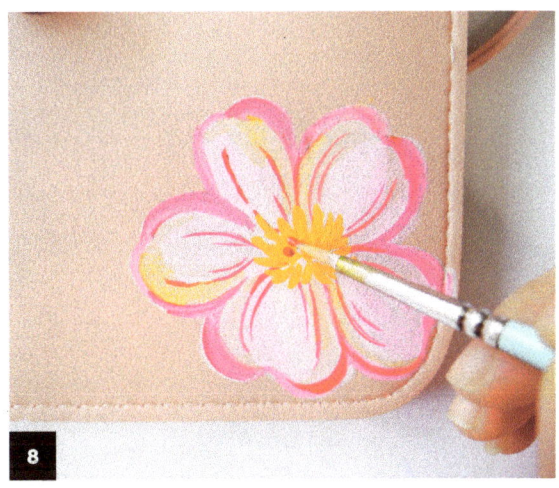

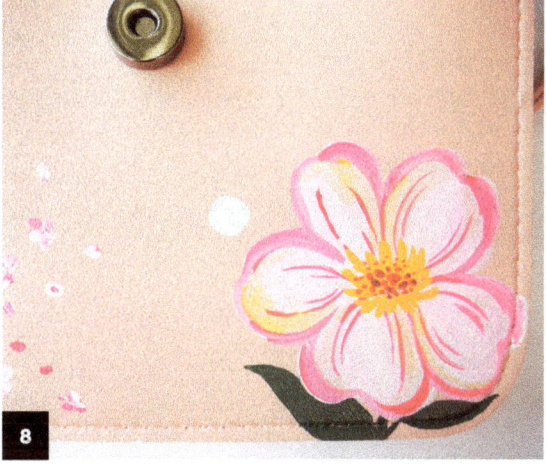

7 With the size 2 brush, add thin curved lines inside the petals, moving toward the center of the flower. The lines don't have to connect to the edge of the petals.

8 Paint the center of the peony with yellow. Make short downward strokes using the size 2 round brush. Allow the paint to dry before adding a layer of tiny red dots to the yellow center. Add more yellow to the tips of some of the petals and paint leaves in green at the bottom of the flower.

(continued)

9 Mix the paints for the humming-bird, blending blue and white to create light blue. Paint a circle for the bird's head with the size 6 round brush and then add an oblong shape below the head for the body. Elongate the shape to create the bird's tail. Add a wing at the top of the oblong shape and a long, semi-thin line on the right side of the circle for the bird's beak. Make sure these shapes are correct before adding details. Allow the paint to dry.

10 Add more blue paint to the light blue mix to use for creating the shadows and details. Paint the hummingbird's wings with this darker color by making short strokes beneath the wing line using the size 2 round brush.

11 With the darker blue, add some shadow to the top part of the body and the head, making sure to blend this shade with the lighter base color. Add the darker blue on the lower part of the beak, blending with the white paint. Allow this layer to dry. Use short strokes to apply white paint on the wing and tail. Create eyes by adding a tiny dot of the darker blue on the head.

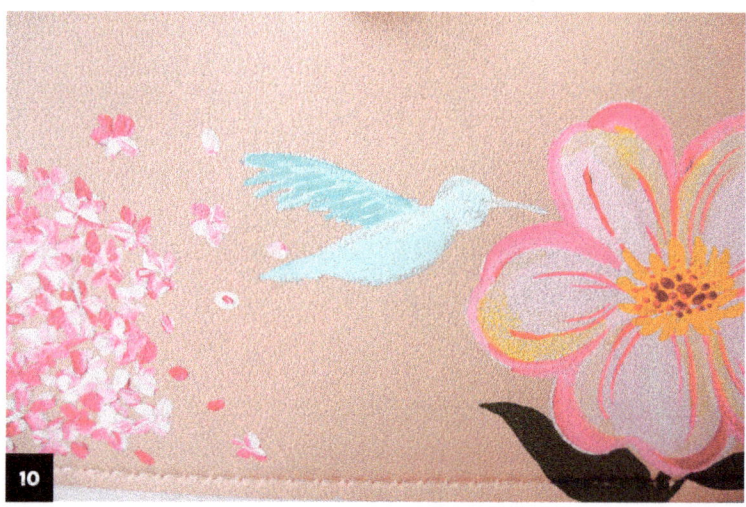

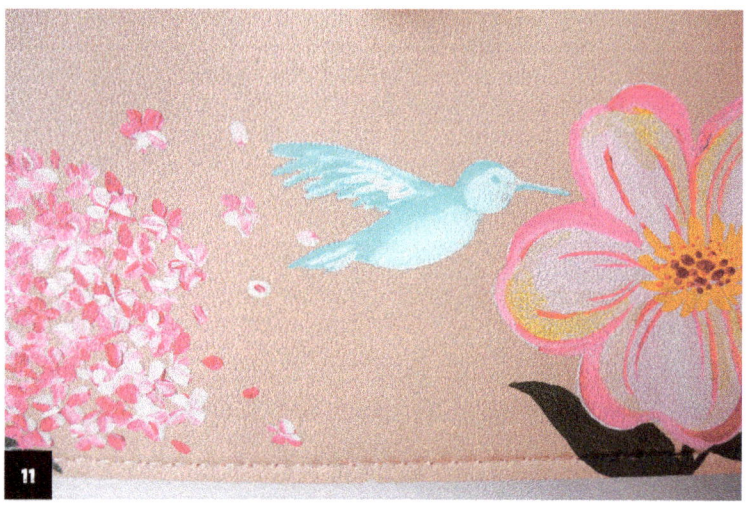

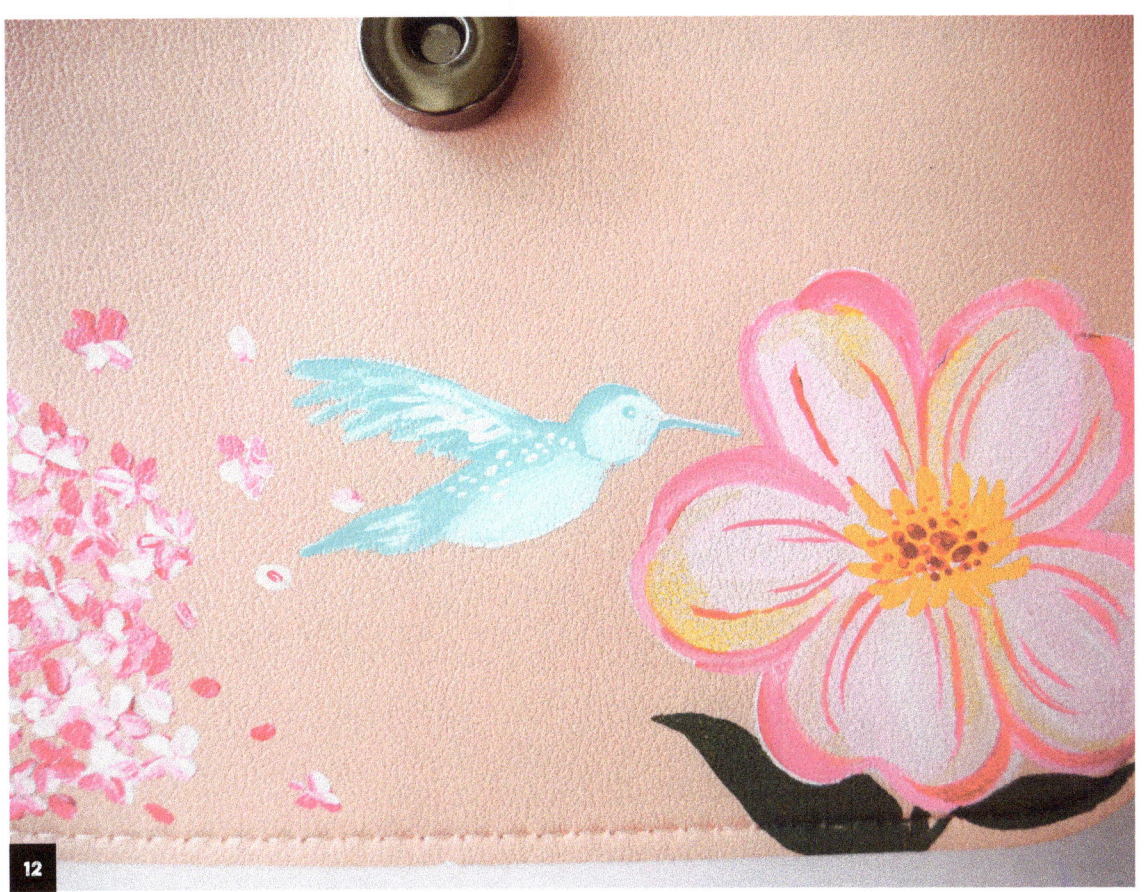

12 As a final touch, paint small white dots on the darker part of the hummingbird's body. Let dry. Seal the paint with the leather sealer, following the manufacturer's instructions.

WOODEN FLORAL BRUSH REST

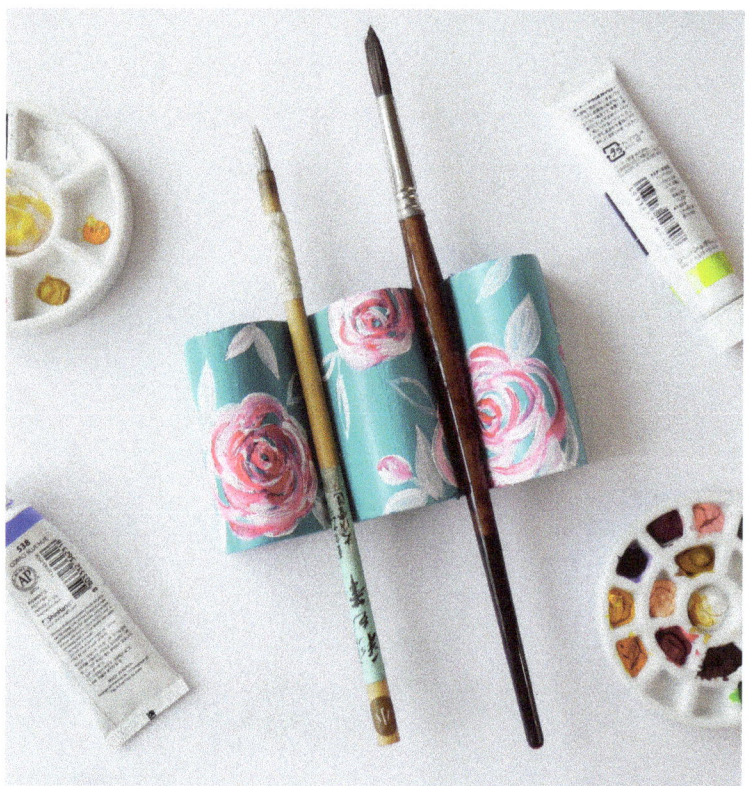

MATERIALS

- - -

Unfinished wooden
    brush rest (you
    can also use these
    techniques to paint a
    small decorative item,
    such as a box or bowl)

Acrylic paint in
    turquoise, white,
    and red

Indoor varnish

Acrylic medium
    (gloss or matte)

Flat brush, size 6

Round brush, size 4

Acrylic paint can be used to decorate wood pieces for home décor, such as bowls, boxes, or ornaments. In this project, you'll give a fresh look to a brush rest made from a carved piece of wood.

1 Prep the unfinished wood if necessary, checking to make sure the surface is smooth and devoid of any rough bumps or splinters. Smooth any rough spots with sandpaper. You can also apply a thin layer of acrylic medium to the wood to help the paint better adhere to the surface. When the medium dries it will be translucent, so it won't affect the color. Allow the medium to dry.

TIP
Painting thin layers enables the paint to dry quickly before more paint is added. If the underlayers are not thoroughly dry, the paint can crack and move when you add details to the surface later.

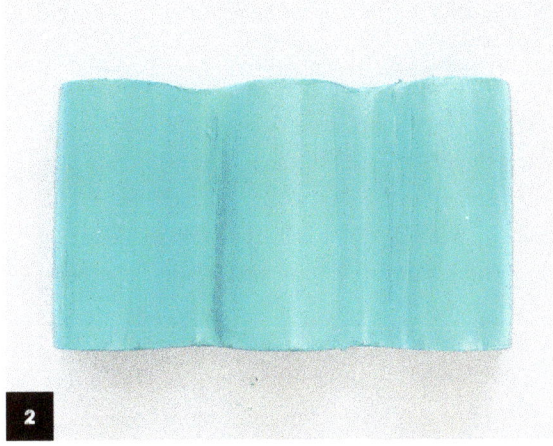

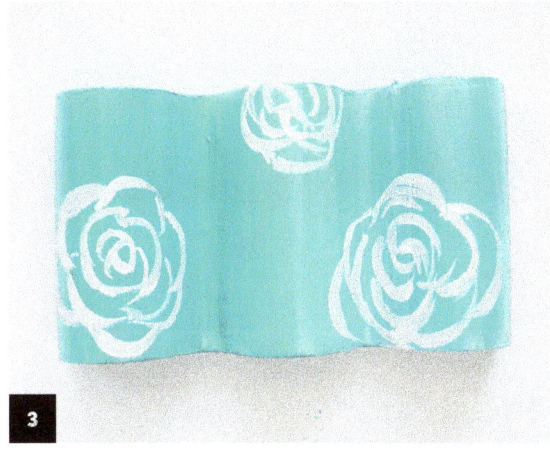

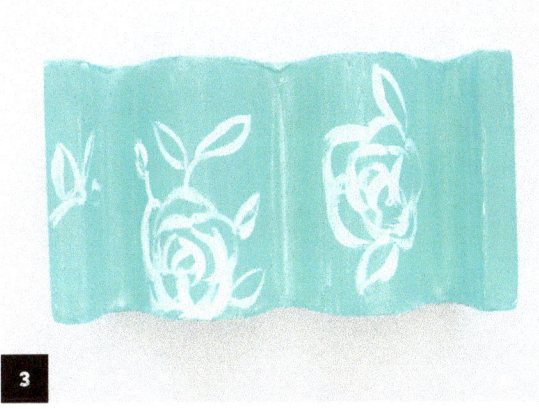

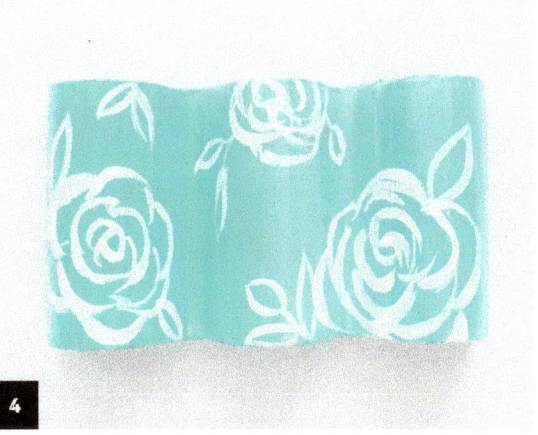

2 Choose a base color for the entire surface; I used turquoise, which reminds me of the beautiful beaches here in the Philippines. Apply a thin layer of paint on the surface with the flat brush, allow it to dry, and then paint another thin layer on top. Continue adding more thin layers, allowing each one to dry, until the bare surface of the wood no longer shows through. Allow the paint to dry.

3 Decide where you want to place the floral designs and what size you want them to be. I painted the largest flower first with white paint and the flat brush. To create the flowers, use the techniques from the roses lesson (see pages 64–67). You don't have to add a lot of details yet; think of the initial design as a guide-line for the rest of the flower. Add the designs to both sides of the brush rest.

4 Paint the outlines of other elements, such as buds and leaves.

(continued)

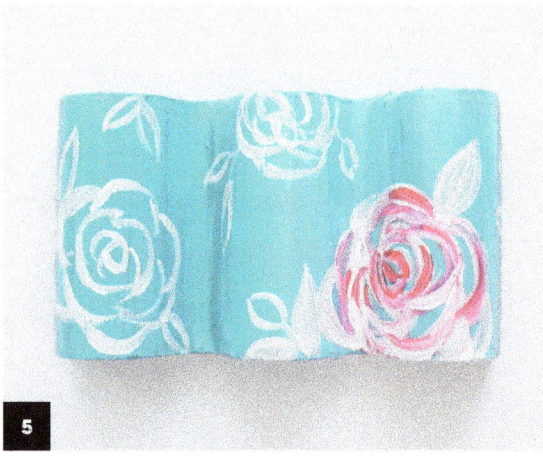

5 Enhance the roses using the round brush. To show more of the beautiful base color, use white acrylic paint to draw leaves near the roses and also on areas where the brush rest seems bare. To make the leaves more interesting, block out the larger ones with white acrylic paint and leave the smaller ones as outlines. Finish painting one side of the brush rest and allow it to dry before turning it over and painting the other side.

6 Lightly brush the surface of the painted area with indoor varnish, following the manufacturer's instructions. This helps protect the paint from moisture.

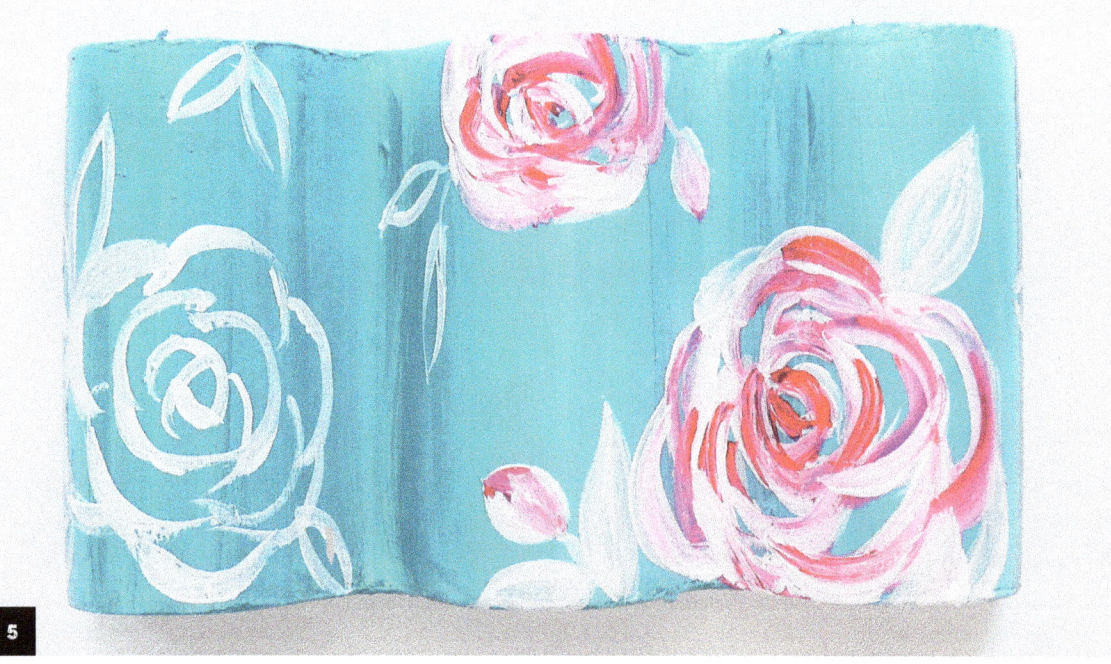

PRESERVING THE DESIGNS

— — —

The shape and size of your piece should determine the placement of your designs. If the underside is flat and rarely seen, it makes sense to add the design to the other side, where it's visible. Think about putting the majority of the design on areas where there is the least amount of friction or contact or where it won't be handled. Using these guidelines will help preserve your painted designs.

TEMPLATES

Purple Grapes

See page 44

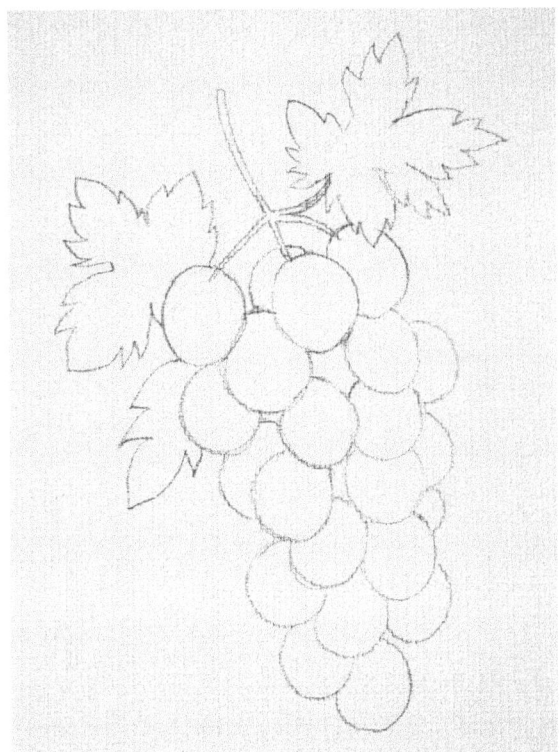

Fluffy Puppy

See page 104

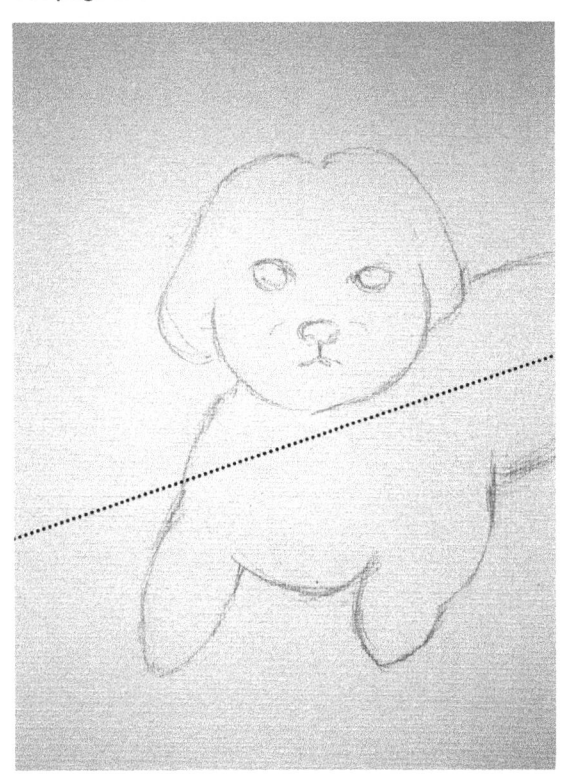

Koi Fish
See page 122

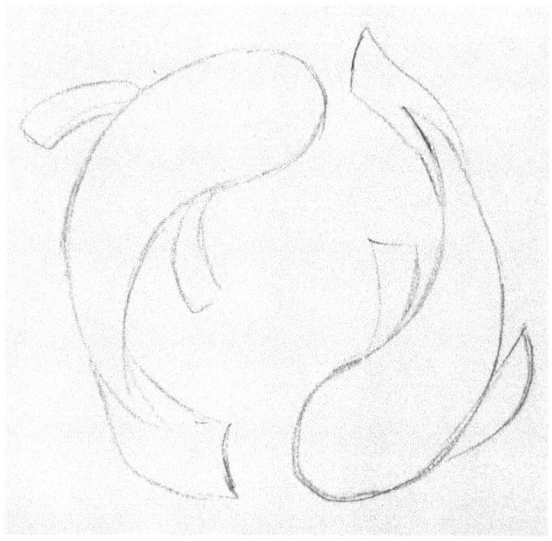

Colorful Parrot
See page 108

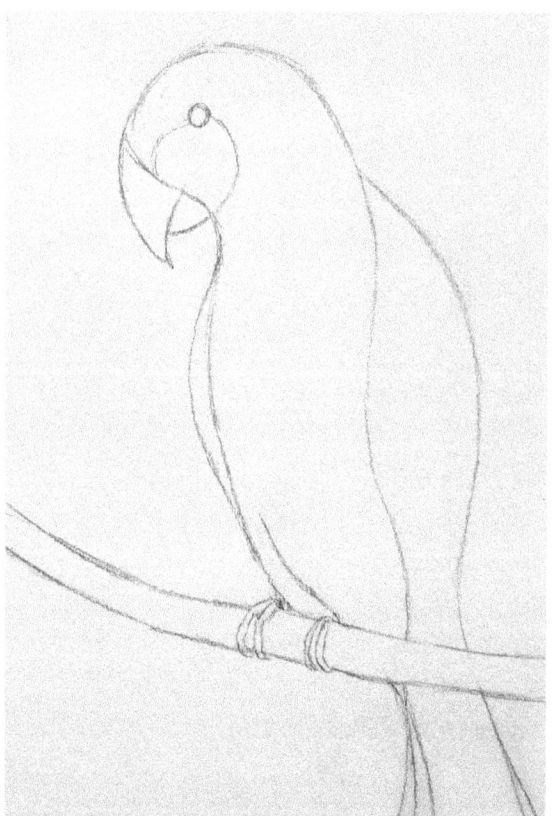

Tiger
See page 112

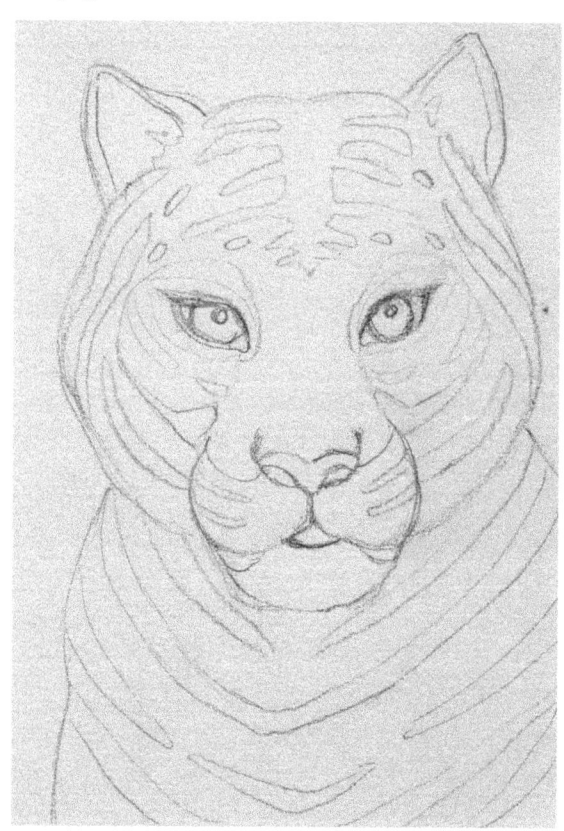

RESOURCES

Art Supplies

Liquitex acrylic paints and inks

liquitex.com

Golden Fluid acrylic paints

goldenpaints.com

HIMI Miya acrylic paints and brushes

miyaarts.com

Winsor and Newton acrylic brushes

winsornewton.com/row/brushes/acrylic-brushes/

POSCA markers

posca.com/en/range/#

Fredrix canvas paper, canvas, and panels

fredrixartistcanvas.com

Canson Montval 300 GSM paper

en.canson.com/watercolour/canson-montval

MT washi tape

masking-tape.jp/en/

ACKNOWLEDGMENTS

Thank you to my mom, Benilda, for letting me lock myself in my room for hours and skip some house chores so I could complete this book. To my brother, Charles, for editing the photos and for cooking the most delicious meals. To my uncle, Dr. Benji, for helping me with the contract and answering my legal questions.

To my dearest friends, Emalin Choi, Kathy Cua, Nikka Unciano, and Bea Francisco, who were the first to hear about this book. Thank you for continually cheering me on in whatever weird and exciting art projects I might have gotten myself into. Thank you for letting me pick your brains, for all the prayers, and for listening to all my anxious thoughts.

To all my students, art friends, collaborators, and the brands that have put their trust in me, especially when I was stumbling through social media sharing my paintings and conducting art classes in various cafés. Thank you for following my art journey.

To the Quarto team, especially to the super nice and patient editor Jeannine, thank you for this life-changing opportunity and for the trust you have given me in the making of this book.

And most importantly, to God who is the source of all blessings, life, and truth in this world. Thank you for allowing me to find my purpose and for giving me the grace to complete this book. That in all things, God may be glorified.

ABOUT THE AUTHOR

Carla Co Chua has loved drawing and painting since childhood, and her earliest influences include popular anime and cartoon shows on Philippine television. She graduated cum laude in information and communication technology management from De La Salle University in Manila and, after several years of navigating the corporate world, she decided to reignite her passion for painting. Through her consistent social media postings on Instagram and YouTube and interactions with her audience, Carla found another calling: teaching. She has hosted several public and private art workshops since 2017 and has collaborated with art supply brands to teach acrylic and watercolor painting at art events around Metro Manila. Carla continues to inspire artists with her beautiful artwork, which includes florals, animals, portraits, landscapes, and still lifes. Carla lives in Manila, Philippines.

Instagram: @carlacochua
YouTube: Carla Chua Art

INDEX